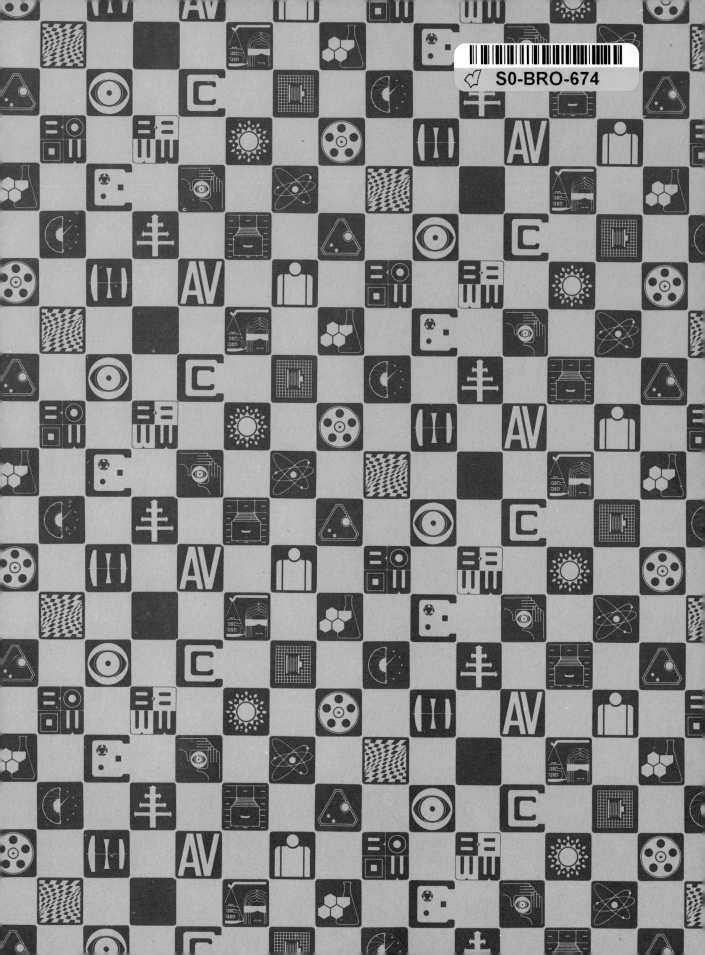

Encyclopedia of Practical Photography

Volume 8
Gum-K

Edited by and published for
EASTMAN KODAK COMPANY

AMPHOTO
American Photographic Book Publishing Company
Garden City, New York

Note on Photography

The cover photos and the photos of letters that appear elsewhere in this encyclopedia were taken by Chris Maggio.

Copyright © 1978 by Eastman Kodak Company and
American Photographic Book Publishing Company, Inc.

Library of Congress Cataloging in Publication Data

Amphoto, New York.
  Encyclopedia of practical photography.

  Includes bibliographical references and index.
  1. Photography—Dictionaries. I. Eastman
Kodak Company. II. Title.
TR9.T34   770′.3   77–22562

ISBN 0–8174–3050–4 Trade Edition—Whole Set
ISBN 0–8174–3200–0 Library Edition—Whole Set
ISBN 0–8174–3058–X Trade Edition—Volume 8
ISBN 0–8174–3208–6 Library Edition—Volume 8

Manufactured in the United States of America

Editorial Board

The *Encyclopedia of Practical Photography* was compiled and edited jointly by Eastman Kodak Company and American Photographic Book Publishing Co., Inc. (Amphoto). The comprehensive archives, vast resources, and technical staffs of both companies, as well as the published works of Kodak, were used as the basis for most of the information contained in this encyclopedia.

Symbol Identification

 Audiovisual

 Biography

 Black-and-White Materials

 Black-and-White Processing and Printing

 Business and Legal Aspects

 Chemicals

 Color Materials

 Color Processing and Printing

 Equipment and Facilities

 Exposure

 History

 Lighting

 Motion Picture

 Optics

 Picture-Making Techniques

 Scientific Photography

 Special Effects and Techniques

 Special Interests

 Storage and Care

 Theory of Photography

 Vision

Guide for the Reader

Use this encyclopedia as you would any good encyclopedia or dictionary. Look for the subject desired as it first occurs to you—most often you will locate it immediately. The shorter articles begin with a dictionary-style definition, and the longer articles begin with a short paragraph that summarizes the article that follows. Either of these should tell you if the information you need is in the article. The longer articles are then broken down by series of headings and sub-headings to aid further in locating specific information.

Cross References

If you do not find the specific information you are seeking in the article first consulted, use the cross references (within the article and at the end of it) to lead you to more information. The cross references can lead you from a general article to the more detailed articles into which the subject is divided. Cross references are printed in capital letters so that you can easily recognize them.
Example: *See also:* ZONE SYSTEM.

Index

If the initial article you turn to does not supply you with the information you seek, and the cross references do not lead you to it, use the index in the last volume. The index contains thousands of entries to help you identify and locate any subject you seek.

Symbols

To further aid you in locating information, the articles throughout have been organized into major photographic categories. Each category is represented by a symbol displayed on the opposite page. By using only the symbols, you can scan each volume and locate all the information under any of the general categories. Thus, if you wish to read all about lighting, simply locate the lighting symbols and read the articles under them.

Reading Lists

Most of the longer articles are followed by reading lists citing useful sources for further information. Should you require additional sources, check the cross-referenced articles for additional reading lists.

Metric Measurement

Both the U.S. Customary System of measurement and the International System (SI) are used throughout this encyclopedia. In most cases, the metric measurement is given first with the U.S. customary equivalent following in parenthesis. When equivalent measurements are given, they will be rounded off to the nearest whole unit or a tenth of a unit, unless precise measurement is important. When a measurement is considered a "standard," equivalents will not be given. For example: 35 mm film, 200 mm lens, 4″ × 5″ negative, and 8″ × 10″ prints will not be given with their customary or metric equivalents.

How Articles are Alphabetized

Article titles are alphabetized by letter sequence, with word breaks and hyphens not considered. Example:

Archer, Frederick Scott
Architectural Photography
Archival Processing
Arc Lamps

Abbreviations are alphabetized according to the letters of the abbreviations, not by the words the letters stand for. Example:

Artificial Light
ASA Speed

Contents
Volume 8

Gum-Bichromate Printing

The process of gum-bichromate printing, which was quite popular at the turn of the century, is today attracting renewed interest because of the wide variety of controlled artistic effects it offers. Although the process seems complex at first, it can be mastered and adapted for personal use with a little time and experimentation. The various materials that can be used all introduce variables that must be worked out to suit individual methods.

Basically, the process consists of contact-printing negatives on a good grade of paper coated with a light-sensitive bichromate solution. This is composed of a water-soluble pigment and potassium or ammonium bichromate suspended in a vehicle of gum arabic.

Gum arabic and potassium or ammonium bichromate are available from many chemical-supply companies. The ammonium bichromate, being more sensitive to light, requires about half the exposure of the potassium bichromate. The pigment can be anything from tube watercolors to tempera paint, just as long as it will dissolve in water. The paper should be strong enough to withstand a good deal of soaking.

The bichromate process is based on the fact that a bichromated and pigmented colloid becomes insoluble proportionately as it has been acted upon by light; specifically, under the different parts of a negative. It is essentially a short-scale process, but by multiple printing, a scale of tones can be built up as long as, or longer than, that of any other process. It affords an unlimited choice in color and in texture of the paper on which the print is made, and in personal control of lines, tones, and masses.

The Paper

Practically any kind of paper can be used, but it is best to choose a fine-linen or drawing paper because of the beauty and permanence of these types. Smooth-surfaced papers are used to render the finest detail, while rougher surfaces give the broad effects to which this process lends itself so beautifully. Tinted paper can sometimes be used to good advantage. In multiple printing, the paper is subjected to many alternate processes of wetting and drying, and as far as possible, a paper should be chosen that will stand this treatment. To reduce difficulty in registration, pre-shrink the paper in hot water (for about 15 min.) and allow to dry.

Sizing

While some papers can be used without sizing, the majority need to be sized. In no case does it do any harm because the purpose of the size is to prevent the pigment from soaking into the paper. A good size is made by soaking 30 grams (1 ounce) of gelatin in 296 ml (10 ounces) of water and then dissolving it by gently heating it in a double boiler. Add an equal volume of 1 percent chrome alum,* and apply the hot mixture to the paper. Next, rub it well into the pores with a small sponge, and allow it to dry. If the paper is very porous, it will need a second coating of the size; two thin coats are better than one heavy one.

A paper can be coated with plain gelatin and then with a 25 percent solution of formaldehyde instead of the chrome alum.

It is not necessary to use photographic gelatin for the size. Equally as good results can be attained by using the unflavored gelatin sold for cooking purposes. As an alternative to gelatin, the paper can also be sized with a paste of laundry starch or by spraying it with household spray starch.

The Gum

Any colloid substance such as egg white, glue, gelatin, or mucilage can be used for this process, but pure gum arabic is the best medium. This should be prepared some time in advance of use by suspending some of the pure "tears" of the gum arabic in a cheesecloth bag in a jar containing about three times their volume of water. This will dissolve after two or three days and will form the stock solution of gum. A few drops of formaldehyde or carbolic acid, or a little bichloride of mercury, should be added as a preservative to prevent fermentation.

The Pigment

Pigment of any color, dry or moist (but not mixed with oil), can be used, but dry pigments must be very finely ground to avoid granularity. Tube

---

*A stock solution of 1% chrome alum is made by dissolving 10 grams of potassium chrome alum in 1 litre of water.

Gum-Bichromate Printing

"Faded Glory" or "All Our Yesterdays" might be an appropriate title for this haunting image made from a continuous-tone negative. The black outline around the sepia-colored area gives a multiple-print effect to the print. Photo by Thomas J. Lindley.

watercolors and tempera paints are ideal for the purpose and present many conveniences in operation. Tube pigments can be squeezed out in a continuous ribbon, the length of which can be measured. This affords a much easier method than weighing for determining an exact amount, and makes it a simple matter to duplicate results.

The Sensitizer

Although ammonium bichromate is sometimes used in this process because of its greater sensitivity to light, the usual sensitizer is a saturated solution of potassium bichromate. A saturated solution would be about 10 percent at ordinary working temperatures, but it is well to put 59 ml (2 ounces) of the potassium bichromate into 296 ml (10 ounces) of water, which may be heated to speed up the solution. When it has cooled, there will be a residue at the bottom of the bottle, indicating that solution decanted from the top is saturated.

Mixing the Emulsion

To secure different effects, the bichromate, the gum, and the pigment are mixed in various proportions, which must be determined to suit individual needs. An average procedure for mixing an emulsion would be as follows:

Mixture for shadow coating
Pigment	10 cm (4 in.)
Gum	15 cc (½ oz)
Sensitizer	30 cc (1 oz)

Mixture for middle-tone coating
Pigment	5 cm (2 in.)
Gum	15 cc (½ oz)
Sensitizer	30 cc (1 oz)

Mixture for highlight coating
Pigment	2.5 cm (1 in.)
Gum	15.0 cc (½ oz)
Sensitizer	30.0 cc (1 oz)

The amount given is sufficient for several sheets of 11" × 14" paper, but the coating mixture is very inexpensive, and it is advisable to have plenty on hand before commencing to coat.

The gum and the sensitizer should first be mixed and then the pigment added; be sure that the mixture is homogeneous.

Coating the Paper. This requires a certain amount of manual dexterity, which is easily acquired with a little practice. The essential thing is to get the coating onto the paper as evenly as possible.

Pin the paper on a flat surface, underlaying it with a piece of newspaper to absorb the excess mixture. Pour the mixture into a saucer so that it can be easily taken up with a wide brush. A flat hog-bristle brush or a camel's-hair mop, about two inches wide, is the best, but any brush with which a smooth wash can be laid can be used. A good-quality brush is recommended because cheaper brushes shed bristles that are difficult to remove from the coating. When the brush is well charged with the mixture, press it out a little against the side of the dish so that it will be thoroughly charged but will not drip.

Beginning at one edge of the paper, make a wide sweep clear across from side to side. Follow this with another sweep in the same direction, slightly overlapping the first, and continue until the whole printing area is covered. It is more convenient to have the paper larger than will be needed for the negative so that it will not be necessary to coat clear to the edges.

This roughly applied wash must be blended in order to evenly coat the paper; the blending must be done quickly as the mixture will begin to set within a minute. The action used to make the coat even must not be too vigorous. Heavy pressure is likely to stir up bubbles in the gum.

The coating mixture is not sensitive to light until it is dry, so all these operations can be carried out in ordinary room light, daylight or artificial.

Drying the Paper. Once the coating has been applied, the paper should be put in a warm, dimly lit place to dry. It will dry within 1 or 2 hours, depending upon the humidity, and may be printed as soon as it is dry or after being kept in the dark for several days.

Printing

When the sensitized paper is dry, contact prints can be made from both normal and high-contrast negatives. Use a printing frame or a heavy piece of glass to hold the negative and paper together during the exposure. Remember, this is a contact-printing process, so the print will only be as large as the negative. Enlarged negatives are frequently used (see DUPLICATE BLACK-AND-WHITE NEGATIVES).

A good starting point for the exposure time is 15 minutes with an ammonium bichromate emulsion, and ½ hour for the slower-acting potassium bichromate emulsion. One 500-watt photolamp makes a good light source, but anything from sunlight to carbon-arc light will work.

No exact time can be given for the printing, as it varies with the density of the negative, the amount of bichromate in the mixture, the amount and color of the pigment used, and the results desired. Light colors print faster than dark ones, and those at the blue end of the spectrum print faster than those at the red end. Browns contain so much red that they print very slowly. A visible image is formed when printing; this is plain enough to serve as a guide to the experienced worker, especially with the lighter-colored pigments.

Developing

Developing consists of simply washing away the soluble gum in water. Light continues to act in the coating after the exposure has been stopped. As this amounts to increased exposure and is very difficult to allow for, it is best to develop as soon after printing as possible. For development, a print is placed face down in a tray of water at 18–24 C (65–75 F). Make sure that no air bells have formed on the face of the print; it can then be left unattended for an hour or so face down in the water. If it has been

Tailoring the variables of gum-bichromate printing to individual situations is fundamental to creative success. In this single-emulsion gum-bichromate print made from a continuous-tone negative, the red pigment required a longer printing time than other colors would have. Photo by Thomas J. Lindley.

Watercolor paints, applied to the surface of this gum-bichromate print after drying, add eye-catching color. Photo by Thomas J. Lindley.

correctly exposed, it will develop automatically. If the image shows plainly in less than ½ hour, it has been underprinted. Whenever it shows very quickly, nothing can be done to save the print, and it is better to hold it under water and wash off all the pigment with a sponge. When the paper is dry, it can be recoated. If the sponge action is very vigorous, it is best to size the paper again before recoating it.

If the paper has been overprinted and shows only a little detail after an hour's soaking, detail can be brought out by gradually raising the temperature of the water to 38–52 C (100–125 F). In extreme cases, a few drops of ammonia added to the water can secure results.

Control

Local control in development consists of taking off more pigment than would naturally come away.

It is accomplished by pouring water over the print for broad areas, or by gently washing it with a tuft of cotton while it is under water, or by spraying water of different temperatures upon it from an atomizer. Small areas can be picked off with a brush while the print is under water. Larger areas on a tough, greatly overexposed print can even be subjected to water sprayed upon it from a hose. In general, though, when the exposure is anywhere near normal, the print is very tender and all work on it must be done gently. A print that has been worked on with cotton or a brush is likely to show more granularity than a print that has been developed normally.

With long developments, the yellow stain of the bichromate is usually discharged, but if it still remains at the end of the development, it can be removed by placing the print in a bath of 5 percent

Three separation negatives were made on Kodalith film from a slide. To produce this gum-bichromate print, one negative was printed on a yellow emulsion layer, the second negative on a magenta emulsion layer, and the third negative on a cyan emulsion layer. Photo by Stanley W. Cowan.

The Gum-Bichromate Process Simplified

All steps can be done in white light.

1. Mix 30 ml (1 ounce) of gum arabic with 59 ml (2 ounces) of water.
2. Mix 15 ml (½ ounce) bichromate with 148 ml (5 ounces) of water.
3. Soak the paper in hot water 65.5 C (about 150 F) for about 15 minutes and then allow to dry.
4. Size the paper by spraying it with any household spray starch. Use the starch sparingly.
5. Mix equal parts—start with 7.5 ml (¼ ounce) of each solution—of the previously mixed solutions of gum arabic and bichromate. This mixture is the emulsion.
6. Mix 1 part pigment with 3 parts emulsion to give the emulsion color.
7. Coat the emulsion on the paper using a flat 6.3 mm (2½-inch) brush and make crisscross strokes to get as smooth a surface as possible.
8. Put the paper in a dimly lit place to dry.
9. Contact-print your negative onto the paper using a printing frame (emulsion to emulsion).
10. Expose the paper to any light source for 15 minutes for the trial exposure. The depth of the final print depends upon the density of the emulsion and the intensity of the exposure.
11. Develop exposed print by placing it face down in a tray of water at 21–26.5 C (70–80 F). Development takes anywhere from 15 minutes to several hours depending on the depth of exposure and the amount of density you desire. When the print looks good to you, stop development.
12. Hang the print to dry.

potassium alum for 5 minutes, after which the print is washed in 2 or 3 changes of water.

When development is complete, allow the print to drain by placing it on an inclined sheet of glass. After a few moments, it should be put in a horizontal position and left there until it is dry. Care has to be exercised in draining a very tender print so that the color will not run.

Multiple Printing

The full richness of the process is not obtained in a single printing. For multiple printing, the sensitizing coating is painted over the dry print and blended exactly as it was upon the plain paper, allowed to dry, and then the negative registered upon it for subsequent printing. Multiple printing is used to build up the whole image, or to give added strength to local areas in the picture. The coating and the printing times can be varied for different effects. For example, great depth and richness can be imparted to shadows by applying the coating only to the parts of the print in which they occur. Warmth can be added to flesh tones by giving one printing in a light red, among other printings of a darker color. The red printing will not show as such but will warm up the flesh tones. The paper should be re-sized before each printing if the previous development has been at all drastic, and it will probably have to be re-sized after two or three gentle developments.

• *See also:* BLUEPRINT PROCESS; CARBON AND CARBRO PRINTING; CYANOTYPE; DUPLICATE BLACK-AND-WHITE NEGATIVES; DYE TRANSFER PROCESS; FABRIC SENSITIZER; KALLITYPE; NON-SILVER PROCESSES; PLATINUM PRINT PROCESS; SILK-SCREEN PROCESS.

A print made with a yellow and a red emulsion layer, and printed from Kodalith film negatives, was left in a tray overnight. Dye in the emulsion floated toward the center, where color concentrated. Photo by Stanley W. Cowan.

Halation

Two kinds of image spreading can be caused by light passing into and through an emulsion. *Irradiation* is a local spreading caused by light being deflected within the emulsion itself as it strikes silver halide crystals. *Halation* is caused by light that passes all the way through and is reflected from the back surface of the film base. Because the light hits the back at an angle, it is reflected outward, forming a halo around a bright spot in the image.

Most films are treated to prevent halation. The most common method is to add a gelatin layer that contains light-absorbing dye to the back of the film.

The local spreading of light being deflected within an emulsion as the light strikes silver-halide crystals is called irradiation. Halation is caused by light that passes through the emulsion and is reflected from the back surface of the film base.

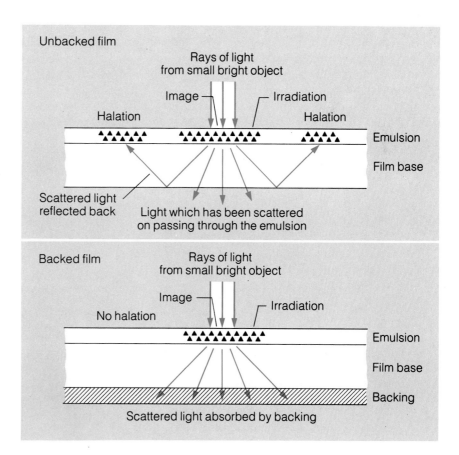

This layer is called a pelloid. The dye dissolves out during processing, although a slight amount may be left in the film; it is often noticeable as a pink or lavender tinge in a used solution. This type of antihalation backing is used on roll and sheet films. A variation of the pelloid backing is called the rem jet (removable jet black) backing, in which carbon particles are used instead of dye to absorb the light. It is used on Kodachrome films, and its removal is the first step in the Kodachrome film process.

Some films have plastic base material that "pipes" or transmits light horizontally through its structure. This light can cause localized effects, or add to overall fog. To overcome light piping, light-absorbing substances are incorporated directly in the base material. This serves to prevent light piping and to minimize halation. These dyes do not dissolve out, and remain as a visible grayishness in the processed material. Because it is evenly distributed throughout the film base, this antihalation density does not affect the image contrast; its only effect is to require a slightly longer printing exposure. This type is common in 35 mm films.

A fourth type of antihalation layer is placed directly beneath the film emulsion. In color films, this may be composed of colloidal silver that is removed in the bleach-fix process step. In a few black-and-white films, a dyed-gelatin layer is placed directly beneath the emulsion. Most of the dye dissolves out through the emulsion during processing.
• *See also:* FILMS AND PLATES; FLARE; REM-JET BACKING.

Half Frame

"Half frame" is a term applied both to a camera and to the image produced by it; specifically, an image 24 × 18 mm on 35 mm perforated film. Originally, this image size was the standard for 35 mm silent motion pictures, and when the 35 mm still camera producing an image 24 × 36 mm was introduced, its format was called "double frame." In more recent times, however, the 24 × 36 mm format has become the standard for 35 mm still cameras and the 18 × 24 mm format a minor one; hence the current term for the former is "full frame" and that for the latter "half frame."
• *See also:* FORMATS.

Halftone

In most types of graphic arts printing, the press can print a full amount of printing ink or none at all. In order to reproduce continuous-tone images, like photographs, the image is broken up into very small dots of various sizes. Light-tone areas are reproduced by tiny ink dots in the white paper, while dark-tone areas are reproduced as tiny white paper dots in a dark ink surround. An image broken up into dots for graphic arts reproduction is called a *halftone image.*

Magnification of a small area of a reproduction of a photograph shows the halftone screen pattern that creates the impression of an intermediate tone. As the tonal value is constant in this area, the dots are uniform in size and density.

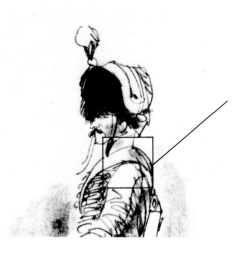

This charcoal drawing was reproduced through the use of a halftone screen. The enlarged portion shows how changes in tonal values are paralleled by shifts in the dot pattern of the halftone.

Halftones are printed from various types of printing plates that require preliminary photographic work. A special screen, called a halftone screen, is usually used to break up the image into dots. When the halftone film image is negative, it is called a halftone negative; when the image is positive, it is called a halftone positive. In some printing processes, positive halftone images are made on photographic paper.

Full-color reproduction requires four halftone plates, one each for the cyan, yellow, magenta, and black printing inks. It is necessary to have the rows of halftone dots of each halftone image at different angles to avoid the formation of moiré patterns.
• *See also:* GRAPHIC ARTS PHOTOGRAPHY; MOIRÉ PATTERN; PHOTOMECHANICAL REPRODUCTION METHODS.

Halide

A salt formed between a metal (such as silver) and one of the halogen elements: bromine, iodine, chlorine, or fluorine. Halides formed with silver are light-sensitive. Silver bromide is the principal component of film emulsions; silver chloride and combined chloride-bromide emulsions are used for printing papers. Silver iodide is primarily a trace additive used in various emulsions. Fluorides have little use in photography. The chemical symbols for the light-sensitive halides are: AgCl (silver chloride), AgBr (silver bromide), AgI (silver iodide), and AgX (sometimes used as a generic symbol for any silver halide, or combination of silver halides).
• *See also:* BROMIDE; CHEMISTRY OF PHOTOGRAPHY; DEVELOPERS AND DEVELOPING; EMULSION.

Halogen Lamp

A halogen lamp is an incandescent lamp having a tungsten filament and a quartz shell, and containing a small amount of iodine or bromine vapor. The ordinary tungsten lamp usually fails because of evaporation of tungsten from the filament; this tungsten deposits upon the walls of the lamp, causing a loss of light, and the filament is eventually destroyed because of the vaporization of the tungsten. In the halogen lamp, the quartz walls are very close to the filament and operate at high temperatures. This, and the presence of the halogen vapor, prevents the tungsten from depositing upon the lamp walls and causes it to return, instead, to the filament. Such action naturally lengthens filament life. Unfortunately, the tungsten does not necessarily return to the same place on the filament from which it originally came. Hence, the lamp eventually fails because of a weak spot in the filament. The lamp tube, however, remains clear and free from tungsten deposits, and the light output and color temperature of these lamps are substantially constant throughout their lives. These lamps are sometimes called quartz-halogen lamps or quartz-iodine lamps because iodine is the halogen gas that is used frequently to fill the bulb.

Because of their many advantages, halogen lamps are gradually replacing ordinary tungsten lamps in nearly every photographic application, such as in enlargers, projectors, and studio lights. They do generate a considerable amount of heat, so that efficient ventilation is necessary. Halogen lamps will produce light at various color temperatures.
• *See also:* LIGHTING.

Hardening Baths

Hardening-bath solutions containing either potassium alum, chrome alum, formalin, or tannic acid have the effect of raising the melting point of the gelatin emulsion, and preventing it from swelling during processing. While the emulsions on most films and papers are hardened during manufacture, it is still good practice to use an acid hardening bath in normal processing.

It is very important to note that most hardeners do not physically harden the gelatin or protect it from scratching or rough handling.* Likewise, hardeners cannot harden gelatin that has already been softened or swollen by immersion in warm water or solutions. A hardener can only prevent further swelling of wet gelatin, or avoid excessive swelling if used before processing.

In general, a hardener is usually incorporated in a fixing bath, and serves to prevent swelling, softening, and reticulation during washing. Fixing baths such as Kodak fixing bath F-5 contain potassium alum and are adequate for most purposes at normal temperatures. For convenience, some photographers prepare a separate hardener and add it to a plain hypo bath as needed. The most usual formula is Kodak hardener F-5a.

Kodak hardener F-5a

Water, about 50 C (125 F). . . 600.0 ml
Sodium sulfite (anhydrous). . . 75.0 g
†Acetic acid, 28% . . . . 235.0 ml
‡Boric acid, crystals . . . . 37.5 g
Potassium alum,
   fine granular
   (dodecahydrated) . . . . 75.0 g
Cold water to make . . . . 1.0 litre

---

†To make approximately 28% acetic acid from glacial acetic acid, add 3 parts of glacial acetic acid to 8 parts of water.

‡ Crystalline boric acid should be used as specified. Powdered boric acid dissolves only with great difficulty, and its use should be avoided.

---

*Tannic-acid hardeners are supposed to harden the gelatin and protect the emulsion against rough handling. An old formula is:

Tannic acid . . . . 1.0 g
Sodium chloride . . . . 10.0 g
Potassium alum (saturated solution) . . . . 85.0 ml
Water . . . . 1.0 litre

Dissolve the tannic acid and sodium chloride in the water. Add the alum solution. Stir and filter. Harden processed film for several minutes, wash well, and dry.

Slowly add 1 part of the cool stock hardener solution to 4 parts of cool 30 percent hypo solution (300 grams of sodium thiosulfate per litre of water), while stirring the hypo rapidly.

For high-temperature processing, chrome alum is usually employed because it has a stronger hardening action than potassium alum. While chrome alum can be used in fixing baths, it is not very effective and has a very short life. It is preferable, therefore, to use it in a stop bath between development and fixing. Inasmuch as it cannot reduce swelling in an already softened emulsion, a developer that has some sodium sulfate incorporated in it is generally recommended to minimize swelling. Then the chrome alum hardener is used and hardens the gelatin so much that no further swelling occurs in the fixing bath or wash. The usual formula for a chrome alum stop bath is Kodak hardener SB-4.

Kodak hardening bath SB-4

Water . . . . 1.0 litre
Potassium chrome alum,
   crystals (dodecahydrated) . . 30.0 g
§Sodium sulfate (anhydrous). . 60.0 g

This solution is used at temperatures above 24 C (75 F). Agitate the negatives for 30 to 45 seconds when they are first immersed in the hardener, or streakiness will result. Leave them in the bath for at least 3 minutes between development and fixing. If the temperature is below 29 C (85 F), rinse the negatives for 1 to 2 seconds in water before immersing them in the hardener bath.

The hardening bath is a violet-blue color by tungsten light when freshly mixed, but it ultimately turns a yellow-green with use; it then ceases to harden and should be replaced with a fresh bath. The hardening bath should never be overworked. An unused bath will keep indefinitely, but the hardening power of a partially used bath decreases rapidly on standing for a few days.

Formalin hardeners are used as prebaths before certain procedures that tend to soften an emulsion severely, such as when using intensifiers, reducers, stain removers, and some toning baths. Since formalin only hardens in alkaline solution, it cannot be added to a stop bath or to an acid fixing bath.

---

§If crystalline sodium sulfate is preferred to the anhydrous form, use 2¼ times the quantity listed.

Kodak special hardener SH-1

Water	500.0 ml
Formaldehyde, about 37% solution by weight	10.0 ml
Sodium carbonate (monohydrated)	6.0 g
Water to make	1.0 litre

After hardening for 3 minutes, negatives should be rinsed and immersed for 5 minutes in a fresh acid fixing bath and then washed thoroughly before they are given any further chemical treatment.

A formalin prehardener is also used when developing films at high temperatures (35 to 43 C [95 to 110 F]). Such a hardener contains an antifoggant to counteract the high activity of a developer at such elevated temperatures. It also contains sodium sulfate to prevent swelling of the film emulsion while hardening is taking place.

Kodak prehardener SH-5

Solution A

Formaldehyde, about 37% solution by weight	5.0 ml

Solution B

Water	900.0 ml
*0.5% solution of *Kodak* anti-fog, No. 2 (6-nitrobenzimidazole nitrate)	40.0 ml
Sodium sulfate (anhydrous). .	50.0 g
Sodium carbonate (monohydrated)	12.0 g
Water to make	1.0 litre

Directions for Mixing. The working solution should be prepared just before use by adding 5 millilitres of Solution A to 1 litre of Solution B and mixing thoroughly.

Directions for Use. Bathe the exposed film in Kodak prehardener SH-5 for 10 minutes with moderate agitation. Then remove the film from the solution, drain for a few seconds, immerse in water for 30 seconds, drain thoroughly, and immerse in the developer. The selection of the proper developer will depend upon the contrast and the time of development desired. In general, at temperatures up to 35 C

---

*To prepare a 0.5% solution, dissolve 1 gram of Kodak anti-fog, No. 2, in 200 ml of water.

(95 F), conventional developers, such as Kodak developers D-76, DK-60a, D-19, and so forth, can be used without modification.

DEVELOPMENT TIMES

Temperature	% of Normal Development Time*
24 C (75 F)	100%
26.5 C (80 F)	85%
29.5 C (85 F)	70%
32 C (90 F)	60%
35 C (95 F)	50%

*Normal development time recommended when the developer is used at 20 C (68 F) without a prehardener.

Following development, rinse, fix in an acid hardening fixing bath, wash, and dry in the usual way.

At Temperatures above 35 C (95 F). Increase the concentration of Kodak anti-fog, No. 2, in the prehardener, using as much as double the normal formula concentration, if necessary, to control fog. Process as before, using a low-activity developer, such as Kodak developer D-76, to avoid excessively short development times. The average development time at 43 C (110 F) after prehardening is about one-quarter of the normal time at 20 C (68 F).

In case the development time at elevated temperatures is too short for practical use, sodium sulfate can be added to the developer to extend the time of development.

Keeping Properties and Useful Capacity. The keeping properties are adequate for ordinary tray and tank practice. Gradual deterioration does occur on standing, but the bath will keep satisfactorily, if unused, in a closed bottle for three to four weeks at 35 C (95 F). For most applications, the useful capacity without replenishment is more than ten 8″ × 10″ films per 946 millilitres (1 quart) without serious change in properties.

Heat Control in Photographic Equipment

Heat can cause special problems with enlargers and projectors of various types because incandescent lamps emit a great deal of infrared and heat radiation as part of their energy output. This heat can be harmful both to the equipment itself, and to the negatives or slides used in the equipment.

Equipment Cooling

Enlargers for the smaller sizes of negatives generally use fairly small light sources, seldom larger than 150 watts, and the amount of heat emitted is not too difficult to eliminate. Some enlargers, for instance, use completely enclosed lamphouses, and depend entirely on radiation from the metal housing itself to carry off the heat of the lamp. If the outside surface of the housing is finned, it will have greater total area exposed to the air, and cooling will be more efficient.

Other enlargers have ventilated lamphouses; here the excess heat is carried off by convection. The air vents must be carefully light-trapped so that there is no leakage of white light from the enlarger that could fog sensitive materials or degrade the contrast of the print being made. Many older enlargers are not adequately light-trapped. Considerable light escapes from the top of the lamphouse through the air vent. It is difficult to design adequate baffling that will not also obstruct the flow of cooling air. Fortunately, most modern machines do have adequately vented lamphouses with good light-trapping capabilities.

Controlling heat in slide and motion-picture projectors is more difficult, since the lamp wattage (which determines the amount of heat to be eliminated) is generally much higher; some 16 mm movie projectors of earlier types use lamps as large as 1200 watts, which emit a great deal of heat.

Such slide and motion-picture projectors always have cooling fans. Inasmuch as they need a motor to drive the mechanism, the fan is usually placed on the motor shaft. Fans for high-wattage lamps tend to be noisy, and little can be done to quiet them, although the blower designs for some slide projectors have been improved in recent years.

More modern 16 mm and 8 mm projectors use lamps of much lower wattage so that getting rid of the heat is much easier. Usually a small, slow-speed blower is used in these machines, and the noise is greatly reduced. Even with moderately high-wattage lamps such as the 150-watt and 250-watt reflector-type lamps used in late-model projectors, a slow-speed fan can often be employed. This is because these newer lamps are of the halogen type, which must be allowed to run fairly hot in order for the halogen regenerative cycle to operate. The fan is only required to carry off the hot air from the lamphouse; it is not required to cool the lamp itself.

Some big enlargers, mainly for negatives in excess of 4″ × 5″, use large lamps for fast printing, and require more cooling than can be accomplished by simple convection. The use of blower fans for cooling these machines poses a special vibration problem. Vibration of the enlarger can cause unsharp prints.

In many cases, vibration is removed from the enlarger by placing the blower on the floor or wall alongside the machine and connecting it to the lamphouse with a length of very soft, flexible hose. To reduce the vibration still further, such blowers are often made as suction devices, drawing warm air from the lamphouse instead of blowing cool air into it. On the other hand, blowing cool air into the enlarger has an advantage, since the cool air can be guided over the negative first, thus helping to keep it from being overheated.

Removing Heat from the Light Beam

While incandescent lamps emit heat in all directions, a very large part of it accompanies the light beam, simply because the infrared radiation is part of the energy emitted. This heat energy, falling upon stationary film in a fairly powerful motion-picture projector, can burn a hole in the film in seconds.

In some cases, no attempt is made to eliminate this heat, because it would involve a loss of light as well; in large, professional motion-picture projectors, the only thing that avoids damage to the film is the fact that each frame of picture is exposed to the light beam for only $1/24$ of a second. Even so, in the biggest projectors (often used in drive-in theaters), some heat filtering is present in the light beam, and a blast of cool air is directed onto the film as it travels through the projection gate.

Whenever a projector has means for stopping the film for a still picture, it must also include means to reduce the heat falling upon the film during still projection so that the film will not be damaged. As far back as the 1920s, portable 35 mm movie projectors were made with provision for projecting still pictures.

Gold-Glass Shutter. The first device used to reduce the light and heat while the film was stationary in the gate was the so-called "gold-glass" shutter used in the Acme projectors of the 1920s. This consisted of a small piece of thin glass, plated on one side with a very thin layer of gold, much like a mirror. This gold "mirror" had the ability to reflect infrared radiation to a large degree, while transmitting most, but not all, of the light. Some red light was lost, and for this reason, the transmitted light had a greenish tinge. While the loss of light in such a filter reached as high as 50 percent, this was balanced by the fact that the motion-picture shutter (which also causes a loss of about 50 percent) was not running. Thus, the still image was approximately as bright as the motion picture.

Heat-Absorbing Glass. The DeVry projectors of the same period used a thick piece of greenish heat-absorbing glass, quite similar to the Corning Aklo and other heat-absorbing glasses still in use today. This worked on a different principle; instead of reflecting the heat and infrared, the glass filter absorbed it, getting very hot in the process.

Water-Filled Glass Cells. Even earlier, at the turn of the century, some lantern slide projectors that used arc lamps had heat absorbers consisting of glass cells filled with water. These usually were connected to a small tank, so that the hot water rose into the tank, and cool water descended by convection. The device worked fairly well, but was best suited to

permanently installed machines because of the danger of spillage. In addition, if the projector was used for any length of time, the water got very hot, often boiling in the cell and causing disturbances in the illumination.

Heat Filters. Most modern, small slide projectors and enlargers have permanently installed heat filters that are generally made of heat-absorbing glass such as Corning Aklo. The modern types of heat-absorbing glass are quite neutral in color, at least in the thin pieces usually used.

Dichroic Filter. A more modern type of heat filter is the dichroic filter. This type of filter is based on the same principle as the coated lens; a number of layers of reflecting material are coated on a sheet of glass and form an interference filter. In this case, however, the thicknesses of the layers are chosen to reflect certain wavelengths and transmit others.

In this way, dichroic color filters to transmit or to reflect specific wavelengths can be made that are more permanent than dye-gelatin filters or other types of colored media. The filters built into color heads of modern enlargers are made in this way.

The coatings on heat-reflective dichroic filters are chosen so that nearly all the visible radiation is transmitted, while infrared radiation is nearly all reflected back to the source. This has the advantage over the usual heat-absorbing glass that the heat is

Incandescent lamps emit very little energy in the ultraviolet region (below 400 nanometres) and the greatest part in the infrared and heat regions (above 700 nanometres). The useful output, in the visible region, is a fraction of the total energy emitted.

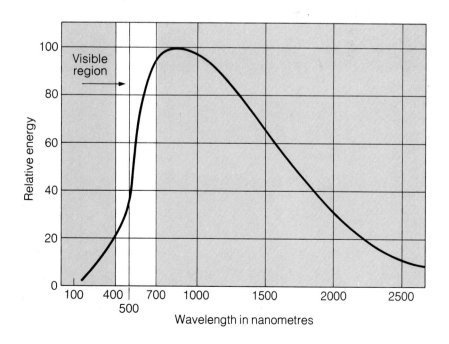

not absorbed by the filter itself, and thus the filter does not get excessively hot in use.

Such filters must be placed in parallel or nearly parallel beams of light, since light striking at an angle would have to pass through a greater thickness of coating materials, and the reflection characteristics would be changed. Dichroic infrared reflection filters are used in most professional color-printing machines, where they can be permanently built in by the manufacturer to maintain their orientation in the light beam. They are seldom used in amateur enlargers, both for this reason and because they are quite costly.

Reflectors. In most older slide projectors, the ordinary heat-absorbing glass was quite adequate, since the heat it absorbed could be removed by the same blower that was used to cool the lamp. In enlargers, there is not as much heat so that the glass does not get very hot.

In modern slide and motion-picture projectors, a different system of heat control is used, which is based upon much the same principle. To begin with, modern slide and movie projectors use smaller lamps, usually containing a built-in ellipsoidal reflector. This reflector concentrates the light on the film, exactly as the condenser lenses in the older projectors did. The optical design of the projectors can be made more efficient by using reflectors rather than condensers. This leads to systems in which a 150-watt lamp produces as much screen illumination as a 500-watt lamp in a condenser system.

The reflectors in these lamps do not need to be made to the same degree of accuracy as imaging lenses. In practice, they are usually molded of glass. They are coated with a multilayered interference coating that is designed to be the reverse of the infrared heat-reflecting filter; that is, the coating is designed to reflect all the visible radiation (light), while transmitting the infrared (heat) radiation. In this way, a "cool" light beam results; nearly all the light reaches the film or slide, while most of the infrared radiation passes backward into the lamphouse.

Of course, this heat must be removed, so a cooling fan is still necessary, but keeping the heat out of the light beam is a great advantage.

Similar lamps are now used in a number of "dichroic" lamphouses or color heads for small enlargers up to 4″ × 5″ in size. In many cases, only a simple convection ventilation system is required to cool these lamps, because of the low wattage involved.

Heliography

Some writers state that the word *heliography* was merely one of several early synonyms for photography. However, it is believed that the word was first applied by Nicéphore Niépce to his process of producing images by the action of light on various bitumens. The exposed parts of the coating became insoluble, while unexposed portions could be washed out with various solvents. Similar processes are still being used by photoengravers to produce acid-proof resist images on metal plates to obtain halftone plates for printing, although photo-offset (lithographic) processes have largely replaced the need for such plates. On the other hand, such photo etching processes are widely used in the manufacture of electronic circuits, especially the tiny "chip" circuits used in cameras, electronic flash units, calculators, and so forth.

• *See also:* HISTORY OF PHOTOGRAPHY.

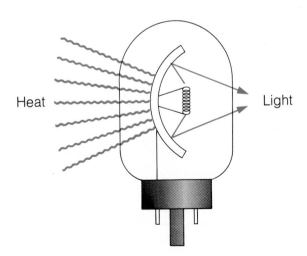

A reflector-type projection lamp, with dichroic mirror, reflects the visible light into the projection lens system, while allowing the infrared and heat radiation to pass out the rear of the lamp. The heat is removed from the lamphouse by its ventilation, cooling fan, or both.

Herschel Effect

If an emulsion that has not been sensitized to red or infrared radiation is exposed to blue or white light, a latent image will be formed in the normal way. In some cases when the emulsion is subsequently exposed to red or infrared radiation before it is developed, some of the effect of the original exposure will be erased. Thus, the long-wavelength radiation is capable of destroying, to some extent, the latent image formed by the blue light. This is the Herschel effect. It is not subject to failure of reciprocity, so far as is known. However, the energy required to destroy a latent image by the Herschel effect is several orders of magnitude higher than that required to form the initial latent image.

This principle is used in the manufacture of some direct-positive acting emulsions. The finished emulsion is flashed with ultraviolet or blue light before coating. When exposed to white light (containing red and infrared wavelengths) and then developed, a positive image results.
• *See also:* IMAGE EFFECTS.

Herschel, Sir John F. W.

(1792–1871)
English astronomer; probably the first photographic chemist

Earlier experimenters had discovered the light-sensitivity of silver salts, but were unable to fix the image after exposure. Herschel had discovered that hyposulfite of soda ("hypo," now known as sodium thiosulfate) would dissolve unexposed silver halides and suggested its use to render the image permanent. He was also the inventor of an experimental method of making photographs on glass, and of several non-silver photographic processes. His most important process was the cyanotype or blueprint, used for many years to reproduce architects' drawings and similar originals. He investigated the light-sensitivity of many iron salts, including the citrates, tartrates, and the double salts such as iron and ammonium citrate (ferric ammonium citrate).

A close friend of Fox Talbot, and well-known to virtually all the early English and French investiga-tors of photography, Herschel coined the word *photography* from the Greek roots *photos* (light) and *graphos* (drawing). He suggested the terms "negative" and "positive" to distinguish the key stages of the photographic image, and coined the word "snapshot." He made studies of the sensitivity of various silver halides to different colors of light, and described the effect of long-wave energy on the latent image.
• *See also:* BLUEPRINT PROCESS; CYANOTYPE; HERSCHEL EFFECT; HISTORY OF PHOTOGRAPHY.

High Contrast

In black-and-white photography, contrast means *tonal difference.* High contrast means that the tonal difference is of a high degree.

When the *subject* tonal difference is high, the photographic process must be controlled to produce a normal, full-scale print.

If an extremely high-contrast print is needed for graphic impact or for expressive effect, the photographic process can be made to produce that effect from a normal or high-contrast subject.

Photographing High-Contrast Subjects

A high-contrast subject for black-and-white photography is one in which the brightest diffuse highlight areas are 250, 500, or more times brighter than the shadow areas. That is, the shadow areas would require eight, nine, or more stops exposure than the highlights to produce an equal negative density. The subject luminance range is eight or nine stops or more. (*See:* BRIGHTNESS RANGE.)

When such a subject is photographed on a film of average contrast and is developed normally, the negative density range may be so great that the negative will be impossible to print on even the lowest-contrast paper grade.

The preferred way to accommodate a high-contrast subject is to expose the film sufficiently to record shadow detail and to reduce development so that highlight densities stay within a printable range. (*See:* BLACK-AND-WHITE PRINTING; CONTRAST; DEVELOPMENT.)

Creating High Contrast

Some techniques will create high-contrast images on normal-contrast film, but these usually do

High Contrast

not produce expressive high-contrast prints. For example, overdevelopment of a normally exposed negative will produce a print in which the contrast in middle tones is somewhat exaggerated and the highlights are areas of white without detail. Underexposing the negative and overdeveloping to an even greater degree will cause loss of shadow detail as well as highlight detail, with some increase in middle-tone contrast. Similarly, printing a normal negative on a very high-contrast grade of paper can produce three variations, depending on the amount of print exposure given. In order of increasing exposure, they are:

1. A print with shadow detail and some middle tones, but no highlight detail.
2. A print with only middle tones, but shadows and highlights without detail.
3. A print with upper middle tones and with highlight detail, but with no shadow detail.

In all the above cases, the middle tones are present, and the result is not a graphic high-contrast effect.

Expressive High Contrast

A true high-contrast print is a black-and-white print with no intermediate gray tones. Without the middle tones, only the essential shapes of the original photograph are reproduced. The resulting solid black and stark white tones combined with sharply outlined subject shapes can make prints with great graphic impact. They are produced by using very high-contrast films and papers such as those commonly used in the graphic arts. With these materials, you can turn cluttered negatives into clean, dramatic pictures, salvage flat negatives and underexposed slides, combine images from several photographs to create a new composition, and turn black-and-white negatives into color prints and slides.

Producing high-contrast negatives and positives is the foundation for many of the special effects and techniques described in other articles. It is very important to develop a basic knowledge of producing good high-contrast images before attempting more sophisticated photo processes such as tone-line images or posterization. In order to produce successful effects, you must be able to control the printing of high-contrast film.

High-contrast films and paper are easy to use because most of them are orthochromatic—they are not sensitive to red light and can be handled under a red safelight. Check the instruction sheet packaged with the material for the safelight recommendation. The obvious advantage to being able to work under a safelight is that you can see what you are doing and can watch the film developing.

High-contrast paper, films, and developer are available from graphic arts suppliers (listed under Printing Supplies in the Yellow Pages of the telephone book), or a photo dealer can order these products. Kodak contact paper is a contact-speed high-contrast water-resistant paper, while Kodak rapid paper is a projection-speed paper of the same type.

Kodalith films are available in a variety of sizes, but the 4″ × 5″ sheets are the most useful. When working with high-contrast films, it is best to make the largest negative that the enlarger will accept because it makes retouching as easy as possible. You can also contact-print negatives and slides onto Kodalith film; this method allows you to reproduce several small images on one sheet of 4″ × 5″ film. Use the contact-printing method only if no retouching is required. By contact-printing, you can also produce bas-relief images.

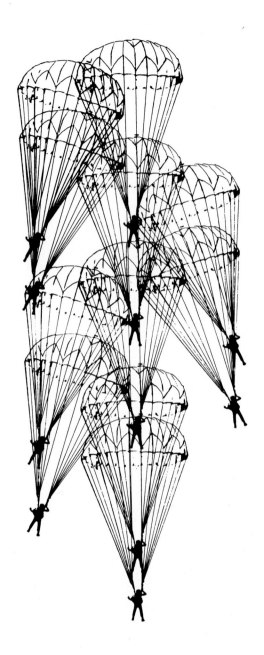

The solid black parachute lines against the stark white background seem to accentuate the vertical drop of the parachutists. It is easy to print multiple images with high-contrast negatives because no dodging is required. The high density of a high-contrast negative is a built-in mask. Photo by Gil Smith.

Using High-Contrast Paper

With high-contrast paper, you can produce a high-contrast print directly from a normal, continuous-tone print. Since most such prints are enlargements, a projection speed, high-contrast paper such as Kodak rapid paper is very useful. It is made for photomechanical reproduction, so it must be obtained from dealers normally supplying Kodak materials for the graphic arts.

If a negative is enlarged onto this paper, and it is processed in a high-contrast, lith-type developer such as Kodalith developer, the image will be a positive image with only two tones, black and white, with all the middle tones dropped out. The length of the enlarger exposure determines the break point at which the tones go from white to black. Shorter exposures produce large areas of white with only the deepest shadows being shown as black. Longer exposures result in large areas of black, with only the lightest tones going white.

If a transparency (slide or black-and-white positive) is used in the enlarger, the print image will be negative—whites and light tones will go black, while the dark tones go white.

Graphic arts papers are usually orthochromatic, and should be handled in the light of a red safelight, such as that provided by a Kodak safelight filter No. 1A (light red). Suitable Kodak developers are Kodalith developer, Kodalith super RT developer and Kodalith liquid developer. Developing time ranges from about 1½ minutes to 3 minutes. This range provides an additional control on the tonal break point between white and black. A shorter developing time provides more white areas —while longer developing times give larger black areas. Combined with the original exposure, this gives the worker an additional control over the effect desired.

Although they are not required, such papers are useful to print high-contrast negatives made on a lith film, such as tone-line negatives, if the two-tone, black-white effect is desired. Conventional moderate-contrast papers should be used when the high-contrast negatives are being used, via posterization, to produce a three- or four-tone print.

Lacking a special paper, an ultra-high-contrast grade of paper such as a Kodabrome RC paper can be used. Although it is not a standard recommendation, the contrast can be increased by use of a Kodalith developer.

Using High-Contrast Films

With extremely high-contrast films such as Kodalith film, you can make negatives directly from slides. Or you can print a negative onto the film to produce a high-contrast film positive, then contact-print the film positive onto another sheet of film to produce a high-contrast negative. Both the high-contrast positive and negative are used for some of the techniques described later.

In this picture, high contrast serves to make an interesting scene positively arresting. A grainy negative on 35 mm film was enlarged onto Kodalith film, then developed in Kodalith fine-line developer. The film was agitated during the first 15 seconds in the developer, and then developed with no agitation for another 2¼ minutes. The resulting positive film was contact-printed onto a sheet of separation negative film, which was then developed for 2½ minutes to produce the negative that made this print. Photo by Conrad G. Houle.

One of the biggest advantages of using such films is that you can eliminate distracting areas of the picture quickly and easily by painting them out with opaque. It is also easy to combine two images from different films or to rearrange the composition of an image by simply cutting the film, rearranging the image into a new composition, and then taping the pieces of film along the edge. By combining these techniques of cutting and rearranging images with the ability to paint out areas of a picture or add details in other areas, an almost unlimited variety of new pictures can be created from existing negatives and slides.

Selecting the Film. There are several high-contrast films available; the one to use depends on the original image and on the desired final result. For general use in making high-contrast positives or negatives from negatives and slides, or for making contact negatives (or positives) from Kodalith film positives (or negatives), use Kodalith ortho film, type 3.

If the original image is in color and has a great deal of red that you want to record in detail, use Kodalith pan film to make the high-contrast negative or positive. Because it is panchromatic, this film will accurately record all the colors in the original as various shades of gray. Ortho films record reds as black, often without much detail.

Processing Kodalith ortho film type 3 and Kodalith pan film. Use a Kodak safelight filter No. 1A (light red) with Kodalith ortho film. Use a Kodak safelight filter No. 3 (dark green) with Kodalith pan film.

1. Develop the film in Kodalith super developer for 2¾ minutes at 20 C (68 F) with continuous agitation.
2. Rinse in Kodak indicator stop bath for about 10 seconds.
3. Fix for 1 to 2 minutes in Kodak rapid fixer at 18.5 to 21 C (65 to 70 F). Agitate the film frequently in the fixing bath.
4. Wash about 10 minutes in running water.
5. Treat in Kodak Photo-Flo solution and hang to dry.

Retouching High-Contrast Films. Because of the extremely high contrast of Kodalith film, when it is exposed, nearly every speck of dust on the film causes a pinhole in the image. Keeping everything clean is a big help, but in spite of everything, most Kodalith images have some pinholes in them. To retouch pinholes, use a marker such as an Eberhard Faber Thinrite Marker 690 black, or Kodak opaque. The opaque comes in red or black, and either color works well. Stir the opaque and then take a small amount on the tip of a brush. Retouch the pinholes by spotting opaque on either the base or the emulsion side of the film.

Opaque can also be used to paint out large areas of a film to eliminate distracting backgrounds. Since the opaque acts as a mask, it is easy to eliminate any clear parts of the image simply by painting them over with opaque. To cover large areas, it may be easier to use a lithographer's tape, which is available

High-contrast film enables the photographer to alter, enhance, and recreate fairly ordinary photographs. Here, the photographer literally changed the direction of this gull in flight. In the original slide, the bird was flying out of the picture. After enlarging it on Kodalith film, the photographer rearranged the composition by cutting the negative apart and taping the gull in this position. Photo by Barbara Jean.

What appears to be a brilliantly executed shot is in reality a montage created with a color slide and Kodalith film. Birds or trees printed on this film can add a foreground or center of interest to sunsets and other scenes. Photo by Barbara Jean.

from graphic arts dealers. Apply the tape over any area that is to be masked out.

To remove density (black areas) from a Kodalith film, treat the area with a strong solution of Farmer's reducer. (*See:* REDUCTION.) This technique is not difficult unless there is an area that must be saved close to the area that is to be removed. Because reducer is a thin liquid and tends to run, it is harder to control than retouching with opaque.

To remove density with opaque, make a positive (or negative) from the original. Since the area to be removed was black on the original, it will be clear on the second film and easy to mask over with opaque. Then the retouched image must be printed onto another sheet of Kodalith film to get back to the original state.

If yellow processing stains appear on the films, they can be removed by immersing the film in a very dilute solution of Farmer's reducer. After the stain has disappeared, wash the film for at least 20 minutes and dry in the usual manner. Use of Kodak hypo clearing agent can reduce the washing time. (Processing stains can be a signal that the chemicals are exhausted. Replace them with fresh solutions.)

The real drama of this scene lies in its vivid colors and abstract beauty. This slide was made by photographing a Kodalith negative on Kodak Ektachrome-X film. Cyan and magenta gelatin filters were placed behind the boats (clear areas in the negative) to record them in different colors. Photo by Barbara Jean.

Uses for High-Contrast Films. Knowing how to produce good-quality high-contrast images is the basis for many of the techniques described in detail in other articles (see the list of cross references at the end of this article). Extremely high-contrast films open new horizons to the photographer. Here are some quick and easy ways to use high-contrast images.

Prints and Slides. It is obvious that you can use a high-contrast negative to make a print. If you print from a positive, you will get a negative print. Because high-contrast images are more graphic than realistic, it often does not matter whether you start with a negative or positive to produce a positive or negative print. In fact, after putting the image through several stages of duplication on Kodalith films, you may completely lose track of whether the image is negative or positive. It will not matter, as long as the final image is visually interesting.

Another way to use high-contrast films is for making slides. Make 4″ × 5″ images, and copy them, using transmitted light on color-slide film. (*See:* DUPLICATE SLIDES AND TRANSPARENCIES for copy methods.) Try different colored filters over the camera lens or cut up pieces of gelatin filters and place them behind the clear areas on the film to produce a multicolored image.

If you have contact-printed 35 mm slides or negatives onto high-contrast film, you can mount the piece of high-contrast film itself and use it as a slide. To add an overall color, mount a piece of gelatin filter material with the film. For the best results, bind high-contrast slides in glass. These slides tend to "pop" more during projection than conventional slides.

You can also add color directly to high-contrast film (and other films too) with water-soluble dyes, such as Kodak retouching colors and dyes made for photographic use. Vegetable food coloring may also produce interesting effects.

To apply one color over the whole film, simply dip the film in a solution of the dye. To add different colors to several areas on the film, use a cotton swab or a brush. The color can be applied to either the emulsion or the base of the film.

• *See also:* BAS-RELIEF; BLACK-AND-WHITE PRINTING; BRIGHTNESS RANGE; CONTRAST; DEVELOPMENT; DUPLICATE SLIDES AND TRANSPARENCIES; EXPOSURE TECHNIQUES; LITHO FILM; MASKING; POSTERIZATION; REDUCTION; RETOUCHING; SABATTIER EFFECT; SILK-SCREEN PROCESS; SPECIAL EFFECTS; TONE-LINE PROCESS.

High Key

A high-key photograph is one that is made up predominantly of light tones, from white to the light middle-gray tones, or of the high values (pastels, tints) of colors. This does not mean that a high-key photograph contains nothing but these lighter tones. For a high-key picture to be effective, there must be some accents or small amounts of dark colors or tones; if they are missing, the light tones seem less brilliant and their tonal separation may suffer.

It should be apparent that the opposite effect—a low-key photograph—is made up mainly of dark to middle tones, or low values (shades) of colors. And a "medium key" photograph contains an average distribution with about equal representation of the dark, middle, and light portions of the scale.

From this, it follows that to make a high-key photograph it is necessary to choose a subject accordingly. It is not possible to make a satisfactory negative of predominantly dark subject matter, nor to obtain a high-key print from a full-range negative

by using less print exposure or a high-contrast grade of paper. The result will only be a bad print.

To make a high-key portrait, for example, choose a blonde or light-skinned subject, make sure that he or she is dressed in light colors or white, and pose the subject in white or light-colored surroundings. Landscape subjects must similarly be predominantly light-toned—whitish sand, snow-covered hills, or fields of ripened grain, for instance.

Judging Exposure

Judging the exposure of high-key subject matter may present a problem. Because light tones or high-value colors reflect more light than the average subject, they will give a higher reading on a reflected-light exposure meter. If the meter indication is followed exactly, the result will be underexposure. The best solution is to use an incident-light meter, or to take a reflected-light reading from an 18 percent reflectance gray card held at the subject position. Giving the exposure indicated by such a reading will properly register the light tones on the film. A negative will seem to have more overall density than usual, but that is quite in keeping with the

Although light tones predominate in this carefully planned high-key photograph, the picture could not succeed without the dark accents throughout the scene: the dark lines of the background paneling, the shadows in and around the can, the black flecks in the flooring, the mouse's eye. The fleshy color of the animal's nose draws the viewer's eye immediately to the mouse. Photo by Dick Faust.

High Key

nature of the subject. Printing can then be done with normal exposure and development on a normal-contrast-grade paper. In a transparency, the light tones will appear light, which is the nature of high key.

Lighting

When the subject is illuminated by artificial light, especially in portrait situations, it is not enough to have a subject that is mostly light in tone. The lighting must be arranged accordingly, so that there are no deep shadows to destroy the high-key effect. The best method is to use mainly frontlighting to make shadows fall behind the subject where they will be hidden from the camera, and to diffuse the light or use soft, broad light sources such as those with umbrella reflectors. The background should be lighted by separate sources so that its brightness can be brought up to the same range as the subject. This also makes it possible to wash out any stray shadows from the subject lighting by directing background light onto them as required.

Outdoor subjects for high-key rendition are best photographed with light that is soft and diffused, such as that under bright, overcast skies. Direct sunlight is likely to produce deep shadows, while a dull day will result in a picture that is dark and gloomy.

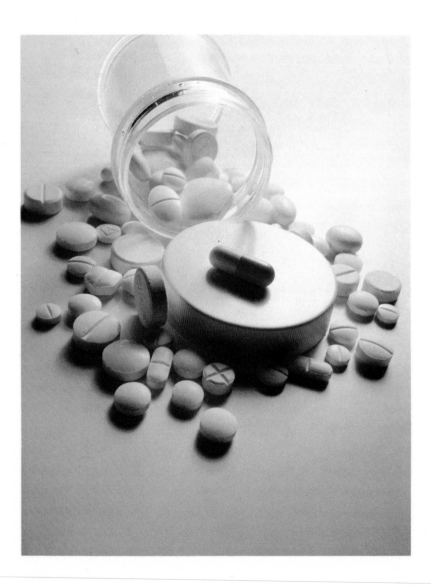

A single red-and-yellow capsule is the only note of color in this white-on-white composition. Distinction of shapes is accomplished by the lighting, which is diffuse enough not to be obtrusive, but strong enough to provide definition. Photo by Viles Studio Inc. for Editorial Photocolor Archives.

In a world teeming with bold, varied colors, this high-key area reflects the beauty found in nature's light-toned elements. The delicate dark lines of branches on snow create a pattern abstract in composition. Photo by Art Young.

Often bright, overcast skies are necessary to make an effective high-key picture, while heavy, overcast skies are required for a low-key picture.

Development of Negatives

Negative development is quite simple. Most high-key subjects, if properly exposed and lighted, require normal development, like any other negative. It is a mistake to underdevelop a high-key negative; this will flatten out local contrast between the light tones to an undesirable degree. Normal contrast, or even slightly high contrast, is needed to maintain tonal separation in the print. At the same time, it is essential to avoid blocking the highlights, which will occur if the negative is overdeveloped to any extent. Probably the best way to process high-

key negatives is to use a compensating developer, or a standard developer such as Kodak developer D-76, diluted 1:1, and to develop the negative fully.

Printing

Printing a high-key picture from a correctly made negative should present no problems. If the negative is normal, then normal exposure and development of the print will produce a picture that is generally light in tone, but in which there is tonal separation right up to the lightest areas, with the few dark accents appearing dark or even black. Actually, they will not be, or need to be, fully black; they will appear darker than they objectively are because of the contrast with the large areas of light tone. The important thing is to expose the print fully so that the lightest tone is just barely off-white. There should not be any blank, toneless areas of white paper within the image except for an occasional specular highlight. Then, if the dark parts are not black enough, try a higher-contrast paper; if on the other hand the middle tones are too dark, try a lower grade of paper.

The paper surface has some influence on the final effect. High-key pictures seldom look their best on a glossy-surface paper, nor on a dead matte surface. The best choice is a smooth surface with some sheen, such as that of a lustre-surface paper, or a very finely stippled surface with a high-lustre finish.
• *See also:* LANDSCAPE PHOTOGRAPHY; LIGHTING; LOW KEY; PORTRAITURE; SNOWFLAKE PHOTOGRAPHY.

High-Speed Photography

One of the most important advantages of motion pictures to a scientist or engineer is the ability to manipulate time. While recording data or action, the motion picture is doing it in relation to a time base —the time base created by the rate at which the film moves through the camera. A motion picture actually consists of a series of still pictures called frames, which are taken at regular intervals and which are subsequently viewed at the same, or at different, regular intervals. Time can be made to appear normal by taking the pictures at the same rate at which they are intended to be projected. To slow down time, the pictures are taken at a rate *faster* than the projection rate will be. Thus actions or movements that occur too quickly for the eye of a human observer to follow, can be slowed down so that all aspects of the action can be studied. Generally, high-speed films are made at rates above 100 frames per second.

(Right) An automobile crash test with an instrumented manikin, testing the actuation of an air-bag safety device. (Center) Selected sections of film showing the spark formation created by a spark plug. (Far right) Selected sections of film showing a stick of propellant which has been ignited by a wire to show its burning characteristics.

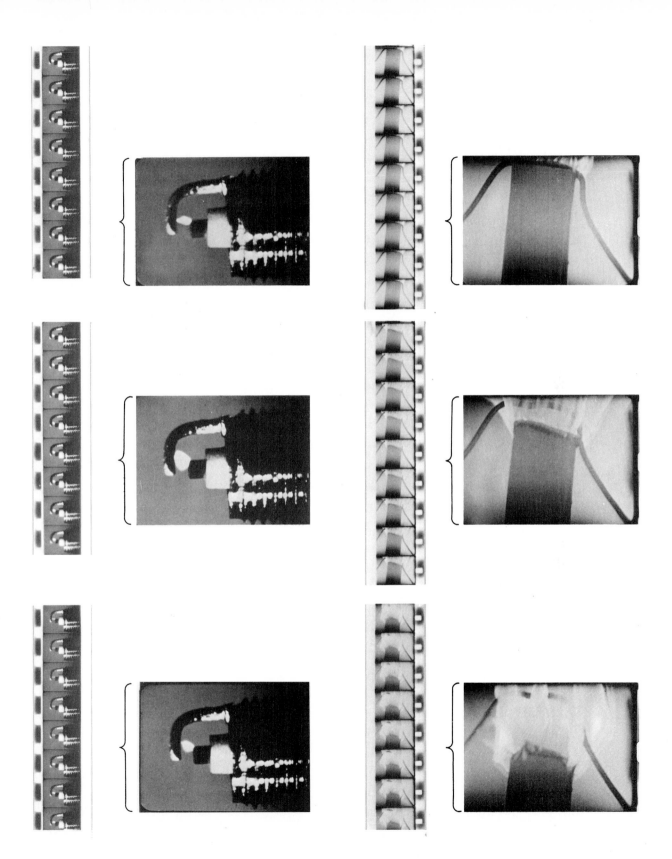

PICTURE FREQUENCY FOR MOTION

Event	Velocity (ft./sec.)	Picture Frequency (frames/sec.)
Man walking	3	16
Type hammer in an accounting machine	16	85
Recoil of an automatic machine gun	40	215
Automobile crash study	100	530
Peripheral speed of a circular saw	150	800
Sound waves in air	10^3	5.3×10^3
22-cal. high-velocity bullet	2.6×10^3	1.4×10^4
Crack forming in glass	5×10^3	2.7×10^4
Detonation front from an explosion	2.5×10^4	1.3×10^5

The accompanying table lists some events along with their average velocities and the picture frequency they require. As the data in the table show, high-speed photography is required for the study and analysis of much of the motion we experience in the world.

Slowing down an event by means of high-speed photography makes possible two methods of analysis in one filming. First, there is the important *subjective* analysis that is obtained when a scientist or engineer simply views the action on the screen. A basic understanding of the action or the problem is augmented by viewing the action in a time frame that is slowed down. This allows the viewer to see individual segments of the action in their relationship to each other. It is then possible to correct the basic understanding of the action or even form a new concept of it.

Second, the film can provide a means of quantitative analysis of the action if the proper steps were taken beforehand to make sure that such data could be obtained. Proper setup of the subject, proper recording of filming data, and, if necessary, the placement of measuring devices in the picture frame or the use of timing devices built into the high-speed camera can provide a wide range of very important measurements.

Many problems can eventually be solved by trial and error, but the use of high-speed photography can often reveal the problem, thereby saving many valuable work hours.

Time Magnification

Time magnification is the term used to describe the degree of "slowing down" of motion that appears on the screen when the film is viewed. Time magnification is defined as the ratio of the picture-taking frequency to the picture-projection frequency, or:

$$\text{Time Magnification} = \frac{\text{Camera Picture Frequency (frames/sec.)}}{\text{Projector Frequency (frames/sec.)}}$$

Normally, the human eye cannot resolve motion that occurs in less than ¼ second, so the application of this equation is important in obtaining some idea of how much the time of the natural action will be expanded. For example, a car traveling at 35 mph is crashed into a barrier in a safety test. The last 5 feet of its travel was photographed at 800 frames per second. What time magnification will occur if the film is projected at 16 frames per second?

$$\text{Time Magnification} = \frac{800}{16} = 50$$

Thus, the real time it takes for the vehicle to travel 5 feet will be magnified 50 times on the projection screen.

$$\text{Vehicle velocity} = 35 \text{ mph} = 35 \times 1.467$$
$$= 51.3 \text{ ft./sec.}$$
$$[1 \text{ mph} = 1.467 \text{ ft./sec.}]$$

$$\text{Time to travel 5 ft.} = \frac{5}{51.3} = 0.097 \text{ or about } 0.10 \text{ sec.}$$

$$\text{Time on the viewing screen} = 0.10 \times 50$$
$$= 5 \text{ sec.}$$

High-Speed Cameras

No single type of camera can satisfy all of the needs of scientists, photographers, or engineers in their quest to capture high-speed action on film. While a large percentage of high-speed studies are done at frame rates between 100 and 500 frames per

High-Speed Photography

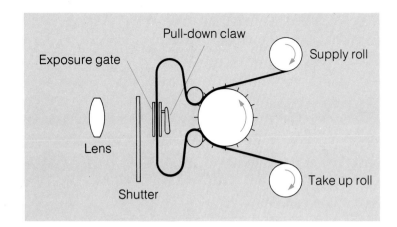

The mechanism of an intermittent pin-registered camera. The film is moved into the gate by the pull-down claw. The claw then retracts, and a pin inserts into one of the perforations to hold the film steady during exposure.

second, there are numerous others that require much higher frame rates.

Most high-speed photography is accomplished with one of four major types of cameras: intermittent pin-registered, rotating-prism, streak, and ultrahigh-speed cameras.

Intermittent Pin-Registered Cameras. An intermittent pin-registered camera uses essentially the same mechanism that a conventional motion-picture camera does. The film is moved into the exposure gate by a pull-down claw that inserts into one of the perforations at the edge of the film. When the film is in position, the pull-down claw retracts, and pins insert into the film perforations in order to hold it steady while the shutter opens to expose the film.

It is the constant stop-and-start (or intermittent) motion that necessitates the use of one or more pins to steady the film for exposure. This kind of mechanical operation does limit the framing rate. Intermittent pin-registered cameras usually operate up to 500 frames per second, although in some equipment the limit has been extended to 1000 frames per second.

Maximum quality and extremely high resolution can be expected from these cameras. They are available in super 8, 16 mm, 35 mm, and 70 mm versions. Super 8 cameras offer a reasonably low-cost approach to general-purpose, high-speed photography. However, although the image quality of super 8 is good, it is not comparable to that of 16 mm, and the maximum frame rate available in the super 8 format is 250 frames per second.

Advantages of the intermittent pin-registered camera are numerous. The image quality is unparalleled when compared with the images produced by rotary-prism cameras. Because of the lower film-transport speeds, the film is used up at a slower rate, allowing a longer recording period. Light-transmission efficiency is high because only the lens is in the image path. The prime disadvantage occurs when short exposure times such as 0.00001 second are used. Then the interval between exposures (about 0.00249 second) may become too long for fast-acting events. Important action may actually occur between frames, or the time magnification may not be great enough.

Rotating-Prism Cameras. In order to attain higher frame rates than are possible with intermittent cameras, the film in a rotating-prism camera is not stopped during exposure. A glass block, or prism, rotates between the camera lens and the film. Light from the subject passes through the prism and intermittently exposes the film. Even though the film and the prism are both moving at a constantly, but commonly, changing rate, this motion is synchronized so that the *relative* motion between the image and the film during the exposure phase is zero. This is accomplished through a mechanical connection between the film drive and the prism drive.

In some cameras, a rotary shutter is employed between the prism and the film plane. Various openings can be obtained with these shutters, and they provide a means of adjusting exposure time as well as more effectively terminating the passage of light

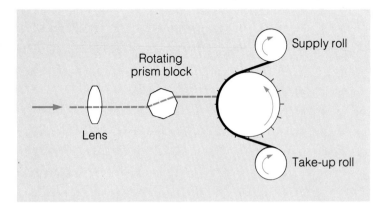

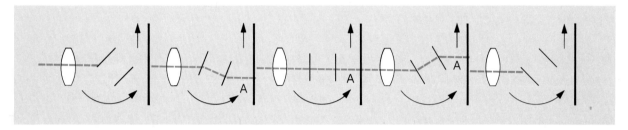

The mechanism of a rotating-prism camera. The film is not stopped during exposure. The rotating-prism block alternately blocks and passes light from the subject to the film. The prism block and the film are synchronized so that the relative motion between the image and film during the exposure is zero.

Only two sides of the rotating-prism block are shown in five successive positions to illustrate how light from the subject at point A is refracted and synchronized with the motion of the film.

to the film. The overall effect of the use of a shutter is an increase in resolution due to shorter exposure times and better definition of frame boundaries.

The advantages of rotating-prism cameras are the higher frame rates (up to 25,000 frames per second) and shorter exposure time, along with a shorter interval between exposures. An interesting feature of some rotating-prism cameras is that by removing the prism assembly and replacing it with a slit, the camera can be converted to streak operation.

Disadvantages of rotating-prism cameras include poorer resolution (30 to 80 lines per mm) than intermittent pin-registered cameras produce, along with short recording times due to the higher frame rates.

Streak Cameras. Intermittent pin-registered cameras and rotating-prism cameras are *framing cameras*. That is, they produce a series of sequential photographs or frames. A *streak camera* does not record discrete pictures of events. Instead, an uninterrupted slit-image is swept across the film. Such cameras are usually used to study self-luminous

events in linear motion. For these studies, they are unmatched by any other instrumentation in their capacity to provide extremely accurate velocity measurements of transient events.

Streak cameras can be divided into two major groups:

1. Moving-film cameras such as those in which a rotary-prism unit is replaced with a slit.
2. Spinning-drum and spinning-mirror cameras that employ a fixed length of film held stationary on the inside of a fixed track or a rotating drum.

Most of these latter types operate at extremely high rates, which classifies them as ultrahigh-speed cameras; they will be discussed in the following section.

In addition to measuring accuracy by means of spatial resolution (lines per mm), the measurement of time resolution is also made possible by use of a streak camera. Time resolution is defined as the minimum interval of time that can be distinguished in the time-displacement record. The time resolution of a framing camera is simply the time interval between two successive frames. With a streak camera, however, time resolution is dependent on the velocity of the film as it passes the slit, the width of the slit, and the resolving power of the film.

Ultrahigh-Speed Cameras. Normally ultrahigh-speed cameras do not produce motion pictures of the variety that are projected onto a screen by a projector. Rather, they are usually a number of sequential pictures or a streak record on a short length of film that may be only a few feet long.

Rotating-mirror and *rotating-drum* cameras operate in the range of about 20,000 pictures per second up to more than a million pictures per second.

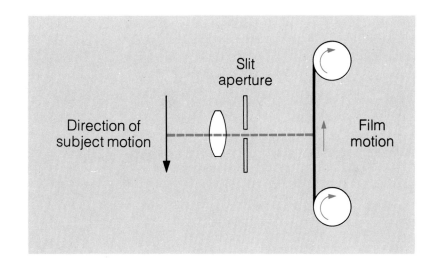

In a streak camera, an uninterrupted slit-image is swept across the film which is moving at a right angle to the motion of the subject. When the subject motion is in a direction opposite to the film motion, a "real" image of the subject is formed when the film velocity equals the image velocity. Such a technique is used in synchro-ballistic cameras to study ballistic projectiles.

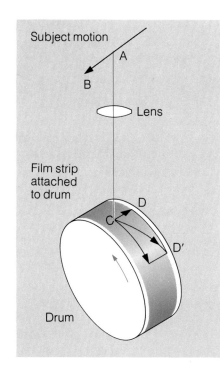

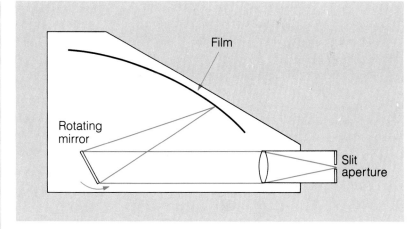

(Left) A simple diagram of a drum camera. As the subject moves from A to B, its image moves along the line CD. During this time, the drum and the film are moving and a trace will be drawn along the line CD'. (Right) A spinning mirror, operated by a gas-driven turbine, "wipes" the image of the subject onto a strip of film, which is held in a stationary position.

In a rotating-prism camera, the maximum speed is limited by the resistance to fracture or flexure of the moving parts. For example, the peripheral speed of the prism cannot be extended beyond its physical capacity, and the linear transport velocity of the film is limited by the strength of the film and the mechanical limits of the transport mechanism. In order to overcome these limitations, a spinning mirror made of a very high-strength material such as beryllium is driven by means of a turbine and compressed air. The image is swept over a piece of film that is fixed in place. In order to attain even higher speeds, the mirror chamber can be evacuated so that the friction of air can be eliminated; the turbine is sometimes driven by compressed helium, which is much lighter than air.

Rotating-mirror and rotating-drum cameras have the advantage that the spinning mirror or spinning drum can be brought up to speed and maintained at a constant rotation before the event begins. Thus, not only is a continuous time-displacement record obtained but the time scale is uniform throughout the record.

Image-converter cameras rely on the formation of an image on a photocathode that is electronically displayed on a larger fluorescent screen at the end of a tube. This amplified image is then photographed by a camera. In essence, these are really electronic cameras insofar as it is an electron beam that forms the useful image. Being an electronic device, the exposure can be controlled down to about 0.001 microsecond, and magnetic deflection of the electron beam makes it possible to move the picture on the screen so that several pictures may be obtained at extremely short durations and intervals. These devices make possible recording rates from 50,000 to 6 million pictures per second.

Image-converter cameras offer the advantages of high light amplification, which means that events of low brightness can be studied, using adjustable frame rates and interval spacing, and extremely high-speed exposures and picture frequencies.

Preparing for High-Speed Photography

Analyzing the Problem. There are several basic considerations in any high-speed photographic situation. Of primary importance to the photographer are the following:

1. *The "what and why" of the test.* Until the photographer knows what is going to occur and why it is to be studied, selection of the proper equipment to do the job cannot be made.
2. *What is the film intended or expected to reveal?* A careful analysis of the overall information that is needed for the project will give the photographer a better understanding of how photography can fulfill those needs.

It is a good practice to make the photographic recording as complete as possible on each job in order to obtain the maximum amount of data, regardless of how narrow the original data requirements may be. This is not being wasteful; there will then be data inherent in the film that can act as a safeguard against those times when the test does not perform as expected or when it becomes evident that unplanned-for data are required. In these cases, the cost of reshooting could possibly be avoided.

Since high-speed photography produces a visual analysis of actions that the unaided human eye cannot resolve timewise, it has a high degree of impact

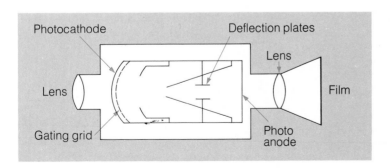

Diagram of an image-converter camera. When an image of the subject is formed on the photocathode, an electron beam forms an amplified image on the phosphorescent screen of the photoanode. This image is then recorded by the camera on the film.

on the casual observer. Modern-day advertising has made a great deal of use of this impact to display the features and benefits of products. This possible use of high-speed film footage can be of very great benefit and should not be overlooked. It is also a good idea to consider including normal-speed motion pictures of the test. This combined coverage provides a complete visual package of the test and is invaluable in explaining the problem and the solution to people who are unfamiliar with the situation.

Analyzing the Subject. In order to determine the number of cameras required to do the job, the proper placement of the camera or cameras, and the picture frequency that will be necessary, the photographer must know certain things about the particular subject.

What kind of motion is involved? Is it linear motion, rotary motion, or angular motion? After these answers are determined, the speed of the event, or of that portion of an event which is to be examined, must be estimated.

Next, what is the size of the field of view in which the subject will move? In addition, it may be valuable to determine what degree of resolution will be required within the field of view. The spatial resolution provided in the finished film is dependent on the resolution capabilities of the camera, the optics, and the film. A common equation that can be used to determine a rough idea is the following:

$$\frac{1}{R} = \frac{1}{r_1} + \frac{1}{r_2} + \frac{1}{r_3} + \cdots \cdots \frac{1}{r_n}$$

That is, the reciprocal of the total system resolution $(\frac{1}{R})$ is equal to the sum of the reciprocals of resolution of each component of the system.

For example, the camera to be used might have a resolution capability (r_1) of 100 lines per mm, the lens (r_2) = 250 lines per mm, and the film (r_3) = 100 lines per mm. The resulting resolution would be as follows:

$$\frac{1}{100} + \frac{1}{250} + \frac{1}{100} =$$

$$\frac{5}{500} + \frac{2}{500} + \frac{5}{500} =$$

$$\frac{12}{500} = \frac{6}{250} = 0.024 \text{ mm}$$

This would mean that two points in the film image would have to be at least 0.024 millimetre from each other to be discerned as two separate points.

Technical Considerations

Frame Rate. When a moving subject is photographed, the image of the subject moves across the film even during the brief duration of the exposure. This produces what is called *image blur.* The degree of blurring is dependent upon the velocity of the subject, the duration of the exposure, and the image magnification. In order to prevent blurring from being objectionable in the finished film, image blur is generally confined to a value of less than 0.002 inch. Image blur of a value greater than this becomes quite noticeable during visual analysis and may hamper making quantitative measurements from the film.

Probably the simplest form of motion to record with high-speed photography is linear motion. To determine the proper frame rate to use to record a subject in linear motion, using a 16 mm camera, and employing the image-blur limit of 0.002 inch, the following equation is used.

$$\text{Frame rate} = \frac{200 \text{ S Cos } \theta}{BW}$$

where:

S = subject velocity in inches per second.
W = field width in inches or the distance of subject movement, whichever is the shorter distance.
θ = the angle in degrees between the film plane and the direction of the subject's motion.
B = shutter ratio—the ratio of the open portion of the camera shutter to the total disc.
200 = constant used for a 16 mm camera.

If the camera is located at a right angle to the direction of motion, the film plane will be parallel to the direction of motion, θ will be 0, and the cosine of θ will be 1. For any other angle, refer to a trigonometric table to find the cosine.

As an example, use the problem outlined in the discussion on time magnification. An automobile is crashed into a barrier at 35 mph. The last 5 feet of the vehicle's travel is to be photographed. Using the equation on the previous page:

S = 35 mph or 616.1 in./sec.
$\theta = 0°$ (assuming that the film plane is parallel to the vehicle's motion). Cos $\theta = 1$.
B = 3 (assuming a camera-shutter ratio of 1:3, or a shutter opening of 120°).
W = 60 in.

then:

$$\text{Frame rate} = \frac{200 \times 616.1 \times 1}{3 \times 60} = 684.5$$

or, about 700 frames per second would be required for this action.

If this same type of linear motion is to be recorded using a 35 mm camera and a minimum image blur of 0.002 inch, the equation becomes:

$$\text{Frame rate} = \frac{500 \, S \, \text{Cos} \, \theta}{BW}$$

In this case, a constant of 500 is used for a 35 mm camera. The significance of this is that the shutter speed must be 2½ times faster than that of the 16 mm camera to produce the same results. This is offset, however, by the fact that for the same field coverage, the magnification is 2½ times greater. Further, if the 35 mm camera was moved farther away from the subject so that the magnification was the same as for the 16 mm camera, then the shutter speeds would be the same for both cameras.

High-speed photography of subjects in rotary motion such as gears, shafts, and wheels present a bit of a different problem when calculating the frame rate. In these cases, the velocity of the subject's motion must be its peripheral speed, which is based on the subject's diameter and the number of revolutions per minute. Many rotating subjects may produce a stroboscopic effect if the rotating part has regularly spaced lines, gear teeth, or spokes on its surface or end view. A frame rate greater than that expressed by the equation:

$$\text{Frame rate}_{(min)} = \tfrac{1}{20} \times \text{number of regularly spaced lines on the revolving part} \times \text{rpm}$$

will be needed to prevent this phenomenon.

For example, a rotating drum is to be photographed. It has 80 longitudinal ribs placed around its circumference and is rotating at 190 rpm. What minimum frame rate will be required to prevent a stroboscopic effect?

$$\text{Frame rate}_{(min)} = \frac{80 \times 190}{20} = 760 \text{ frames/sec.}$$

Since this is the minimum frame rate required, it would be best to use a frame rate of 800 to 850 frames per second.

Exposure Time. When the necessary frame rate has been determined, the resulting exposure time should be recorded. Exposure time is dependent on the frame rate and the shutter opening according to the equation:

$$\text{Exposure time/sec.} = \frac{\text{Shutter opening (in degrees)}}{360 \times \text{frames/sec.}}$$

One of the accompanying tables shows the exposure times that result from various shutter openings and frame rates.

Camera Running Time. Since high-speed photography depends upon moving film through the exposing plane of a camera very quickly, the length of time that can be covered by the photography can be quite limited. For instance, the figures in one of the accompanying tables show a range of running times for 16 mm film for various frame rates and roll lengths. These figures are based on 40 frames per foot of 16 mm film.

Camera Position. The position of the camera relative to the subject may, of course, be limited by the physical surroundings. While it would be desirable to position the camera at a right angle to a subject moving in a linear fashion, walls or other obstructions may prevent this. An experienced photographer is always ready to employ such things as mirrors or temporary camera mounts to accomplish desired objectives.

Basically, the camera should be positioned so that the image size on the film will be large enough to provide easy and accurate analysis. This is determined by the camera-to-subject distance and the focal length of the lens. A good camera position will yield a picture of the subject encompassing its full

EXPOSURE TIMES*

Shutter Opening (in Degrees)	48	64	72	100	200	300	400	500	600	700	800	900	1000
5	1/3456	1/4608	1/5184	1/7200	1/14400	1/21600	1/28800	1/36000	1/43200	1/50400	1/57600	1/64800	1/72000
10	1/1728	1/2304	1/2592	1/3600	1/7200	1/10800	1/14400	1/1800	1/21600	1/25200	1/28800	1/32400	1/36000
20	1/864	1/1152	1/1296	1/1800	1/3600	1/5400	1/7200	1/9000	1/10800	1/12600	1/14400	1/16200	1/18000
30	1/576	1/768	1/864	1/1200	1/2400	1/3600	1/4800	1/6000	1/7200	1/8400	1/9600	1/10800	1/12000
40	1/432	1/576	1/648	1/900	1/1800	1/2700	1/3600	1/4500	1/5400	1/6300	1/7200	1/8100	1/9000
50	1/345	1/461	1/518	1/720	1/1440	1/2160	1/2882	1/3600	1/4320	1/5040	1/5760	1/6480	1/7200
60	1/288	1/384	1/432	1/600	1/1200	1/1800	1/2400	1/3000	1/3600	1/4200	1/4800	1/5400	1/6000
70	1/247	1/329	1/370	1/514	1/1028	1/1543	1/2060	1/2570	1/3086	1/3600	1/4114	1/4629	1/5143
80	1/216	1/288	1/324	1/450	1/900	1/1350	1/1800	1/2250	1/2700	1/3150	1/3600	1/4050	1/4500
90	1/192	1/256	1/288	1/400	1/800	1/1200	1/1600	1/2000	1/2400	1/2800	1/3200	1/3600	1/4000
100	1/173	1/230	1/259	1/360	1/720	1/1080	1/1440	1/1800	1/2160	1/2520	1/2880	1/3240	1/3600
110	1/157	1/209	1/235	1/327	1/654	1/982	1/1310	1/1600	1/1964	1/2291	1/2618	1/2945	1/3273
120	1/144	1/192	1/216	1/300	1/600	1/900	1/1200	1/1500	1/1800	1/2100	1/2400	1/2700	1/3000
130	1/133	1/177	1/200	1/277	1/554	1/831	1/1130	1/1390	1/1662	1/1938	1/2215	1/2492	1/2769
140	1/123	1/164	1/185	1/257	1/514	1/771	1/1030	1/1285	1/1542	1/1800	1/2057	1/2314	1/2571
150	1/116	1/154	1/173	1/240	1/480	1/720	1/960	1/1200	1/1440	1/1680	1/1920	1/2160	1/2400
160	1/108	1/144	1/162	1/225	1/450	1/675	1/900	1/1125	1/1350	1/1575	1/1800	1/2025	1/2250
170	1/102	1/135	1/152	1/212	1/425	1/635	1/850	1/1060	1/1271	1/1482	1/1694	1/1906	1/2118
180	1/96	1/128	1/144	1/200	1/400	1/600	1/800	1/1000	1/1200	1/1400	1/1600	1/1800	1/2000
190	1/91	1/121	1/136	1/190	1/380	1/568	1/760	1/950	1/1137	1/1326	1/1516	1/1705	1/1895
200	1/86	1/115	1/130	1/180	1/360	1/540	1/720	1/900	1/1080	1/1260	1/1440	1/1620	1/1800
210	1/82	1/110	1/124	1/172	1/340	1/514	1/690	1/860	1/1029	1/1200	1/1372	1/1543	1/1714
220	1/78	1/105	1/118	1/164	1/328	1/491	1/655	1/820	1/982	1/1145	1/1309	1/1472	1/1636
230	1/75	1/100	1/113	1/157	1/312	1/470	1/635	1/780	1/939	1/1096	1/1252	1/1409	1/1565
240	1/72	1/96	1/108	1/150	1/300	1/450	1/600	1/750	1/900	1/1050	1/1200	1/1350	1/1500
250	1/71	1/92	1/104	1/144	1/288	1/432	1/576	1/720	1/864	1/1008	1/1152	1/1296	1/1440
260	1/66	1/89	1/100	1/138	1/276	1/415	1/555	1/692	1/831	1/969	1/1108	1/1246	1/1385
270	1/64	1/85	1/96	1/133	1/266	1/400	1/535	1/667	1/800	1/933	1/1067	1/1200	1/1333

*Based on 40 frames per foot of 16 mm film.

RUNNING TIMES FOR 16 MM FILMS (IN SECONDS)

Frames per Second	Length of Film Roll (in Feet)								
	100	125	200	250	400	450	500	1000	1200
48	84	104	168	208	330	375	420	834	996
64	62	78	126	156	252	281	312	624	750
72	56	69	111	139	222	250	278	556	667
100	40	50	80	100	160	180	200	400	480
200	20	25	40	50	78	90	102	198	240
300	13	17	27	33	53	60	67	133	160
400	10	13	20	25	40	45	50	102	120
500	8	10	16	20	32	36	40	78	96
1000	4	5	8	10	16	18	20	40	48
2000	2	3	4	5	8	9	10	20	24
3000	1.3	1.7	2.7	3.3	5.3	6	6.7	13.3	16
4000	1	1.3	2	2.5	4	4.5	5	10	12
5000	.8	1	1.6	2	3.2	3.6	4	.8	9.6

motion, or that part of its motion that must be studied. If a gear train on a machine is to be studied, the gear train, not the whole machine, should fill the camera view.

Care should be taken to protect the camera from sprays, flying sparks or particles, or any other products of the environment in which the camera is being operated. It may be necessary to build a camera enclosure with a piece of clear glass or plastic to protect the lens.

Rigidity of the camera mount is also very important to the usefulness of the final film. The mount or tripod must be substantial enough to support the camera without vibration or movement.

Time Measurement. The measurement of motion using high-speed photography is of little value unless the time spectrum within which the motion occurred is known. The most common method of recording a time base on a photographic film is by the use of a small timing lamp built into the high-speed camera. This lamp is positioned so that its image is recorded on the film. It is flashed at a constant, known rate so that the spacing between the flashes on the film is inversely proportional to the lamp's flashing rate and directly proportional to the rate of film travel past the lamp.

For example, if the distance between two flashes on the film equals two inches, and the lamp was flashing at a rate of 100 flashes per second, then the film's rate of travel was equal to $2 \div \frac{1}{100} = 200$ inches per second.

In some cases, the electronic driving circuit for these lamps is built into the camera. For other cameras, a *timing light generator* is an accessory item that supplies the signal voltage for producing the timing marks. Usually, three frequencies of timing marks are available: 10, 100, and 1000 pulses per second.

The location of the timing lamp within the camera may place a timing mark on the film quite a number of frames from the frame actually in the exposure gate at the instant the mark is made. This displacement is caused by mechanical and space limitations within the camera. This is a very important point; if the camera changes speed during the time between the exposure of the timing mark and the exposure of the image alongside the work, the marks will not represent a true timing reference. Once a camera reaches its peak speed, this variation

may not be important. However, it is vital to use the correct timing offset for the camera being used. This requirement does not exist with rotating-drum and rotating-mirror cameras because the rotating elements provide a highly accurate and constant speed of recording.

The displacement of the timing marks from the subject frame, once determined for a particular camera, is easy to apply in all data reduction operations. In some industrial studies, however, film that has been exposed in a wide variety of cameras may have to be analyzed. In this case, it is important that the timing-mark displacements be known beforehand for each camera used.

Recent developments of data blocks, which can produce a digital or binary display of data on the film at the exposure aperture, have simplified the problem of data reduction. Many of these blocks use light-emitting diodes (LED) or fiber optics to enable these displays to be used in areas of very limited space.

It is important that timing displays be used at all times even though there is no predetermined need for this type of data. Subsequent problems or questions may arise after the test is over that may require this information.

Recording Data. In order to obtain useful data or measurements from the finished film, it is important to record all the pertinent data involved in the test so that they are available during the analysis operation. Of the greatest importance are a description and measurements of the subject, and a sketch showing the camera or cameras and the lights in relation to the subject. On the next page is a list of important parameters that should be recorded. It is a simple matter to arrange these items into a worksheet that can be duplicated and used when a large amount of high-speed work is contemplated.

Lighting. Whether sunlight is being used in outdoor photography, or artificial light is being employed in the studio or in some other location, high-speed photography demands a great degree of care because exposure times can range from thousandths of a second to millionths of a second.

As in portrait photography, the control of light and shadow areas of the subject are important to produce the most natural and revealing representation on film. While it is true that in most cases the ultimate aim of a high-speed film is a technical

```
Date
Subject
Description of the problem

        Motion
Linear: Velocity
Rotational: R.P.M.
          Diameter of subject
          Divisions in subject
Vibrational: Frequency
          Amplitude

     Camera information
Camera used
Field width
Distance (camera to subject)
Angle of camera to subject
Frame rate
Exposure
Time magnification
Lens used
Timing light frequency
Type of illumination

      Film information
Film used
Roll length
No. of rolls
```

analysis and not an aesthetic display, it should be remembered that good lighting techniques result in the best images for analysis. The main lighting problem that is faced by the high-speed photographer is the high level of illumination that is required. In some cases, because of space limitations or available power for lighting, the photographer may be forced to use techniques that produce deep shadows.

Photoflash. A special type of photoflash lamp used for high-speed photography is represented by the Sylvania FF-33. This lamp is designed to provide a high level of light output over a relatively long period of time. These bulbs are usually used in a reflector and, at a distance of 12 to 18 inches from the subject, will illuminate an area about 1 to 2 square feet. One lamp will expose 37 feet of film when the camera is operated at 1000 frames per second. When slower camera speeds are used or when longer film lengths are required, several lamps can be fired in a sequence of 1.75 seconds. To do this, a sequence timing device is required. The advantages of photoflash are low total heat radiation, low voltage (4.5 to 45 volts), and constant color temperature independent of power-line variations.

Xenon Flash. This type of light source, or "electronic flash," produces a brief, but very intense flash of light caused by ionization of the gas contained in the tube. Xenon gas is preferred for the flashtube because of its high efficiency of conversion of electrical energy into light. In addition, the spectral distribution of the light produced approximates that of daylight.

Laser. In recent years, the laser has been found to be a useful light source in some applications in high-speed photography. High-density lighting of small areas is possible and hundreds of millions of watts per square centimetre can be obtained. Although the coherent nature of this light source may not be essential in many applications, it does provide the ultimate degree of control in aiming and focusing the light precisely on the subject area being photographed in some situations.

Use of Exposure Meters. A conventional exposure meter, such as the type used for still photography or normal-speed movie photography, has limited usefulness for high-speed photography because of the very short exposure times usually encountered. This means that readings from conventional meters have to be extrapolated. In addition, most films will exhibit some reciprocity failure at the extremely short exposure times encountered in high-speed photography. That is, although a meter reading can be extrapolated to mathematically equivalent exposure settings at very high speeds, the film will not respond in an equivalent manner; more exposure will be required for proper results than the calculations indicate. (*See:* RECIPROCITY EFFECT.)

The surest way to determine accurate exposure is to make a series of tests at various lens apertures and with various levels of illumination, at operating speed. Such tests are also valuable for checking the placement and balance of the illumination.

Films for High-Speed Photography

Both black-and-white and color films are used for high-speed photography. Film selection depends not only on the requirements of the job itself, but also on a number of characteristics of the films.

A common mistake is the selection of the fastest films possible to use on all jobs. In some cases, a slower-speed film may have adequate speed for the exposures involved, and in addition, its graininess and resolving-power characteristics will produce a better quality picture.

Color and Black-and-White Films. For most studies, black-and-white film is the most satisfactory choice. It is economical to use and duplicate, and special lighting conditions are not always necessary with it. However, color film is the logical choice if color is an important characteristic of the subject, or if the film is to be used for public presentation or for other uses where good appearance and quality are important.

Retrieval time is faster for black-and-white films if users process the film themselves, and black-and-white film processing is easily accomplished. Most color films, however, must be processed by commercial color-processing laboratories, due to the cost and the complexity of processing equipment for color motion-picture film.

Black-and-White Negative and Reversal Films. Of all the black-and-white films available for high-speed photography, reversal films are the most widely used. This is due to their fine-grain characteristics, and the economy and convenience of using the same film that was used in the camera as the projection film for analysis. In addition, the positive images obtained with reversal films maintain the same brightness relationships that are seen in the subject itself.

Reversal films are not without shortcomings, particularly when used in high-speed photography. These films usually have a shorter exposure latitude than most negative films. This means that the film is less forgiving when the exposure is not correct. Reversal films also are usually slower in speed than negative films. Both of these characteristics can pose problems because, in many cases, sufficient lighting is a difficulty.

The convenience of reversal films should not overshadow the consideration of negative films for many high-speed photographic applications. Negative-film processing is easier and less critical than reversal processing. Shorter processing time can be important in situations where the quickest access possible to the film data is required. Even though most people are unaccustomed to viewing negative films, it is possible to become quickly accustomed to viewing and analyzing a film in this form. After the analysis is made using the negative film, a positive copy can be made for more conventional viewing if necessary.

Negative films can also be push-processed so that higher effective speed ratings can be used. When lighting conditions do not permit normal exposure, it is often possible to obtain acceptable quality by underexposing by 1 stop and then push-processing the film by increasing the recommended development time by 50 percent. This is only a general rule, however, because the limit for push-processing varies according to the film/developer combination and the contrast of the scene. The quality of push-processed films will not be as good as that of pictures exposed and processed in the recommended manner. They will have increased contrast and graininess overall, and some shadow detail may be lost. However, the overall quality is usually acceptable.

Another advantage of negative films occurs when a film is underexposed. Underexposed areas in a reversal film may be too dense in the final film for the projection light to penetrate. Hence, detail is lost at the viewing screen. Underexposed image areas on a negative film, however, are low in density, and projection illumination is not a problem.

Physical Properties of Films. It is common to select a film for a given purpose according to its photographic characteristics: speed, spectral sensitivity, contrast, resolving power, granularity, and related properties. In high-speed photography, a film is subjected to great physical stresses at the very high transport speeds required in the camera. In addition, high-speed photography is often carried out in extreme environmental conditions of heat, cold, or humidity. For these reasons, the physical characteristics of a film—and especially of the base material—are extremely important.

In addition to not tearing, cracking, or breaking, a film must have dimensional stability. If the spacing between frames, sprocket holes, or timing marks changes because of expansion or contraction due to temperature, humidity, or processing, it may be impossible to derive accurate information from the film.

Film bases are of two major types: Cellulose triacetate combined with solvents, a plasticizer, and stabilizers; and polyester plastic. In most high-speed applications, films with a polyester base, such as Kodak Estar base, are superior in their major physical characteristics. These characteristics include degrees of dimensional stability, thermal expansion, humidity expansion, processing dimensional changes, aging shrinkage, tear strength, and brittleness.

The following are *Kodak* films for high-speed photography:

Kodak RAR film 2495 (*Estar-AH* base)
Kodak RAR film 2498 (*Estar-AH* base)
Kodak RAR film 5498
Kodak RAR film 2479 (*Estar-AH* base)
Kodak Linagraph Shellburst film 2476 (*Estar-AH* base)
Kodak pan film 2484 (*Estar-AH* base)
Kodak recording film 2475 (*Estar-AH* base)
Kodak high speed recording film 2485 (*Estar-AH* base)
Kodak Tri-X reversal film 7278 (16 mm)
Kodak 4-X reversal film 7277 (16 mm)
Kodak Ektachrome EF film (daylight) 5241 (35 mm) and 7241 (16 mm)
Kodak Ektachrome EF film 2241 (*Estar* base) 16 mm and 35 mm
Kodak Ektachrome EF film (tungsten) 5242 (35 mm) and 7242 (16 mm)
Kodak Ektachrome MS film 5256 (35 mm) and 7256 (16 mm)
Kodak Ektachrome MS film 2256 (*Estar* base) 16 mm

Film Perforations and Pitches. A vitally important physical characteristic of a motion-picture film is the kind and pitch of its perforations. There are four major types of perforations. The Bell and Howell and the Kodak standard perforations are the most common, but those developed by Dubray-Howell and Cinemascope are used by some equipment. The distance between perforations is called the pitch. Films may have perforations along one or both edges.

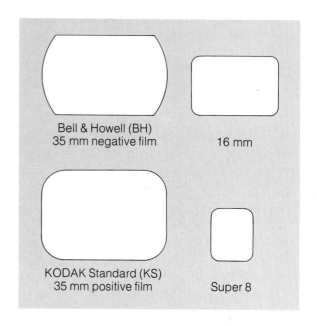

Comparative size and shape of standard film perforations.

Location and alignment of film perforations. (A) Film width; (B) pitch: distance from bottom edge of one perforation to bottom of the next; (E) distance from outside edge of perforation to film edge; (F) width between opposing perforations, maximum possible frame width; (G) skew: maximum permissible offset between opposing perforations.
NOTE: Film specifications are given as 1R (perforated one edge) or 2R (perforated two edges), followed by pitch in decimaliinches, for example, 2R–2994.

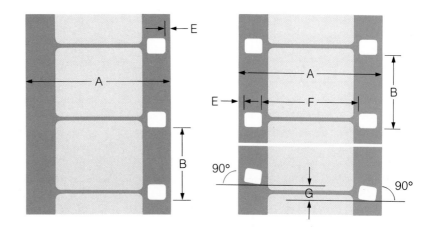

It is essential to use film with the correct perforation type and pitch. Otherwise the film will not travel at a uniform speed and will not seat securely in the exposure gate of the camera or optical printer. The almost sure result is damage or destruction of the film, jamming, and damage to the equipment. High-speed cameras require film with high-speed perforation pitch. The diagrams on the preceding page illustrate the major factors in perforation types, pitch, and alignment. The camera instruction book should indicate what kind of films must be used. The specifications for individual films are given in their data sheets, or are available from the manufacturer.

Analyzing the Film

A high-speed film is made in order to analyze an event. Two types of analysis—qualitative and quantitative—are possible. A film may be designed only to provide a visual or qualitative view of the action, or it may be designed to provide accurate measurements of the action in a quantitative manner.

Visual analysis of a film can usually be accomplished by simply projecting the film onto a screen before the person or persons doing the analysis. If 16 mm film is used, a stop-motion projector is very helpful. This type of projector is capable of projection rates from 1 to 24 frames per second. It can also be stopped to project a single frame. The projector must be designed so that there is no loss of brightness on the screen, while at the same time the film is protected from blistering or burning up in the projection gate by the high-output projection lamp. Another very handy feature of these projectors is a digital frame counter that allows the analyzer to know exactly where a particular frame is in a film roll; it is also necessary to determine the time frame of the action.

Streak-camera records are normally analyzed directly from the original negative, or they are enlarged on a viewer for more accurate measurements. One form of measurement made from a streak record is a quantitative measurement of optical density as a function of image distance. This type of measurement is usually made with a recording microdensitometer, which consists of a traveling-stage microscope that is focused on the film sample and projects its image onto a slit aperture. The slit image is read by a phototube and the result is plotted by a chart recorder. In this way, the film image can be scanned to determine the variation of optical density in reference to the distance between points of the image.

Quantitative analysis of film designed to provide data on subject size, shape, location, and orientation is accomplished on film readers. These are instruments that consist of a viewing screen upon which the film is projected in combination with a flying spot or movable cross hairs visible on the screen. The spot or cross hairs are positioned at a particular place on the image of the subject; their relative movement from frame to frame quantitizes the image position and either displays it visually, or provides punched cards or some other output suitable for computer processing.

Determining the type of data reduction equipment needed or the extent of the investment that will be required depends upon an analysis of the volume of data reduction that will be carried on, the type of analysis that will be required, and the quality or the accuracy of the data that is needed.

• *See also:* Cathode-Ray Tube Recording; Electron Imaging; Laser; Motion Study; Oscillograph Recording; Reciprocity Effect; Schlieren Photography; Scientific Photography; Time-Lapse Photography.

High-Temperature Processing

Certain photographic materials are intended to be processed at temperatures well above the common recommendation of 20 C (68 F). For example, most modern color materials and some black-and-white products are designed to be processed at a nominal 38 C (100 F). The high temperature reduces total processing time and causes various chemical reactions to take place with maximum efficiency. Automatic machines in processing laboratories often use high temperatures to achieve high-speed operation.

However, unless specially protected, gelatin emulsions will swell excessively and become extremely soft in high-temperature solutions. In that condition, the gelatin is highly susceptible to damage, even when handled in a way that would be virtually troublefree at a lower temperature. In addition, processing times may be so short that they

ADDITION OF SODIUM SULFATE TO DEVELOPER SOLUTIONS

| Kodak Developers | Range of Temperatures | | Sodium Sulfate (Anhydrous) Per Litre |
	Celsius	Fahrenheit	
D-11, D-19 D-61a, D-76	24 to 26.5	75 to 80	50 g
	26.5 to 29.5	80 to 85	75 g
	29.5 to 32*	85 to 90*	100 g
DK-50 DK-60a	24 to 26.5	75 to 80	100 g
	26.5 to 29.5	80 to 85	125 g
	29.5 to 32*	85 to 90*	150 g

*If necessary to develop at 32 to 35 C (90 to 95 F), decrease the time by about one-third.

cannot be precisely controlled, resulting in uneven and excessive development, and overfixing.

When black-and-white films not designed for high-temperature processing must be processed at a high temperature—for example, in hot weather or in tropical climates—the following procedures should be used.

Whenever possible, the temperature of the processing solutions should be held at 18.5 to 24 C (65 to 75 F). When this is not practical, special precautions must be taken to avoid excessive swelling and softening.

At higher temperatures, the use of Kodak prehardener SH-5 (or the equivalent) before development will harden the emulsion sufficiently to allow use of normal solutions and processing procedure, even at temperatures as high as 43 C (110 F). Full instructions for use, including adjustment of developing time for various temperatures, are given with the formula in the article HARDENING BATHS.

The use of the prehardener is the simplest and safest procedure for processing at high temperatures. When the prehardener is not available, however, the addition of sodium sulfate to the developer solution will permit operation at temperatures up to 32 or 35 C (90 or 95 F). Addition of the quantities of sodium sulfate shown in the accompanying table will maintain approximately normal developing times at the higher temperatures. In using any of these developers, it is necessary to observe the following precautions:

1. Developer, stop bath, fixing bath, and wash water must be at the same temperature to within approximately 2.5 C (5 F) of each other.

2. After development, the film should be treated in a freshly prepared hardening rinse bath, such as Kodak hardening bath SB-4. (*See:* HARDENING BATHS.) The film should be agitated for several seconds when first immersed in the stop bath, and then left for 3 minutes.
3. The film should be fixed in a fresh acid hardening fixing bath, such as Kodak rapid fixer (2 minutes) or Kodak fixing bath F-5 (5 minutes).
4. The film should be washed for 10 to 15 minutes in running water or in several changes of water. Longer washing may cause trouble.

• *See also:* FIXERS AND FIXING; FORMULAS FOR BLACK-AND-WHITE PROCESSING; HARDENING BATHS; RAPID PROCESSING.

History of Photography

Photography is a technological invention that has become the most universal means of communication and artistic expression that the world has known. It overcomes the barrier of language difference. It can be specific and realistic, where music and related media can only be general or abstract. In the form of motion pictures and television, it can far outshine theater in the variety, precision, and complexity of the subjects it presents. As a medium of visual art, it has at least as wide a range of unique expressive capabilities as painting, etching and engraving, and the other hand arts. As a tool of scientific investigation, it has unequalled precision in making visual records of phenomena beyond the perception of the human senses.

The history of photography is a matter of technical growth and of simultaneous communicative growth; both aspects are discussed here to some extent. These accounts are supplemented and amplified by a great number of other articles, as indicated in the text and the list of cross references at the end of this article. A complete list of references relating to this topic will be found under HISTORY OF PHOTOGRAPHY in the *Index to the Encyclopedia of Practical Photography.*

Background to the Invention of Photography

As with most technological inventions of the eighteenth and nineteenth centuries, the necessary preliminary discoveries and advances had been completed long before photography itself was invented. When accumulated knowledge finally coincided with a cultural readiness, and even an unconscious social expectation—in the first quarter of the nineteenth century—photography was an idea whose time had come. As a result, it was invented or reinvented almost simultaneously by several people working more or less independently in a number of European locations. Of these people, only a few made contributions from which truly workable processes evolved; they are rightly considered to be the true inventors of the medium.

Equipment. By 1700, the camera as it was first to be used in photography was already in existence:

Fig. 383.

It was the *camera obscura,* a box fitted with a focusing lens and a mirror that reflected images onto drawing paper laid over a glass surface in the top. Artists used the camera obscura to make drawings quickly with accurate perspective and scale. (*See:* CAMERAS.)

Chemicals. Between 1725 and 1777 the light sensitivity of silver-nitrate and silver-chloride solutions had been discovered and investigated to some degree. Thus, roughly half a century before its invention, the equipment and chemicals necessary for photography were in existence.

Early Experiments. The first known experiments in obtaining images with light-sensitive materials were carried out in England in about 1800 by Thomas Wedgwood and Humphry Davy. They obtained silhouettes of the type today called photograms by placing an opaque object such as a shell or a leaf on paper or white leather sensitized with silver-nitrate solution and exposing it to sunlight. They also obtained images projected by a solar (sun-illuminated) microscope on such materials. However, none of this work was permanent, for they lacked the knowledge to fix an image by removing the unexposed light-sensitive compounds once the image was formed. Their work could be viewed only by candlelight to limit additional exposure; the images soon disappeared as the previously unaffected portions accumulated exposure and darkened from repeated viewings.

True Photography. The invention of true photography—the permanent recording of images formed by a lens in a camera—was accomplished by three men: Joseph Nicéphore Niépce, Louis Jacques Mandé Daguerre, and William Henry Fox Talbot.

Technical Evolution of Photography

The following chronology summarizes the major technical developments in the invention and growth of photography.

1816, France. Niépce obtains camera images on paper sensitized with silver-chloride solution;

In the camera obscura, *the image formed by the lens and reflected by the mirror on the ground glass is traced on drawing paper laid over the glass. Reproduction courtesy International Museum of Photography, Rochester, N.Y.*

however, the fixation is only partial. Niépce regards the results as "imperfect, failures" because they are reversed in tonality (negatives). (*See:* NIÉPCE, JOSEPH NICÉPHORE.)

Early 1820's, France. Niépce produces "heliographic drawings"—contact-print images of engravings or other line copy on glass, paper, or metal coated with a bitumen varnish that hardens when exposed.

1826, France. Niépce achieves the first permanent photograph in a camera, on a pewter plate coated with light gray bitumen. After an 8-hour exposure, a direct-positive image results when oil of lavender dissolves away unexposed, unhardened bitumen to let the dark metal plate represent shadows. Various amounts of hardened bitumen remain to form highlights and middle tones.

1829, France. Niépce uses silver plates in place of pewter, and devises a way to remove bitumen from highlights after darkening shadow areas with iodine, to produce an image entirely in silver. Daguerre forms a partnership with Niépce to perfect this invention. (*See:* DAGUERRE, LOUIS JACQUES MANDÉ.)

1833, France. Niépce dies; Daguerre takes over actual experimentation.

1835, England. W.H.F. Talbot obtains negative images on silver-chloride paper by long "printing out" exposures in a camera obscura; they are imperfectly fixed. (*See:* TALBOT, WILLIAM HENRY FOX.)

1835, France. Daguerre discovers that mercury fumes will develop an invisible (latent) image on a silver plate that is sensitized with iodine fumes before exposure.

1839, England. Talbot points out the basis of modern photography: A negative on suitable material (such as paper) can be used to produce as many positive copies as desired by contact printing. Sir John F. W. Herschel coins the word "photography" (suggests "negative" and "positive" in the following year), and points out that images can be made permanent by dissolving away unexposed silver compounds with a solution of hyposulfite of soda ("hypo" or sodium thiosulfate), which he had discovered in 1819. (*See:* HERSCHEL, SIR JOHN.)

1839, France. On August 19, "Daguerreotype," the first practical photographic process, is given to the world. Exposures are uncomfortably long for portraiture, but images are made permanent by the use of hypo. The precision of details and exquisite beauty of these direct-positive images on silver plates make the daguerreotype an immediate world-wide success, although the complex procedures and cost put it beyond the reach of most people. (*See:* DAGUERREOTYPE.)

1840, England. Talbot discovers a method of developing paper-negative images that greatly reduces the exposure required in the camera. (*See:* PAPER NEGATIVE.)

1840, U.S. J. W. Draper is one of the first to produce photographic portraits using a lens with a diameter of five inches and a focus of seven inches. (*See:* DRAPER, JOHN WILLIAM.)

1840, Austria-Hungary. J. M. Petzval designs the first lens specifically for photographic use; its maximum aperture of $f/3.6$ makes possible portrait exposures of less than one minute, launching the most widespread use of the daguerreotype. (*See:* PETZVAL, JOSEF.) The lens is produced the following year by Voigtlander for use in the first all-metal, unitized camera. (*See:* CAMERAS; VOIGTLANDER, PETER WILHELM FRIEDRICH.)

1841, England. Talbot patents the calotype process, later called the Talbotype. Negatives on paper sensitized with silver iodide, silver nitrate, and gallic acid are developed in gallic acid; positives are made by printing out contact exposure on similarly sensitized paper. Use of the process is greatly restricted by its inferior tonality and resolving power (as compared to the daguerreotype) and by Talbot's stringent patent enforcement and expensive licensing requirements. (*See:* CALOTYPE.)

Major achievements with the paper-negative process are made in 1843–1848 by Hill and Adamson (see the section on Portraiture in this article), and by various photographers on the Continent, beyond the reach of Talbot's legal agents.

1842, England. Herschel invents the ferroprussiate (blueprint, cyanotype) process. (*See:* BLUEPRINT PROCESS; CYANOTYPE.)

1848, France. Abel Niépce de Saint-Victor perfects the use of albumen to hold light-sensitive compounds on a glass plate to make negatives on an absolutely smooth and transparent material—the two major qualities lacking in a paper negative. (*See:* ALBUMEN.)

1850, France. L. D. Blanquart-Evrard invents albumen printing paper to retain the delicate tonality and high resolution obtainable with glass-plate negatives.

Gustav Le Gray invents the waxed paper process, which treats paper (to make it nearly transparent) before sensitizing and exposure, rather than after as is the common practice.

1851, England. F. S. Archer publishes a method of using collodion in place of albumen for negatives on glass. It comes to be called the "wet plate" or "wet collodion" process because the plate must be coated, sensitized, exposed, and processed before the collodion dries to a tough, waterproof, transparent sheet (far superior in handling qualities to albumen) that can even be stripped from the glass to form a flexible, plastic negative; typical working time is a maximum of 20 minutes under normal conditions. (*See:* ARCHER, FREDERICK SCOTT; COLLODION; WET COLLODION PROCESS.)

A variation of the process produces positive-appearing images called ambrotypes, in which the glass-plate negative is backed with black material. (*See:* AMBROTYPE.)

Talbot demonstrates the possibility of flash photography, using an intense electric-spark discharge to get a sharp image of a moving subject; the apparatus that is required is not suitable for practical application.

1852, U.S. Collodion direct positives—like ambrotypes, but produced on dark metal—are introduced as ferrotypes; they are commonly called tintypes because of the thin metal base material. (*See:* FERROTYPE; TINTYPE.)

1853, England. J. B. Dancer makes the first model of a twin-lens camera for stereo photography, working from designs suggested in 1849 by Sir David Brewster; production begins in 1856. (*See:* BREWSTER, SIR DAVID; STEREO PHOTOGRAPHY.)

1858, France. Nadar takes the first aerial photographs over Paris from a free balloon. (*See:* NADAR.)

1861, Scotland. James Clerk Maxwell publishes research in color perception and the three-color separation of light. His work builds on that of Thomas Young who, in 1801, had explained the production of colors by interference and diffraction in ruled gratings and thin films, and had proposed a three-color theory of vision. (*See:* DIFFRACTION; MAXWELL, JAMES CLERK; VISION; YOUNG, THOMAS.)

Maxwell demonstrates additive color synthesis, using hand-colored materials in lantern slide projectors; photographic materials of the day cannot be used for color photography because their sensitivity is limited to the blue region of the spectrum. (*See:* ADDITIVE COLOR SYNTHESIS.)

1862, U.S. Reversal process to obtain positive images is first demonstrated by bleaching out the negative, and then exposing and developing previously unused halides in emulsion.

1865, U.S. Building on a demonstration of photography by the light of burning magnesium in 1859, by Roscoe and Bunsen, William White suggests the use of a stream of magnesium powder constantly igniting in a gas flame to form a continuous high-intensity artificial light source. The idea is finally commercially exploited in 1883 with the introduction of flash powder.

1868, France. Ducos du Hauron publishes methods for both additive and subtractive color synthesis of images by photography, and suggests the use of a three-color monopack plate; he demonstrates some results obtained by diffraction and interference effects. (*See:* SUBTRACTIVE COLOR SYNTHESIS.)

1871, England. Richard Leach Maddox invents the first truly practical dry-plate negative process, using gelatin in place of collodion to bind silver halides to glass plates. (*See:* GELATIN; MADDOX, RICHARD LEACH.)

1872, U.S. Eadweard James Muybridge makes the first attempts to photographically analyze a horse's gallop, for Leland Stanford. Results are imperfect because collodion wet plates do not permit short enough exposures. He resumes motion study for Stanford in 1877 and achieves excellent results in the next two years, using a battery of cameras to make sequence photographs on gelatin dry plates. (*See:* MOTION STUDY; MUYBRIDGE, EADWEARD JAMES.)

1873, Germany. Professor H. W. Vogel discovers the use of dye substances to extend the sensitivity of photographic emulsions from the blue into the green region of the spectrum, making possible orthochromatic plates (meaning "correct color," although they are still red-blind). (*See:* VOGEL, HERMANN WILHELM.)

1875, England. Leon Warnerke invents a roll holder for use with studio and field (view) cameras; a roll of sensitized paper provides for up to 100 exposures. (*See:* WARNERKE, LEON.) The idea does not catch on, however, until the introduction of the Eastman-Walker roll holder in 1885, in the U.S. This contains a device for automatically marking each exposure, and maintains tension on the film to keep it flat in the exposure plane. (*See:* EASTMAN, GEORGE.)

1876, England. Commercial manufacture of gelatin dry plates begins.

1879, U.S. E. J. Muybridge invents the zoopraxiscope to project continuous movement from photographic images. Lantern slides (positives) of a motion-study sequence are mounted around the circumference of a circular glass plate; this setup is coupled with a revolving shutter and a projector to throw intermittent images on a screen at a rate at which the human eye can blend the images into a continuous flow. (*See:* ZOOPRAXISCOPE.)

1880, England. Sir William Abney discovers the use of hydroquinone as a developing agent. (*See:* ABNEY, SIR WILLIAM DE WIVELESLIE.)

1882, France. Etienne Marey begins chronophotography to record stages in the flow of movement by recording successive images on a single plate at constant rates of 12 per second and faster. (*See:* MAREY, ETIENNE JULES.)

1882, England. Sir William Abney produces silver-chloride gelatin emulsion for printing-out paper; it takes more than ten years for this and similar materials to supplant albumen paper.

1884, U.S. Eastman negative paper is introduced; it consists of a light-sensitive emulsion or paper which, after development, is made transparent enough for printing by treating it with hot castor oil. (*See:* EASTMAN, GEORGE.)

1888, U.S. John Carbutt begins manufacture of celluloid-base sheet film.

The Eastman Dry Plate and Film Company introduces the number one *Kodak* camera, the first self-contained roll-film camera. It is small enough (6½″ × 3½″ × 3½″) to be hand-held, and is easy to operate: A fixed-focus (3½ feet to infinity) lens, single stop, and single speed (about 1/40 sec.) produce 100 exposures, 2½ inches in diameter without the need for technical skill. This simplicity, coupled with the developing and printing service offered by the manufacturer, ushers in the era of amateur photography on a mass scale.

1889, U.S. The first commercial transparent roll film, perfected by Eastman and his research chemist, is put on the market. Using a flexible base of cellulose nitrate, the film is coated on glass-topped tables 200 feet long. The availability of this flexible film makes possible the development and achievement (1891) of Thomas Edison's motion-picture camera and projector.

1890, England. Hurter and Driffield publish the results of 20 years of research into the response of photographic materials; their methods of measuring density and graphing the results in a characteristic curve lay the foundations for the fields of photometry and sensitometry. (*See:* CHARACTERISTIC CURVE; DENSITOMETRY; DRIFFIELD, VERO CHARLES; HURTER, FERDINAND; SENSITOMETRY.)

1891, U.S. Metol and Glycin are first used as developing agents. (*See:* GLYCIN; METOL.)

Thomas Edison produces motion pictures on a continuous length of Eastman celluloid film in his Kinetoscope camera and projector. (*See:* EDISON, THOMAS ALVA.)

1892, U.S. Frederick E. Ives invents a camera to take three-color separation negatives, and a Photochromoscope viewer that optically combines single or stereo color-separation positives to produce full-color images. The process is patented in 1894

1907, France. A Lumiere color process, the Autochrome plate, becomes the first commercially manufactured practical color process in photography; it is an additive process using a panchromatic emulsion coated over a layer of red, green, and blue dyed starch grains on a glass plate. (*See:* LUMIERE COLOR PROCESS.)

1910, France. Dioptichrome color materials are produced, based on patents of Louis Dufay. Later products based on similar principles include Dufaycolor. (*See:* DUFAYCOLOR.)

1912, Germany. Friedrich Deckel invents the Compur shutter, which uses gears to control slow speeds and a clockwork movement to control fast speeds. It is a great improvement over his Compound shutter of 1902, which was the first to use a series of overlapping leaves to open and close the path through the lens aperture. (*See:* DECKEL, FRIEDRICH.)

1914, U.S. Eastman Kodak Company introduces a two-color subtractive process called Kodachrome; it is dropped after a few years, but the name is used again, 21 years later, for a three-color process based on different principles.

1921, U.S. Radio transmission of photographs is demonstrated; the method is eventually used as widely as phototelegraphy ("wirephoto"), invented in 1904. The first major use of such methods is by photo agencies such as Underwood & Underwood, the initiators of a news-picture service in New York, in 1896.

1923, U.S. Amateur movie-making becomes possible with the introduction of 16 mm reversal black-and-white film, by Eastman Kodak Company.

1924, Germany. E. Leitz begins production of the Leica camera, designed by Oskar Barnack. Although not the first to use 35 mm film, it succeeds in establishing a new kind of photography, and in introducing the "system" concept in which the capabilities of a basic camera body are greatly extended by a group of coordinated attachments and accessories. (*See:* BARNACK, OSKAR.)

and later manufactured as the Kromscop. (*See:* IVES, FREDERICK EUGENE.)

1893, Ireland. John Joly invents the additive color process using regular line screen, checkered with red, green, and blue squares. The screen is placed in contact with the plate in the camera for exposure, and then bound in register with the developed plate. (*See:* LINE SCREEN SYSTEMS.)

1895, Germany. W. K. Roentgen discovers X-rays, and devises methods for recording their effects on photographic emulsions: radiography. (*See:* RADIOGRAPHY; X-RAYS.)

1898, U.S. Reverend Hannibal Goodwin is granted a patent covering roll film composed of a silver-bromide gelatin emulsion on a celluloid base.

1900, France. Auguste and Louis Lumière invent the Photorama, which takes and projects 360-degree panoramic photographs. (*See:* LUMIÉRE, LOUIS.)

1901, France. Cellulose acetate is invented; its nonflammable properties promote its adoption as a safety base for still films. Flammable cellulose nitrate continues to be used for motion-picture films as late as 1951.

1904, Germany. B. Homolka and E. König, who had studied with H. W. Vogel, invent dye sensitizers that extend emulsion sensitivity into the yellow and red regions of the spectrum.

Wratten and Wainwright begin commercial production of panchromatic ("all-color") plates two years later in England.

1927, U.S. A full-length film, "The Jazz Singer," is a Vitaphone production with synchronized sound on disc. Later the Bell Labs/Fox-Movietone process produces integral sound on film.

1928, Germany. Modern twin-lens roll-film reflex camera, the Rolleiflex, is introduced by Francke & Heidecke.

1928, U.S. Eastman Kodak Company introduces two new motion-picture films—Cine-Kodak 16 mm panchromatic film for amateur use and Kodacolor film, which is an additive three-color film with a lenticular system. (*See:* LENTICULAR SYSTEMS.)

1929, Germany. J. Ostermeier produces the first commercially acceptable self-contained flash-bulb: aluminum foil sealed in an oxygen-filled bulb.

1932, U.S. The first photoelectric exposure meter is produced by Weston Electric Instrument Company.

1934, Holland. The first wire-filled flashbulb is introduced by Philips.

1935, U.S. A gas-discharge tube emitting white light is introduced for electronic flash photography. (*See:* ELECTRONIC FLASH.)

Mannes and Godowsky, working with the staff of the Kodak Research Laboratory, invent Kodachrome film. It is the first successful three-layer, monopack subtractive color film; it uses dye-forming compounds that are introduced during the separate development of the reversal image in each layer. Appearing first as a 16 mm movie film, it is supplied in 135-size in 1936. (*See:* GODOWSKY, LEOPOLD, JR.; MANNES, LEO.)

1936, Germany. Agfacolor reversal film is introduced; it is the first three-color monopack film in which subtractive dye-formers are incorporated in each emulsion layer.

1939, Germany. Negative-positive subtractive color cine materials are developed using Agfa tripack emulsions; they are first used for a full-length feature in 1941.

1939, Germany. A. Rott and E. Weyde independently develop diffusion transfer processing of negative images; Rott establishes the principles of diffusion transfer reversal processing in 1942. (*See:* DIFFUSION TRANSFER PROCESS.)

1940, U.S. and England. Multiple-contrast black-and-white printing paper is introduced in the U.S. by Defender Photo Supply, and in England by Ilford, Ltd.; the effective contrast grade of the paper is changed by using filters over the printing light.

1942, U.S. Kodacolor negative film is introduced.

1942, England. A new developing agent, Phenidone, is patented by Ilford; it is similar to Metol, but much more active, and makes possible a new class —P-Q (Phenidone-hydroquinone)—of developers.

1943, U.S. Reversal print material, Ansco Printon, for making color prints from slides or transparencies, is introduced for user processing.

1945, U.S. Films with incorporated color couplers, developed during World War II, are available to the public: first Anscocolor film in 1945, then Ektachrome film in 1946.

1946, U. S. Kodak dye transfer process is introduced; it is a commercial process that represents the culmination of various printing methods utilizing dyed or pigmented bichromate-gelatin emulsion that hardens on exposure and development in a tanning developer. The first such processes were a three-color method by du Hauron in 1869, and carbon printing, invented by J. W. Swan in 1864. (*See:* CARBON AND CARBRO PRINTING; DYE TRANSFER PROCESS; TANNING DEVELOPER.)

1947, U.S. Edwin H. Land introduces Polaroid "one-step photography" with a self-processing black-and-white film that yields a positive print by the diffusion transfer reversal method. (*See:* LAND, EDWIN H.)

1950, U.S. Color couplers for self-masking color correction are introduced in Kodak color negative films.

1950, U.S. The first modern wide-screen motion pictures are produced using an anamorphic system, which optically squeezes the 2.1:1 image so it can be recorded on a standard 2:3 35 mm motion-picture frame, and restores it to full width upon projection. (*See:* ANAMORPHIC SYSTEMS.)

1955, U.S. Kodak Tri-X (ASA 200) and Royal-X pan (ASA 650) films, and Kodak Ektacolor paper for prints from color negatives, are introduced.

1960, U.S. The laser is invented, making possible holography by the principles developed in 1947 by Dennis Gabor. (*See:* HOLOGRAPHY; LASER.)

1960, U.S. A self-processing color-print material, based on the Polaroid diffusion transfer system, is demonstrated; it is marketed as Polacolor film in 1963.

1963, U.S. A modern dye destruction, or silver-dye bleach, reversal color-print material—Cibachrome—is introduced in both professional and home-processing versions. (*See:* DYE DESTRUCTION COLOR PROCESS.)

1963, U.S. The loading of film in still cameras is greatly simplified with the production of a film cartridge made with a built-in, prethreaded take-up spool, and a family of Kodak Instamatic® cameras is designed especially to hold this cartridge. The camera is loaded by simply dropping the cartridge into the back of the camera.

1972, U.S. Polaroid Corporation demonstrates a new camera and film as the SX-70 system; the camera is a unique single-lens reflex design and the film is an integral diffusion transfer material that produces a full-color print without any peel-away, discardable component.

1976, U.S. Kodak instant print film PR10 is introduced.

1978, U.S. Polavision self-processing color movie film is marketed; it combines a self-processing diffusion transfer emulsion with an integral additive-color line screen.

The Growth of Photography as a Medium of Expression

There have been two major lines of development in the use of photography to communicate information and express feelings or reactions; these are generally distinguished as the *straight* and the *pictorial* approaches or styles.

Straight Photography. This style prizes the straightforward, unmanipulated use of the medium; it concentrates on letting the subject speak for itself, in its own terms. Thus, the emphasis is on those methods and techniques that add to the sense of reality—and, by implication, the literal truth—of the image.

Filtration, burning-in, dodging, and similar techniques are acceptable when used to clarify the actual appearance and qualities of the subject. Filters that change color arbitrarily, matte or textured-surface papers, soft focus, optical distortion, and other "expressive" devices that direct attention away from the subject and toward the methods or qualities of the photographic medium are avoided. The aim is to present the subject, not to interpret it, nor to express the photographer's feelings or reactions to the "mood" or other subjective qualities. In essence, the photographer works to produce an image in which he is completely anonymous and the subject is able to communicate for itself, about itself, in the most effective way.

Pictorial Photography. This style is concerned first with the visual beauty of the image made of a subject, rather than the beauty (or other inherent aspects) of the subject itself. It concentrates on the way the medium is used to make an interpretation of the subject, and essentially asks the viewer to pay attention to and admire "the picture" rather than "the subject." This approach draws upon all the expressive techniques of the medium in order to find ways to present the photographer's subjective reaction to the subject, or his interpretation of it. To the degree that technique itself becomes an expressive element in the picture, attention is directed to the photographer's skill and taste in *making* rather than *taking* a picture.

The kinds of photography that embody the straight approach include: amateur snapshots, record and informational pictures, news reportage and photojournalism, documentary photography, realistic illustration, and realistic "art" photography. The pictorial approach underlies "high art" photography, advertising and editorial illustration of the interpretive and dramatic type, abstract pictures, and design and decorative photography.

A Matter of Choice. Any kind of subject matter can be photographed with either a straight or a pictorial approach. For example, a building can be photographed to show the details and character of its materials and construction, or to emphasize the expressive drama of its design. A portrait can be an identification card picture, or a head-on candid view; or it can use soft focus, carefully arranged lighting, costumes, props and settings, retouching, and other devices to glamorize or idealize the subject. The determining factor is the intent and style of the photographer, not the nature of the subject or the medium. The straight and pictorial approaches have grown side-by-side through a large part of the history of photography, and are equally represented in the masterpieces of the medium. The following summaries can touch only some high points.

The Natural Scene. Photography began in 1839 with the straightforward recording of the world. At first, only fixed subjects in bright sun could be photographed, which meant landscapes and architecture; the technical limitations of the medium eliminated the possibility of manipulating the results for expressive effect. It was apparent from the beginning, however, that interpretation was not necessary, the reality of the world was far more fascinating. Outstanding early photographs include those of Maxime du Camp who made paper negatives in the Middle East in 1849–1851 for the folio *Egypt, Nubia, Palestine and Syria,* published by Blanquart-Evrard. During the 1850's, Henri Le Secq made outstanding paper-negative views of French cathedrals and monuments for the same publisher. In the 1860's, the Bisson Frères made magnificent, large wet-plate photographs in the Alps, many of which were used in presentation albums for European royalty.

In the 1870's, a number of photographers accompanied government geological and mapping ex-

Fascination with the exotic pervaded all aspects of European art in the mid-19th century. Maxime du Camp's calotype negative of the Colossus of Abu Simbel, Egypt, was taken for the folio Egypt, Nubia, Palestine and Syria, *published in Paris in 1852. Photo courtesy International Museum of Photography, Rochester, N.Y.*

peditions or worked for the expanding railroads in the American West. Timothy H. O'Sullivan and William Henry Jackson produced pictures that far surpassed those of most of their contemporaries. Jackson's photographs of the Yellowstone Valley helped move Congress to designate it the first National Park in the United States. Carlton E. Watkins and Eadweard Muybridge were both known for the beauty of their large-format views of the California landscape, as well as stereographic views of the West.

In the first half of the twentieth century, the work of two men marked the topmost achievement in photographing nature: Edward Weston and Ansel Adams. Weston's work ranged from close-up studies of vegetables, shells, and other natural forms, to broad views of dunes and the sea coast; in all of his pictures there is a concern with the sense of life in organic form, and absolute clarity and reality in every textural detail. Adams' masterpieces are sweeping views of the grandeur of the valleys and mountains of the American West. These photographs are unmatched examples of the straightforward use of photography to achieve maximum pictorial effect.

Others who have achieved significant results in this area include Eliot Porter, who has mastered large-format color photography of nature, and Bradford Washburn and William Garnett, whose aerial photographs have a clarity and beauty that often borders on the abstract.

Reporting. Every straightforward photograph is a direct report on its subject. But the use of photographs to record events of a newsworthy character effectively dates back to 1855, when English photographer Roger Fenton outfitted a wet-plate darkroom van to photograph the prolonged war in the Crimea. This was not news photography by any strict definition, for the pictures were not even printed for several months while Fenton was recuperating from illness contracted during a year in the Crimea. However, this project marks the first significant use of photography to document a major event.

A decade later, photographers in the field units of the Mathew Brady organization were providing a steady flow of photographs of the American Civil War that were immediately copied by wood engraving for publication in periodicals. Brady's most notable photographers were T. H. O'Sullivan, James and Alexander Gardner, and George Barnard. Al-

Alexander Gardner's albumen print, "Home of a Rebel Sharpshooter," Gettysburg, Pa., 1863, appeared in his Sketchbook of the Civil War. *Gardner was working with a field unit of Mathew Brady's organization when this photograph was made. Photo courtesy International Museum of Photography, Rochester, N.Y.*

Henry Peach Robinson's staged composition, "Fading Away," is a composite print made from several negatives. The heavy bathos of this scene is typical of Victorian taste at its most sentimental. This is one of two versions, both made in 1858. Photo courtesy International Museum of Photography, Rochester, N.Y.

though it was still not possible to take action pictures, the work of the Brady photographers for the first time showed the world the destruction and devastation of war with a reality that was almost too much to bear. It is a grim achievement that has been repeated by photography in each succeeding war.

The direct reproduction of photographs became possible in the 1880's, with the invention of the halftone process. But it was not until World War I that news photography grew significantly. In the period from 1915 to 1940, photojournalism was born and came to maturity. It stemmed largely from the work of Erich Salomon, who excelled at getting pictures of "closed" diplomatic sessions and business conferences, and André Kertész, whose pictures revealed that the stream of everyday activities of ordinary people was full of visual moments that summed up the quality of their lives. In the 1930's and after, Brassai and Henri Cartier-Bresson were the very next generation of this same tradition.

In the 1940's, the tradition of war reporting was maintained most brilliantly by Robert Capa, David Seymour (Chim), W. Eugene Smith, and David Douglas Duncan. The role of the hard-pushing domestic newspaper reporter was epitomized in the work of Arthur Fellig—Weegee—in New York.

The growth of television from 1948 onward caused the death of photojournalistic magazines and greatly reduced the number of newspapers throughout the world. Today, papers use more and better photographs than ever before, but the work of individual photographers receives less notice, perhaps because papers are no longer the primary source of the news.

Documentary photography is a major area that parallels reportage and photojournalism; often the distinction between documentary and news photography is impossible to make. The growth of this field, and the work of such people as Eugene Atget, August Sander, Jacob Riis, Lewis Hine, Dorothea Lange, and many others, is discussed in the article DOCUMENTARY PHOTOGRAPHY.

Pictorial Art Photography. From its first year, photography was used to take studies and reference pictures of landscapes, architecture, and posed models from which painters and sculptors could work. From its third or fourth year, various attempts at illustration were made—usually staged scenes from stories in the Bible. But the real beginnings of the art movement in photography came in the late 1850's, and the aim was to make photographs like paintings.

Two images mark the beginnings of pictorial photography: "The Two Ways of Life" by Oscar Rejlander (1857) and "Fading Away" by Henry Peach Robinson (1858). Both were created by preplanning a composition and assembling individual elements in what was thought to be the way artists achieved paintings. The finished pictures drew their themes, their compositions, and their styles from the tenets of established, middle-of-the-road painting.

History of Photography

Robert Demachy's gum-bichromate print "Struggle" (c. 1900), is representative of the exquisite delicacy afforded by that process. Photo reproduced courtesy of Aperture, Inc.

The aim was to show that photographs could be art, and the mistaken assumption was that they would be art if they were made by the principles of established visual art—which was painting.

The example set by these two pictures—which met with a high degree of approval—was copied by hundreds, and eventually thousands of others. The pictorial movement grew rapidly, in part because it was a fertile field for imitators whose work unfortu- nately tended to obscure that of some genuinely cre- ative photographers. The growth was spurred by H. P. Robinson's *Pictorial Effect In Photography* (1869), perhaps one of the most misleading books on photography because it led the uninformed to be- lieve that there were definite rules for selecting the theme and subject of a picture, and for arranging the composition of the picture elements. The implica- tion was that if these rules were mastered, the picture would be a work of art. This belief flourished because the "artistic" segment of any medium is largely composed of casual followers.

The assumption that painting could define what visual art should be, caused photographers to develop more and more ways to make their images appear to be paintings. From cut-and-paste montage work and multiple printing, they progressed to a variety of techniques that enabled them to make the final print look like an etching, engraving, pastel drawing, lithograph, or some other product—anything but a photograph. This concern with technique led to an overemphasis on surface appearance, with a consequent lack of attention to meaningful subject matter. The result was that a few safe or sure-fire subjects came to be repeated so often that they became clichés: country lanes, an old person holding a newborn child, sailboats at anchor, a cottage in the snow, and so on.

Two printing methods were especially prized by pictorialists because of the exquisite results that were possible—the gum-bichromate process, and the platinum print or platinotype. And it was with these processes that the true masters of pictorialism achieved their best results at the turn of the century. In France, Robert Demachy and Emile Puyo produced gum-bichromate images that have never been equalled for delicacy and subtlety of effect. In the United States, Clarence White, Gertrude Kasebier, Edward Steichen, and a few others created pictorial masterworks. Their photographs are characterized by a sensitivity in the use of technique that makes even the most familiar subject matter seem to be newly interpreted in a meaningful way.

Unfortunately, the first peak of pictorialism was soon obscured by an ever-rising flood of imitations. The original masterpieces were soon submerged by hackneyed variations; clichés came to dominate the standards of camera clubs and exhibitions, and pictorialism lapsed into a decadence that was submerged by the socially concerned photography of the 1930's and 1940's. Its agonies were seen in the pictures of William Mortensen.

As with any medium, the problem was not with the mode of expression, but with those attempting to use it. This is borne out by the revival of the pictorial approach—though not specifically identified as such —in the 1960's and 1970's. After two generations in which photojournalism and documentary photogra-

phy were dominant, a new group of young photographers began to re-explore the interpretive uses of photography.

The combination images of Jerry N. Uelsmann are directly in the tradition of Robinson and Rejlander, as he acknowledges with good humor in a double-exposed self-portrait. The austere surrealism of the images of Ralph Gibson follow a new pictorial path first marked by Bill Brandt after 1945. The territory of psychic and spiritual fantasy is explored in the pictures of Les Krims and Arthur Tress and the narrative sequences of Duane Michals. Emmet Gowin has stayed on the realistic side of the surrealistic borderline, while Ralph Eugene Meatyard and Frederic Sommer have plunged across. Bea Nettles and Betty Hahn have rediscovered the gum-bichromate process and the assembled image. There is an energy and diversity and a freshness of subject matter that mark this new wave of pictorialism. It is the first new exploration of the potentials of the medium in 50 years.

Abstract Photography. In the first several decades of its growth, pictorial photography was largely undermined by the attempt—conscious or, much of the time, unconscious—to imitate painting. But, interestingly, some of the first truly original images within the pictorial tradition arose from the influence of a major, even revolutionary, change in painting: abstraction.

The abstract style may take one characteristic of a subject and make that the major aspect of the image, or it may do away with recognizable subject matter to deal only with expressive qualities inherent in the medium.

Some examples of the first type of abstract photography are:

1. Silhouettes, in which only the overall shape of the elements is clearly stated, without details of texture or internal contour;
2. The tone-line process, which emphasizes the expressive quality of the subject edge as a free-standing line rather than the border of a shape area;
3. Extreme high contrast, in which only black and white (or solid color and no color) are used, without intervening modulations of tone;

History of Photography

4. Extreme close-ups or fragmentary views, which make the end of a broken matchstick look like a mountain peak, or the curve of part of a painted letter a dramatic sweep of color or tone;

5. Views so distant that a sandy plain becomes a shimmering sea, and a sunny, forested hillside becomes an undulation of feathery velvet.

Abstract pictures that do not represent actual objects are commonly called non-representational or non-objective. They deal with the flow and interaction of sheer form unrelated to object shapes and with changing tones or colors. They are most often created by photographing with such a high degree of distortion that recognizability is lost, by photographing moving subjects or light sources, by exposing photo materials to light without using a camera, and by interrupting processing procedures or modifying solution formulas so that accidental chemical reactions produce visible effects in the emulsion.

Although it is possible to look back at photographs produced before about 1915 and discover qualities that appear abstract to the eye, or even totally abstract images, that is a matter of imposing something on the pictures that was not intended; the abstraction comes from the viewer, not the photographer. Purposeful abstraction in photography began about 1916. Early attempts included photograms—images of objects placed on film or paper that was then exposed to light. Christian Schad, one of the founders of the Dada movement in art in Zurich, used torn bits of paper and other flat materials to produce "Schadographs." Man Ray used three-dimensional objects and translucent materials to produce "Rayographs."

The first non-objective images made with a camera were the "Vortographs" of Alvin Langdon Coburn, in 1917. Coburn argued that black-and-white photography was nothing but abstraction—what seemed real in a representational photograph was nothing more than essentially arbitrary shapes of black, white, and gray tones on the paper. Yet, such patterns could move people to true emotional response. That being the case, it should be possible to move them to respond by the power of the shapes and tones alone, without reference to recognizable objects in the image. To explore this idea, he arranged three mirrors in a kind of triangular tunnel which, when placed over the camera lens, broke up the subject into hundreds of fragments with no coherent arrangement. A kaleidoscopic pattern resulted, which might be as repetitive as the motif in a tiled floor, or as free-flowing as the elements of a Cubist painting, a style that had only recently been developed in the work of Georges Braque and Pablo Picasso.

Francis Bruguiere produced a large number of images of light patterns thrown on cut-paper sculptures of non-objective shapes, in the 1920's and 1930's, as well as multiple prints with fantasy or surreal subject elements, and images with reversed tonalities. Some of the most graceful and lyrical images, which were produced by a moving light source directly exposing a film or print paper, were created

Francis Bruguiere's "Cut-Paper Abstraction" (1927) shows images of light patterns cast on nonrepresentational cut-paper sculpture. Photo courtesy International Museum of Photography, Rochester, N.Y.

"Abstraction, Bowls, Connecticut" (1915), by Paul Strand, is one of the photographer's best-known realistic abstractions. Photo reproduced courtesy of Aperture, Inc.

by Lotte Jacobi. The creation of expressive qualities by the manipulation of processing procedures and solutions has been raised to new levels in the work of Todd Walker.

Laszlo Moholy-Nagy explored the photogram, photomontage, and collage with his design students first at the Bauhaus in Germany, and later at the New Bauhaus in Chicago. Semi-abstract photomontages with a political or propaganda purpose

were created in the 1920's and 1930's by John Heartfield, often in combination with graphic elements added by the painter George Grosz.

"Realistic abstraction" in which recognizable subject matter was interpreted or presented in an abstract manner grew in parallel with the examples already given. Paul Strand's pattern images of Wall Street shadows and workers, and of a white fence, a house, and a barn, in 1915 and 1916, mark the begin-

Peter Henry Emerson's "Gathering Waterlilies" expresses the photographer's belief that only real subjects could generate beautiful photographs. Photo reproduced courtesy of Aperture, Inc.

ning of this growth. So too, do his close-ups of a stack of kitchen bowls, and the shadows of a porch railing on an upturned table. Although Strand was to turn to completely non-abstract straight photography, the direction of his early work was followed by many others. Some of the most interesting pictures in this vein have occurred in the work of Aaron Siskind and, more closely tied to reality, that of Harry Callahan.

An area that bridges between abstraction and more conventional pictorial photography is made up of images that try to explore the world of dreams, psychological fantasy, mythology, and fictional reality or surreality. The successful wedding of surrealistic themes and modes of expression begins most fruitfully in the work of Bill Brandt in the late 1940's and early 1950's. His nude studies, done with high-key tonal simplification and wide-angle distortion that turn the subject into sculptures like those of Brancusi or Arp, are a unique and important body of work in abstract photography of the 1960's. They are very much in the tradition of liquid forms photographed in distorting mirrors by André Kertész, in the 1920's.

Among contemporary photographers, surreal images of fascinating ambiguity have been produced by Ralph Gibson, and disturbing satirical narratives by Les Krims. The "sequences" of Duane Michals are photo narratives of psychic or spiritual experiences. Arthur Tress' pictures seem to be an inward look at a struggle between narcissism and psychotic fear. The many other realities that may exist simultaneously with those of the everyday world—forces within the earth, creatures in dimensionless space-time, the world in limbo between sleep and waking—have been pictured in the images of Jerry N. Uelsmann with a great mastery of combinatory techniques.

Naturalistic Photography. It was inevitable that as the pictorial approach established itself as a definite aesthetic attitude, a reaction should set in against it. By the late 1870's, pictorial-art photography was swamped with imitators and cliché-makers who were photographers with third-rate talent at best, and egocentric poseurs at worst. The first and most forceful opposition to this was raised in England by Peter Henry Emerson. His criticism was not in terms of the aims of photography, but in terms of subject matter and method. He agreed with the pictorialists that photography could be art, and could produce pictures of great beauty. However, true beauty existed only in the real world, not in works of art that had been already produced. Since the camera dealt with reality better than any other medium, only real subjects—natural subjects in their natural surroundings—could generate beautiful photographs. Contrivance, scenes staged with models, combination printing, imitation of the surface effects of painting—all the techniques prized as essential by pictorialists—could only lead to failure, he claimed, because they were methods of distorting reality, and thus beauty, not of recording it. His attitude immediately won him the ridicule and even hatred of the established art movement in photography, partly because of the passion with which he stated his views and the vehemence with which he replied to those who disagreed with him.

Emerson's basic point was best exemplified by his own pictures of life and scenes among the marsh farms and fishing villages of the Midland Broads in England. His platinum prints and photogravures had an exquisite beauty achieved by a straightforward use of the medium that pictorialists strived to achieve—usually unsuccessfully—by roundabout, artificial methods. Although the straight approach in photography had existed as an unquestioned manner of working from the very beginning, Emerson's creed of naturalistic photography raised it to the level of a conscious aesthetic attitude for the first time in any significant manner.

As the center of an enthusiastic band of followers, Emerson waged intellectual and artistic war with the pictorialists for a number of years. He wrote the text *Naturalistic Photography* to counteract what he considered to be the pernicious effect of H. P. Robinson's *Pictorial Effect in Photography;* he lectured, wrote magazine articles, and judged photographic competitions, in an effort to lead creative photographers to what he was sure was the only right road in photography. Then, to the astonishment of everyone, Emerson reversed his stand in the 1890's. In a pamphlet dramatically bordered in funereal black, he announced "The Death of Naturalistic Photography." For shadowy intellectual/artistic reasons of his own, he had concluded that photography was a science and a craft but could never be art. Ostensibly, he withdrew, leaving the field to others. Emerson continued to watch developments in photography, and to react to them even to the point of eccentricity. He took it upon himself to send commendations or awards to photographers whose work he admired, long after his name had been forgotten to all but a few older practitioners of the medium. As late as 1922, Brassai was startled to receive a congratulatory letter and an award in Paris from a certain P. H. Emerson about whom he knew nothing.

Emerson's turnabout did not destroy the straight approach as an artistic attitude in photography, although the stylistic term "naturalistic photography" soon lapsed into disuse.

Some of the finest images in the expressive development of photography were done at the turn of the century in this tradition by Frederick H. Evans. His quiet, glowing, affectionate studies of English forests and cathedrals in England and France have never been surpassed. His method consisted of becoming completely immersed in the emotional

Frederick H. Evans's platinum print "A Sea of Steps," Wells Cathedral, Stairs to Chapter House and Bridge to Vicar's Close (c. 1898), is one of the photographer's glowing tributes to a lovely old English cathedral. Photo reproduced courtesy of Philadelphia Museum of Art.

(Left) Alfred Stieglitz's "The Steerage" (c. 1907), is representative of his unposed, snapshot-like aesthetic which was so heavily influential on later photographers. (Right) Stieglitz's "Equivalent: Mountains and Sky, Lake George" (1924), is an example of his attempt to engage the viewer, on an emotional level, to react as deeply as the photographer himself to what is essentially a neutral subject. Photos reproduced courtesy of Aperture, Inc.

feeling of his subject over a long period of time, and then making the photograph to the most demanding standards of perfection. Evans photographed from about 1895 to 1915, when he gave up photography because rising prices in World War I had driven platinum paper off the market and nothing else would allow him to make his prints with equal expressiveness.

Straight "Art" Photography. The aesthetic movement that commenced with Emerson's naturalism was carried forward in a number of ways; one of the most significant was its protection and nurturing in the United States by Alfred Stieglitz. As a young man, Stieglitz had won first prize in a photo

competition for having submitted the only "spontaneous" picture—a snapshot-like view of young people around the well in a square of an Italian city. The judge had been P. H. Emerson.

Between 1900 and 1930, Stieglitz promoted the cause of serious expression in art, which he insisted included photography, in spite of the opposition of art critics, museum curators, and others who constituted the fine arts establishment. In three successive galleries and in "Camera Work," the finest art magazine of its time (1902–1915), Stieglitz showed the work of outstanding contemporary photographers, the photographs of newly-rediscovered historical masters such as Hill and Adamson, and Julia

History of Photography

Margaret Cameron, and the newest and best of modern painting and sculpture. Through Stieglitz's efforts, Americans first saw the work of Picasso, Braque, Matisse, Arp, Brancusi, Arthur Dove, John Marin, Georgia O'Keeffe, and others. And they saw the work of master photographers such as Clarence White, Edward Steichen, Gertrude Kasebier, A. L. Coburn, F. H. Evans, and many more. Although most of these were top-ranking pictorialists, in his own photographs Stieglitz carried the straight approach to new levels. And he recognized the potential of the first mature work of Paul Strand, who was to become one of the main forces in carrying the straight approach into the mid-twentieth century.

Stieglitz was something of an intellectual beacon in the straightforward aesthetic movement. Others helped to develop the tradition in their own work: Edward Weston, Ansel Adams, Minor White, Wynn Bullock, Harry Callahan, Paul Caponigro, and many more.

In his efforts to achieve sublime expression in realistic photography, Stieglitz created a kind of picture that makes an intellectual, and perhaps artistic, bridge between straight photography and abstraction: the "equivalent." A completely realistic, straightforward picture of emotionally neutral subject matter (clouds, for example), the equivalent photograph's intent is to engage the viewer on a level that causes an emotional reaction as deep as (though not necessarily the same as) the feeling that moved the photographer to make the picture. The "meaning" or identity of the subject matter is not impor-

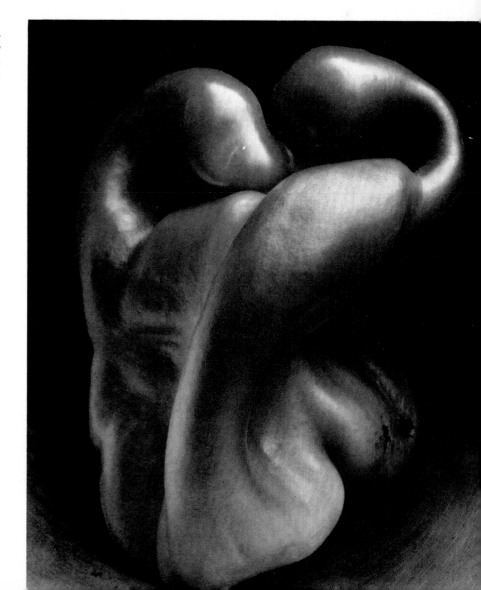

Edward Weston's photographs of common objects, such as this wonderfully contorted green pepper, transformed the mundane into abstractions of pure form. Photo reproduced courtesy of Cole Weston.

tant; the experience of viewing the photograph is. There is a significant degree of intellectualism in the concept, which is one of the factors that attracted Minor White to attempt to work in the same vein.

Portraiture. As noted previously, any kind of subject matter can be photographed with a straight or a pictorial approach. And as the foregoing discussions have shown, there are many variations possible within either approach. The portrait has been the most common kind of photograph (except the snapshot) since the second year of the medium; it has also been the subject of the widest stylistic variations.

In every period there has been an accepted and an expected style for a portrait. It is the style evident in studio photographs with almost monotonous regularity. Changes may be seen in what was considered the proper pose, expression, dress, background, and composition of a portrait from period to period, but the differences among studio portraits in any given period are few. However, there are some significant bodies of work that represent major achievements in portraiture. Several are worth noting.

In 1843–1844, David Octavius Hill and Robert Adamson photographed some 400 Scottish clergymen to obtain reference material for a giant commemorative painting planned by Hill. Although lim-

Minor White's "Moon and Wall Encrustations" makes an abstract design from small details of a commonplace subject. Photo reproduced courtesy of Aperture, Inc.

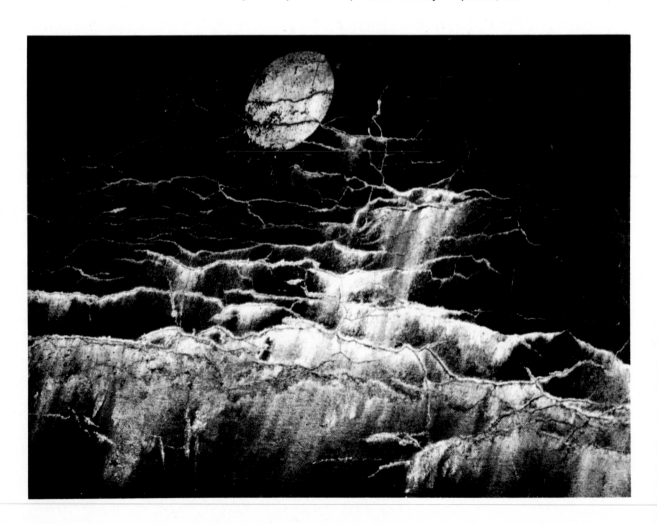

History of Photography

This double portrait by David Octavius Hill and Robert Adamson, of the 19th-century sculptors John Henning and Alexander Handistyle, represents an unusual portrait style for the period: a preference for the real rather than the ideal. Photo courtesy International Museum of Photography, Rochester, N.Y.

ited by the high contrast and coarse texture of the calotype (paper-negative) process, they produced the first portraits in which poses were used to express engaged activity and something of the outward character of the individual. The subjects did not stare into the camera in conventional style, but were involved with other activity—either their own thoughts, or something occurring outside the picture area. (In the intended painting, the central activity was the signing of the Deed of Demission, which separated the Scottish Free Church from the Church of England.) This gave the photographs an air of the subjects' having been observed without attracting undue attention, which heightened the sense of actuality—not of the person, but of the

moment. The painting was not completed for 20 years; the photographs were nearly lost, and did not come to be appreciated on their own terms until the negatives were discovered and reprinted in the late 1880's.

Nadar (Felix Tournachon) photographed celebrities in government, science, and the arts in Paris in the1850's and 1860's. Although he worked with only a dark gray background in the studio, Nadar was able to capture a sense of life and vitality that makes his pictures true portraits—images in which real individuals are encountered, and not representations of individuals.

By far the most outstanding achievement in nineteenth-century portraiture was that of Julia

The human quality of unusual people formed much of the subject matter of Diane Arbus's work. This 1965 photograph is entitled "Young man and his pregnant wife in Washington Square Park, N.Y.C."

Margaret Cameron from 1865 to about 1870. Cameron brought the physical and psychological close-up to photographic portraiture. Using a long-focal-length lens to fill her wet-plate negative with the subject's head, she worked to capture the inner spirit of the person, not just the outward aspect. The sense of intimate psychological mood that emanates from her best work was far ahead of its time—timeless, in fact—for her subjects live in unguarded, introspective, revealing moments as vividly to the viewer of her portraits as they did before her lens.

In the twentieth century, the O'Keeffe "portrait" by Alfred Stieglitz is a landmark. Acknowledging that no one picture could capture a human being—any more than one frame could sum up a motion picture—Stieglitz photographed Georgia O'Keeffe hundreds of times over a period of 20 years in their life together. Taken as a group, the best pictures form a complex and intimate portrait of a woman of infinite aspect. The achievement lies not in sheer volume, but in the repeated depth of perception of the photographer.

Paul Strand was one of the first to see true portraits—studies of individual human character—in street shooting, taking pictures of those he encountered on the basis of immediate reactions. It was an approach he later surrendered in favor of a straightforward, unconcealed approach that resulted in direct portraits of great intensity. But the idea that portraits of significance were to be found outside the studio was raised to great power by Lisette Model, and used with gentleness and a tender appreciation for the expressiveness of seemingly insignificant moments by André Kertész from the 1920's onward, and by Henri Cartier-Bresson, beginning a decade later.

Of all those who met subjects in real life on their own terms, Diane Arbus stands out. Her portraits in the 1960's of the human qualities of unusual people —dwarfs, giants, the retarded, nudists, circus "freaks"—have a directness that forces an involuntary choice. Either communication and understanding is established, or the viewer must turn away, rejecting the picture in order not to come to grips with his own feelings.

The studio photographs of Yousuf Karsh of Ottawa are notable for making legendary images of legendary subjects—or those who aspire to legend. His pictures of Presidents, Nobel Prize winners, and other celebrities are characterized by an obtrusive lighting style that converts the subjects into sculptures, medallions, or perfect illustrations of their consciously contrived public images.

By contrast, the portraits of Richard Avedon deal with the person behind the public image. Although he is perfectly capable of taking the public illustration when required, it is the private person he excels at making visible.

Conclusion

Technical invention and innovation have continued unceasingly from the inception of photography. Each new development has made it possible to see more, and to communicate what is seen in new ways. The expressive development of photography has grown alongside the technical. Each new mode of expression has broadened the medium, for it has been added alongside, not in place of, what already existed. The various aesthetic attitudes did not replace one another, they became part of a wider range of continuing choices. And in any period, the aesthetic use of the medium has always been a much smaller part than the informative and investigatory applications. Photography is virtually unique in the scope of the functions it can masterfully fill.

• *See also:* CAMERAS; DOCUMENTARY PHOTOGRAPHY; NEWS PHOTOGRAPHY; PHOTOJOURNALISM.

Further Reading: Beaton, Cecil and Gail Buckland. *The Magic Image: The Genius of Photography from 1839 to the Present Day.* New York, NY: Little, Brown and Co., 1975; Coe, Brian. *The Birth of Photography: The Story of the Formative Years 1800–1900.* New York, NY: Tapplinger Press, 1977; Gernsheim, Helmut and Alison Gernsheim. *The History of Photography from the Camera Obscura to the Beginning of the Modern Era,* 2nd ed. New York, NY: McGraw-Hill Book Co., 1969. Muller-Brockmann, Josef. *History of Visual Communication.* New York, NY: Hastings House, 1971; Newhall, Beaumont. *The History of Photography: 1839 to the Present Day.* Boston, MA: New York Graphic Society, 1974; Rotzler, W. *Photography as Artistic Experiment from Fox Talbot to Moholy-Nagy.* Garden City, NY: Amphoto, 1976; Willsberger, Johann. *The History of Photography.* New York, NY: Doubleday, Inc., 1977.

Hoegh, Emil von

(1865–1915)
German lens designer

Emil von Hoegh worked at C. P. Goerz and Co. for many years. His most outstanding design is that of the Goerz Double Anastigmat, later trademarked "Dagor." He also designed the first extreme wide-angle lens, the Goerz Hypergon, which had an angle of view of nearly 130 degrees.

Holography

Holography is often conveniently described as a kind of three-dimensional, lensless photography. Technically, it is a method of recording the interference fringes caused by the interaction between two coherent wave fronts—one from an object and the second from a reference beam—and subsequently reconstructing the original wave front so that the object appears to exist in three dimensions. The record of the set of fringes, usually on a photographic film or plate, is called a hologram. The word hologram stems from the Greek root *holos*—which means whole, complete, or entire—and the word *gram,* which means message. Thus, a hologram is a complete record of a scene or object.

The principle of the hologram was introduced in 1948 by Professor Dennis Gabor, who was then at the Imperial College of Science and Technology of the University of London. He was trying to find a way to improve the resolution of the electron microscope by reducing the spherical aberration of the electron lenses. For several reasons Gabor's original goal was not realized, but his work and that of several other scientists laid the foundation for an investigation that was to begin in 1962 at the University of Michigan. At Michigan, Emmett Leith and Juris Upatnieks developed the method of two-beam interferometry now used to make most holograms, and David Falconer is credited with giving the new field its accepted name—holography.

In recognition of his pioneering work in holography and his distinguished contributions in the field of optics, Dr. Gabor was awarded the 1971 Nobel Prize for Physics.

Holography versus Conventional Photography

In conventional black-and-white photography, light from an object or scene is focused by the camera lens onto the photographic emulsion, point by point. The resulting exposed and developed film or plate is readily identified as a negative image of the original subject. This process converts a three-dimensional subject to a two-dimensional image. Variations in the amount of light (light-intensity distribution) reaching the photographic emulsion appear on the negative as varying amounts of silver density. To make a more recognizable image, the negative is printed onto photographic paper to produce a positive image.

A hologram, on the other hand, is unlike any ordinary photograph. To begin with, it may be produced without a camera lens, and the appearance of the developed plate or film rarely gives an indication of the subject matter it represents. Holograms generally have an overall gray appearance with a random scattering of whorls and circles. A hologram is different from a conventional negative or print in that it has captured all the amplitude and phase information about the wavefront of light from the subject.

Making and Viewing Holograms

A verbal description of how a hologram is made invariably oversimplifies the many problems and

One arrangement for producing a hologram. In this case the transparent objects are backlit. The object beam and the reference beam intersect to produce interference fringes within the emulsion layer of the holographic film or plate. The elements are explained in the accompanying diagram.

technical details that must be considered before a satisfactory hologram is produced. Because the literature, as well as the manuals prepared by manufacturers of holographic systems, include considerable theory and how-to information, coverage here is deliberately limited.

The accompanying diagram shows the basic elements required for making one type of hologram (a lensless Fresnel hologram) and for reconstructing an image of the original object in three-dimensional realism. The narrow, collimated beam of light from the laser is focused by a lens and passes through a pinhole. One portion of the expanded beam is reflected from a plane, front-surface mirror to form a reference beam that is directed to a photographic plate or film. The second portion (the object beam)

(A) Basic elements for making a lensless Fresnel hologram. (B) Returning the hologram to its former position in the hologram-making arrangement, and then illuminating it by the same reference beam, to reconstruct an image of the original scene. (C) Viewing conditions under which a real image can be observed, suspended in space on the observer's side of the hologram plate.

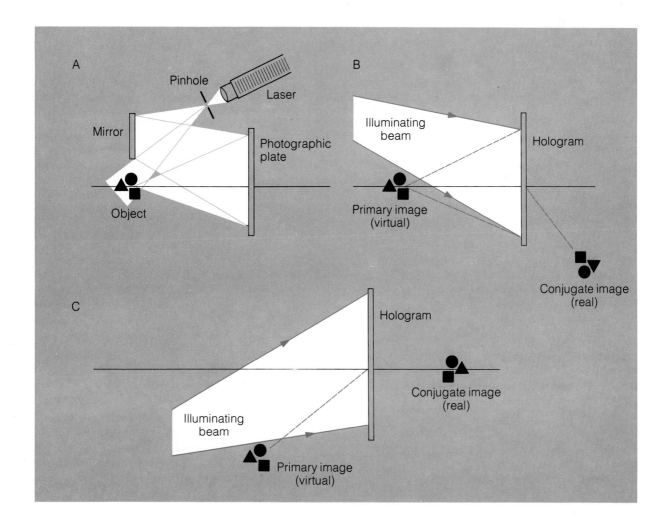

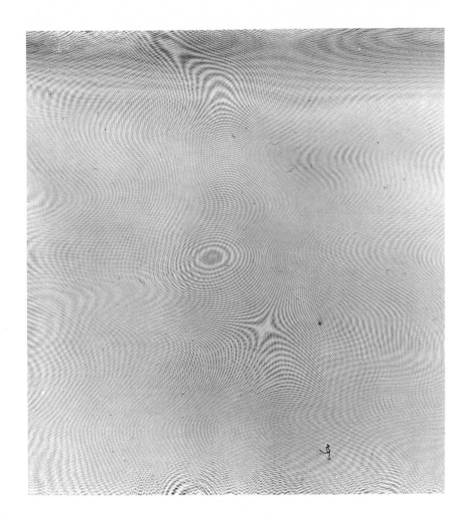

A photographic print of a typical amplitude hologram gives no indication of the original scene. The hologram image is a record of the interference pattern of the wavefronts from the reference beam and the object beam. The whorls are caused by dust particles and do not appreciably affect image quality on reconstruction.

illuminates the subject, which may scatter, reflect, or even transmit light. Light rays from the subject interfere with light rays from the reference beam. As the diagram shows, the photographic plate intercepts the interfering object and reference beams, and records the resulting interference fringe pattern. The photographic plate literally slices through space and captures in real time all of the information about the subject that can be seen at the vantage point of the plate. Holographic fringes are extremely fine—usually 500 fringes per millimetre or more.

After the hologram is exposed and processed, it may look very much like that pictured in the accompanying photograph, except that it is usually transparent enough that one can read a newspaper while looking through it. One method of reconstructing an image of the original scene is to return the hologram to its former position in the hologram-making arrangement (see preceeding diagram *B*), and then illuminate it by the same reference beam. The observer looks through the hologram as if looking through a window, and sees a virtual image. Under the right viewing conditions (see preceeding diagram *C*), a real image can also be observed, suspended in space on the observer's side of the hologram plate. If the original subject is three-dimensional (it does not have to be), the hologram image is also three-dimensional and exhibits parallax proportional to the size of the window.

Holography, therefore, is a two-step imaging process, while conventional photography can be considered a one-step imaging process. It is sometimes convenient to think of the hologram not only as a record, but also as a "lens" in an otherwise

Holography

lensless system, which is subject to the same types of aberration as a conventional photographic lens.

The Role of the Laser

The laser is a light source possessing very special qualities that play a key role in holography. Lasers are possible because variations—ultra-high frequency vibrations—can cause emission of electromagnetic vibrations. In the laser (an acronym for light amplification by stimulated emission of radiation) these vibrations occur at the atomic level. The result is a light beam of highly constant frequency and the sharp concentration of the emitted radiation into a beam. (*See:* LASER.)

Lasers are classified by type (gas, liquid, or solid-state), by their lasing material (argon, helium-neon, krypton, and others), the principal wavelength(s) they emit, and the duration of the radiation emission.

Applications of Holography

Word of the initial successes of Leith, Upatnieks, and other investigators in the early and mid-1960s soon spread from technical papers in scientific journals to the pages of the popular press. With this additional coverage, many claims were advanced for future uses of this new scientific tool—many of them of the science-fiction variety.

Today, holography is being applied in a number of practical ways, having emerged from the research laboratory to commercial importance. Active, growing companies have been formed to develop and promote holographic systems for recording and communication applications that cannot be served by any other means. Some of the more promising uses of holography are briefly described here, followed by a listing of those applications that are receiving considerable attention by investigators.

Display and Advertising. Costly or unique objects that are not easily duplicated or transported can be effectively displayed through the use of holograms. Similarly, models of complex three-dimensional objects can be made economically available to students in the form of holograms bound into texts. Examples of such objects are unusual pathological specimens and models of organic molecules. Holograms intended for mass distribution are constructed in such a way that they can be viewed conveniently without the use of a laser. The most impressive holograms of this type, called "reflection," or Lippmann-type, holograms can be reconstructed with any small-filament tungsten lamp.

Holographic Nondestructive Testing (HNDT). The engineer, especially, has found practical opportunities to use holography in the area of interferometric testing. Several types of holographic interferometry—single- double- or, multiple-exposure, real-time, and time-average—are being used in flaw detection; vibration and strain analysis; and to measure surface deformations of all kinds, including thermal expansion and contractions, swelling caused by absorption, and the growth of biological specimens. Holographic interferometry is uniquely applicable to the study of objects with diffuse surfaces.

In all of these methods, the investigator can study and measure (sometimes quantitatively) the interference fringe patterns that are superimposed on the object under study. A complete three-dimensional representation of the interference phenomena is available to the viewer, permitting post-exposure focusing and examination from various directions. If desired, the scene may be photographed in order to obtain hard copies for further study or for record purposes.

Information Storage and Retrieval. A variety of applications are being studied that involve the storage of information on holographic plates or film, and its rapid retrieval for visual display or reproduction. The interest in using holograms in computers and as memory storage banks in photocomposing, associative-memory, and other optical-memory systems stems from the extremely high packing density or storage capacity that holograms offer. It has been estimated that 15 million bits of information can be stored per square centimetre of emulsion area. With such capacity, a $4'' \times 5''$ plate (129 cm²) is capable of storing the same amount of information that can be stored on several hundred rolls of magnetic tape.

Because of its unusual capacity plus its ability to store patterns of information, pictures, and diagrams, holography can be adapted for use in library retrieval systems, voice recognition, fingerprint retrieval, and automatic translation of such character languages as Chinese, Korean, and Japanese.

One important property of such a storage system on film is that careless handling of the film (surface abrasion or even folding) will not destroy

Photograph of a hologram reconstruction where the camera has replaced the eye for viewing through the hologram "window." The quality of the photograph—resolution, depth-of-field, and graininess—is a function of the size and quality of the original hologram, the method of reconstruction, and the photographic technique. Of course, the photograph fails to capture the three dimensional aspects of the image.

the retrievability of the information it contains. This is because the information elements are stored as patterns that cover a larger area of the film than they would if reduced by conventional microphotography to the same average storage density.

Particle Size Determination. One of the earliest practical applications of holography was in the study and measurement of particle size in a sample volume of an aerosol. By making a hologram of the aerosol by means of a pulsed laser, it is possible to obtain a stop-action record that can be examined in detail at a later time. The useful depth of field that can be recorded on a hologram far exceeds that obtainable on a conventional photograph. Furthermore, the observer can shift viewing position while looking through the hologram window and see particles that would otherwise be hidden by larger particles on an ordinary, two-dimensional photograph. If desired, the hologram image can be formed on a vidicon and displayed (with substantial magnification) on a closed-circuit television monitor.

Other Applications. Following is a list of other applications or types of holography, some of which have already progressed from the research and development stage to commercial use.

Surface contouring
Correction of lens
    aberration
High-resolution
    microscopy
Holographic deblurring
    of conventional
    photographs
Hologram lenses
Side-looking airborne
    radar
Ultrasonic non-
    destructive testing
    (acoustical
    holography)

Dynamic process
    recording in
    medicine
Portraiture
Color holography
Computer-generated
    holograms
Encoding
High-speed holography
Holographic sonar
Production of diffraction
    gratings
Teaching aid in optics
Panoramic holography
Sonoradiography

Unusual Properties of Holograms

Some of the unusual characteristics of holograms have been alluded to in describing commercially promising applications for holography. Grouping these properties together will serve to explain why the term "unique" is aptly used when holograms are described and compared with conventional photographs or transparencies. Quite apart from the fact that holograms bear no visible resemblance to the object they represent and that nearly all conventionally processed holograms "look alike," holograms possess other unusual properties. The principal reason is that they contain information about both the amplitude and phase of the wave front that is recorded. In ordinary photography, only variations in intensity (amplitude squared) are recorded.

Holograms Record All the Information. A three-dimensional object can be considered as consisting of an infinite number of individual points, each of which becomes a point light source when irradiated by the coherent light of the object beam. Each point, therefore, supplies information about itself to the entire area of the hologram plate, thereby introducing a high degree of redundancy. Upon reconstruction, the observer can see only those portions of the original scene that were illuminated *and* recorded by the hologram plate. If a processed plate is partially destroyed, or if it is broken into small pieces, any one of the pieces contain all of the information necessary to reconstruct the original scene, as "seen" by that particular segment. The smaller the portion available for reconstruction, however, the poorer the resolution and information content of the hologram image. It follows that the larger a hologram can be made (within certain limits), the more information it can record about the object. Wrap-around, or cylindrical, holograms on flexible film have been made that permit 360-degree viewing of the object image.

Holograms Are neither Negative nor Positive. It is convenient to think of a hologram as a negative, especially if it has been processed in a conventional manner in a normally negative-producing chemical process. The fact is, however, that a hologram is neither negative nor positive in the usual photographic sense. If a hologram is contact-printed onto a second plate or film (only holograms having suitable fringe patterns will work), the resulting print still produces a positive image even though the original image has been reversed by the printing step. This feature of holograms is used to advantage in making duplicate holograms in a single step by one of several methods.

The infinite number of individual points of a three-dimensional object become point light sources when irradiated by the coherent light of the object beam. Each point source supplies its information to the entire holographic plate, causing redundancy. When reconstructed, the observer sees only the parts of the original object that were illuminated and recorded by the plate.

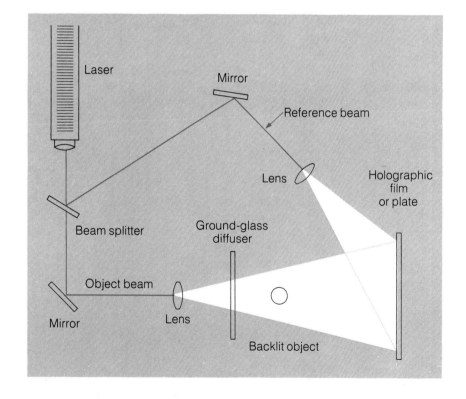

Holograms Exhibit Parallax, Perspective, and Depth of Field. Parallax is quite evident when viewed through a hologram window at the virtual image, or when a white-light hologram is viewed by reflected light. Close one eye and the original scene is viewed from one vantage point; shift to the other eye and it is seen from a different viewpoint. The same effect is achieved by holding a pencil at arm's length and alternately observing the scene beyond with one eye and then the other. An object in the background that is hidden from view with only the left eye open, for example, is clearly seen with only the right eye open. A conventional photograph does not exhibit parallax, while stereoscopic photographs or transparencies (which require special optical viewing aids) offer this capability only from the single camera position from which the stereo photos were made.

Returning again to the concept of looking through a window, the number of different views available to the observer is limited by the size of the hologram and by the illumination the object received during the recording step. A 360-degree cylindrical hologram, for example, allows the observer to view the hologram image from all sides; the height of the hologram (determined by the film width determines the angular viewing capability in the vertical direction.

Reconstructed virtual images of three-dimensional objects are seen in proper perspective; that is, features of the object are seen in their proper size and position. Furthermore, every feature from foreground to background is in sharp focus; no lens is used, objects at all distances are in focus, and there is infinite depth of field. Under different viewing conditions, reconstructed images may be pseudoscopic. That is, close objects look farther away than far objects—the image gives the appearance of reversal relief.

It is also significant to note that a hologram is capable of recording and playing back a very wide range of brightness from the original scene. In ordinary photography, the production of a print that captures the brightness range of an original scene in proper perspective is a real challenge to the photographer. A camera lens must be selected on the basis of the size of the final print and on the probable distance from which the print will be viewed. Furthermore, it is increasingly difficult to keep foreground and background in sharp focus for close-up pictures. (*See also:* LASER.)

Some Manufacturers and Suppliers of Holographic Apparatus

Assembled helium-neon and other gas lasers can be obtained from the following sources. For more information about available holographic supplies, see *Laser Focus Buyer's Guide,* 385 Eliot St., Newton, MA. 02164 Tel. (617) 244–2939.

Ardel Kinamatic
125–20 18th Avenue
College Point, New York 11356

The Ealing Corporation
Optics Division
2225 Massachusetts Avenue
Cambridge, Massachusetts 02140

Gaertner Scientific Company
1201 Wrightwood Avenue
Chicago, Illinois 60614

Jodon Engineering Associates, Inc.
145 Enterprise Drive
Ann Arbor, Michigan 48103

Metrologic Instruments, Incorporated
143 Harding Avenue
Bellmawr, New Jersey 08030

Newport Research Corporation
18235 Mt. Baldy Circle
Fountain Valley, California 92708

Oriel Corporation of America
One Market Street
Stamford, Connecticut 06902

Further Reading: Cathey, W.T. *Optical Information Processing and Holography.* New York, NY: John Wiley and Sons, 1974; Collier, R.J., C.B. Burckhardt, and L.H. Lin. *Optical Holography.* New York, NY: Academic Press, 1971; Dowbenko, George. *Homegrown Holography.* Garden City, NY: Amphoto, 1977; Klein, H. Arthur. *Holography.* New York, NY: Lippincott, 1970; Lehmann, Matt. *Holography: Technique and Practice.* New York, NY: Pitman Publishing Corp., 1977; Outwater, Christopher and Eric Van Hamersveld; *Guide to Practical Holography.* Beverly Hills, CA: Pentangle Press, 1974; Smith, Howard M. *Principles of Holography,* 2nd ed. New York, NY: John Wiley and Sons, 1975.

Home Movies

Home movies are taken for the same general reasons amateur slides and snapshots are—to preserve occasions involving family and friends, and to obtain truly personal souvenirs of experiences such as travel and vacations. Almost all home movies are now made in the super 8 format, although some 8 mm equipment is still in use. An increasing number of home movies also have matching sound, recorded on the film at the time of shooting.

Super 8 Cameras

Super 8 home-movie cameras accept cartridges containing 50 feet of film. At a standard operating speed of 18 frames per second (fps), this is enough for 3⅓ minutes of filming. (Some super 8 cameras accept 100- or 200-foot film cartridges, which are necessary for some kinds of uninterrupted professional filming, such as television news coverage.) Speeds of 9 fps (for fast-motion effects, or shooting in very dim light) and 24 fps (for slow-motion, and for professional-speed sound recording) may also be available. The motor of the camera is powered by batteries.

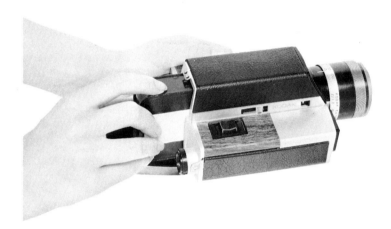

Super 8 home-movie cameras come in side-loading and rear-loading varieties. To load the rear-loading type, insert the film cartridge with its notches aimed at the front of the camera and its label facing the side window.

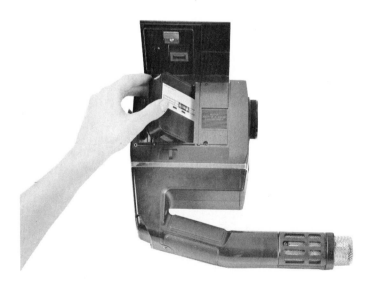

A side-loading sound movie camera requires tilting the sound film cartridge as shown for ease of insertion. The sound-recording mechanism is automatically actuated as the cartridge is snapped in place.

(Left) A super 8 camera with automatic exposure control sets the lens openings for you. However, with cameras such as the one shown here, it is possible to "fine-tune" the controls to suit personal taste. (Right) Individual filmmaking needs will determine the selection of movie-camera equipment, particularly in terms of lens capability. While fixed-focus lenses are popular, a zoom lens can add versatility to photographic efforts, especially if it offers macro focusing as this one does. Photos courtesy Minolta Corp.

Super 8 sound-movie cameras have a built-in microphone and magnetic recording system, or accept a plug-in accessory microphone. Sound cameras will accept cartridges loaded with magnetically striped super 8 film, *and* with silent (unstriped) film. *Silent movie cameras will accept only silent-film cartridges.*

Exposure Control. If the camera has an automatic exposure-control system, it is set to the proper film speed (exposure index, or EI) by a notch in the film cartridge. The exposure-control systems of most modern super 8 cameras, such as Kodak XL movie cameras, are designed to operate with both medium-speed (EI 40) and high-speed (EI 160) films. However, some camera systems do not couple with a high-speed cartridge notch. In that case, they will overexpose a high-speed film unless the exposure setting can be manually corrected (see the camera manual, or inquire of the manufacturer). Many exposure-control systems incorporate in the camera viewfinder a signal light that warns when the scene illumination is too dim for filming.

Cameras without automatic exposure-control systems must be set at the *f*-stop required for proper exposure in a given situation. Settings for various subjects and light conditions are given in film instruction sheets and in other sections of this article.

Lenses and Viewfinders. The lens of a super 8 camera may be a single-focal-length lens with fixed or adjustable focus, or it may be a focusing zoom lens. With a fixed-focus lens, all subjects more than about 4 feet from the camera will be in focus in bright sunlight; check the camera manual for the exact minimum distance. Adjustable-focus lenses may be focused by a distance scale on the lens, by a coupled rangefinder, or through the lens (single-lens reflex). Cameras that accept high-speed films usually have scale or rangefinder focusing so that a maximum amount of light reaches the film. Through-the-lens systems divert part of the light to the viewfinder, which may restrict camera use under very low light conditions.

Sports-type viewfinders show not only what the film format takes in, but some of the surrounding area as well. Some finders are coupled to a zoom lens so that, as the lens coverage changes, the scene in the viewfinder changes correspondingly. Through-the-lens viewfinders show the same image that falls onto the film. They are especially useful with a zoom lens because they show the change in lens coverage at all times.

The focal length of a lens determines its angle of view, or how much of a scene it includes. Single-focal-length lenses on super 8 cameras are usually somewhat wide-angle; that is, they take in more of the scene than a lens of normal focal length would. The coverage of a lens of only one focal length can be changed only by moving the camera closer to or farther from the subject or by adding a supplementary lens in front of the camera lens to change its focal length. (*See:* CLOSE-UP MOVIES.)

Zoom Lenses. A zoom lens has a variable focal length. Its coverage can be changed from wide-angle to normal to telephoto without adding attachments. The zoom movement is smooth and can be operated continuously to change the focal length while a shot is being made. In this way a shot can change from a distant view to a close-up (or vice versa) without the camera having to be stopped or relocated. Some zoom lenses are manually controlled by a ring or lever. Power-zoom lenses are controlled by a battery-operated motor built into the camera.

A zoom lens should be focused critically on the center of interest in a scene. With a scale-focusing lens, it is necessary to determine the camera-to-sub-ject distance accurately and set the scale accordingly. With through-the-lens viewing or coupled-rangefinder focusing, use the following procedure:

1. Before beginning a shot, zoom the lens to its maximum telephoto setting. This will provide the largest image of the subject for easier and more accurate focusing. In addition, it will allow you to preview the depth of field at the telephoto setting to determine how much area in the scene will be in acceptable focus.
2. Focus the lens on the center of interest.
3. Before beginning the intended shot, zoom back to the area you want to cover. Do not change the focus setting.
4. Begin filming.

Zooming during a shot can be very effective *if used sparingly*. Too much zooming, however tempting, becomes distracting and annoying, and may induce a sense of motion sickness. The real advantage of a zoom lens is that it permits the moviemaker to frame a subject in any of a variety of ways from a given camera location before a shot begins. It also makes it easy to adjust the shot if the subject starts to move out of range.

A zoom lens makes it easy to achieve a number of precise framings from a distance without having to move the camera. The best choice can be determined before the shooting begins.

The unique feature of a zoom lens is the ability to make a smooth transition from wide-angle, to normal, to telephoto coverage of a subject—and vice versa. This three-frame illustration of the zooming-in technique draws much of its impact from the skillfully framed close-up shot that ends the sequence.

Home Movies

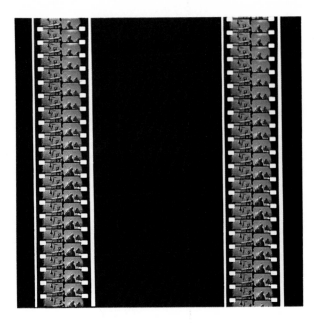

(Above) The perforations in these strips of processed but unslit 8 mm film are larger and greater in number than those in super 8 film; consequently, the frame size is smaller. (Right) A projector such as this is designed to accept both super 8 and single 8 mm film. Photo courtesy Ehrenreich Photo-Optical Industries, Inc.

8 mm Film, Cameras, and Projectors

The film used in 8 mm cameras has different perforations and records a smaller picture than super 8 film does. Cameras that use 8 mm film may have many of the same features found in super 8 cameras. In addition, some spool-loading 8 mm cameras permit rewinding of the film for intentional double exposures or other special effects. However, such shots are seldom necessary to make interesting home movies, and most people consider the larger image size of super 8 more important. In general, the most advanced features for home movie-making are found on super 8, rather than 8 mm, cameras.

Although there are projectors that can show both super 8 and 8 mm movies, there are no cameras that are interchangeable. Only 8 mm film can be used in an 8 mm camera and only super 8 film in a super 8 camera.

Films for Home Movies

Super 8 and 8 mm films for home movies are reversal films. This means that the film exposed in the camera is developed to a positive image for projection. There is no negative. As the tables on the next page show, most movie films are color films, although some black-and-white film are available.

Color films for home movies are supplied in three types—G, A, and Daylight. The designation indicates the type of illumination with which the film is designed to achieve proper color balance. Type G is available only in super 8 silent film and will provide pleasing color balance under most indoor and outdoor lighting conditions. Type A is available in super 8 sound and silent film and 8 mm silent film; it is balanced for tungsten illumination (movie lights and most common household lamps). With a type A conversion filter, this film can be readily adapted for use in daylight situations. Most super 8 cameras have a built-in type A conversion filter. Daylight-type film is designed specifically for daylight illumination and is available only in 8 mm film.

Super 8 film is 8 mm wide. It is most commonly supplied in 50-foot cartridges, although some emul-

Kodachrome 40 silent movie film (left) and Kodak Ektachrome 160 sound movie film (right). Note the differences in shape and size of the cartridges. The sound cartridge is designed to engage the sound recording head of the movie camera.

sions are available in longer lengths and in double-width for use in professional cameras. Super 8 film has narrower sprocket holes than 8 mm film, providing a frame size 52 percent greater in picture area. Super 8 sound-movie film has a magnetic stripe that runs along the unperforated edge of the film and is used for recording synchronized sound within the camera. A very narrow strip runs along the opposite edge just outside the sprocket holes and balances the effect of the sound stripe on the thickness of the film roll.

Films of 8 mm format are supplied in 16 mm width (double 8) and 25-foot length on daylight loading spools or in magazines. In use the film is exposed along one half its width; it then must be turned over and exposed along the other half. After

	Film Speed		Super 8 Cartridges		Double
Film	Tungsten (3400 K)	Daylight (with 85 Filter)	Silent	Sound	8 mm
Ektachrome 160 movie film (type A)	160	100	X		
Ektachrome 160 sound-movie film (type A)	160	100		X	
Type G Ektachrome 160 movie film	160	160*	X		
Kodachrome 25 movie film (daylight)		25*			X
Kodachrome 40 movie film (type A)	40	25	X		X
Kodachrome 40 sound-movie film (type A)	40	25		X	

KODAK COLOR FILMS FOR HOME MOVIES

*No filter is required for daylight exposure.

KODAK BLACK-AND-WHITE FILMS FOR HOME MOVIES

Film	Film Speed Tungsten	Daylight	Super 8 Silent Cartridges
4-X reversal*	320	400	x
Plus-X reversal	40	50	x
Tri-X reversal	160	200	x

*Available through dealers in audiovisual products.

processing, it is slit down the middle and the two pieces are joined to form a 50-foot length of film for projection.

What Makes Interesting Movies

Home movies that capture viewer attention have a number of things in common; among them are the following.

Movement. Movies have built-in interest because they are realistic. The subjects move, just as they do in real life. There are, however, certain things that can be done to make movies even more interesting. For one, people should be included in scenes and should be photographed moving about naturally. Standing in front of Old Faithful geyser staring at a camera is hardly the natural thing to do. Subjects might instead be photographed walking up to a sign about the geyser and reading it. Such a scene would best be followed by a close-up of the sign in order to tell viewers what was being read. Next, the subjects might be shown turning and walking toward Old Faithful, just as they would be expected to do naturally. This approach can be applied to all movies, whether they depict gardening, a picnic, or a trip to the playground.

Story-Telling. If an event is photographed exactly as it happens, chances are a movie story will result.

To make an effective, complete movie story, a photographer should decide in advance what he or she wants to include. Suppose, for instance, the movie is to depict a day at the beach. The photographer might begin by showing the hustle and bustle of preparation, loading the car, and everyone piling in. A few transition scenes might also be filmed along the way to the beach. At the beach, the subjects could be shown spreading out colorful beach towels, playing in the sand and surf, and having lunch—things that normally would be photo-graphed. Packing up, and ultimately a tired crew getting out of the car back at home, would wind up the story. These scenes tell the key aspects of the whole experience—and that adds up to a good movie story.

There is an interesting movie story in almost any event. A Christmas movie might begin with buying a tree; a movie of a fishing trip might begin with preparing the gear at home; and a birthday party movie might begin with putting up the decorations. Remember, everyday events like washing the dog, playing ball, and a backyard game of croquet are also appropriate subjects.

Variety. Changing the *viewpoint,* the subject *distance,* and the *length* of the scenes helps keep movies interesting and audiences alert.

Changing viewpoint and changing subject distance go hand in hand. Imagine a movie of children playing in a sandbox. A long shot from about 20 feet showing the kids building a sand castle is a good opening, but an entire sequence filmed from that distance would be boring to watch. Instead, follow the long shot with a medium-distance shot or two taken from a different viewpoint. You might aim over the children's shoulders to show the castle's construction, and then move in for some close-ups, changing viewpoint again. For example, expose some footage from a low viewpoint, looking up at the children's faces; or show the movements of each child separately.

Move in, move back, aim the camera up, aim it down, film from the side. This will liven up any movie sequence—if it is done with purpose, not haphazardly.

Just as it is effective to vary the distance and the viewpoint, it is also good to vary the scene length. How long should a scene be? At the normal camera speed of 16 or 18 frames per second, it takes the same time to show the movie as it does to film it. So decide how long a scene should be on the screen, and film for that length of time. Some scenes need to be long, some medium in length, and some short. An overall shot of a beach to establish location may last only a few seconds, but the more interesting close-ups may deserve a much longer filming time.

Color. The most colorful movies result from combining colorful subjects with correct lighting and exposure. One way to provide color for a movie is to ask people to wear their most colorful clothing;

red sweaters and yellow skirts or slacks can really enliven a movie.

Colorful subjects look their best in bright sunlight, although shadows are undesirably harsh. Overcast or cloudy days can be good for close-up movies of people because colors become softer and more pastel, shadows disappear, and people stop squinting. Bright colors are more important on overcast days to keep movies from looking dull.

For best portrayal of colorful subjects, correct exposure of each shot is essential (exposure techniques are covered in later sections of this article).

Technique. Hold the camera steady, keep the camera lens clean, and focus properly for sharp movies.

Steady Camera. A movie camera takes a series of separate still pictures that give the appearance of motion when they are projected. For these separate pictures to be sharp, the camera must be held steady. If it is jiggled, the individual pictures will be out of focus, and the projected movie will look blurred. The use of a tripod avoids this problem, but it is often impractical to carry one. The next best thing is a very steady stance, with feet planted firmly and slightly apart, and the camera braced firmly against the face; film with as little camera movement as possible.

Sometimes a photographer will want to make a "pan" shot in which he or she slowly swings the camera through an arc while filming. A pan shot is

A keen eye will spot the makings of a good home movie in the simplest everyday occurrences. The challenge of a somewhat tricky spare and the thrill of victory for the girl who makes the mark are captured in this sequence.

Home Movies

The bright colors of the flags catch the viewer's attention in this pageant scene. Diffused light from overcast skies softens shadows and intensifies the colors.

useful with a view that is too big to be included in one straight-on shot. It is generally best to pan from the least important area to the most important area of the scene (the order can sometimes be reversed to provide a different emphasis). Follow these tips:

1. Film several seconds of the main part of the scene without moving the camera.
2. Then pan the camera slowly to take in the rest of the scene.
3. Finish by holding the camera still on the last view for a few seconds.

Steadiness is important in panning, too. If the pan is too fast, the pictures will be blurred. Use a tripod or unipod, or hold the camera firmly and pivot your body at the hips.

Sometimes it is necessary to follow a moving subject with a camera. In this type of pan, keep the subject centered in the viewfinder so that it remains sharp and the background becomes blurred.

For best results, the subjects should move around within the scene, and the camera should remain still. Panning should be kept to a minimum; pan only in wide, expansive scenes or with subjects traveling across a large area.

Clean Lens. For bright, sparkling pictures, the camera lens must be clean. Lenses gradually become dirty from fingerprints and dust. A movie made through a dirty lens will look like a scene viewed

High speed can be indicated by how rapidly the subject crosses the frame or, as in this shot, how fast the background moves past. Panning the action, by keeping the subject centered in the camera viewfinder while following its path of motion, can prove an exciting ingredient in a good movie.

through a very dirty window. When it is necessary to clean a lens, first blow away any grit or dust, or brush it away with a camel's-hair brush; then gently wipe the surface of the lens with a clean, soft, lintless cloth or lens-cleaning paper. If the lens is really dirty, use a few drops of lens cleaner on the paper.

Focus. Many movie cameras have fixed-focus lenses. With this type of lens, do not film subjects closer than the minimum distance, unless a close-up lens is used. If the lens has a focusing scale, be sure to set it for the distance from the camera to the subject. With cameras that feature a rangefinder, follow the instructions of the manufacturer to obtain good focus. To focus a zoom lens, remember to move it to the maximum telephoto setting, focus, and then zoom back to the desired view before starting the camera.

Movies in Daylight

Good home movies can be made outdoors in direct sunlight or open shade, or under bright overcast skies. As explained in the section on films, most color films for home movies have a type A emulsion and require an 85 filter at the lens for daylight expo-

sure. Most super 8 cameras have a built-in filter for this purpose.

The following suggestions are for daylight filming with automatic-exposure-control cameras:

> For most situations, just aim and photograph. If possible, have the sunlight shining on the front of the subject. Make sure that the camera's meter and lens are not exposed to direct sunlight during filming.

Since the automatic-exposure control sets the lens for the average brightness of the subject, well-exposed movies will result if:

1. the subject is all in sunlight or all in shade.
2. very light subjects in dark surroundings, and very dark subjects in light surroundings are avoided.
3. the sky is excluded from movies on overcast days. On these particular days the sky is much brighter than most subjects.

For manual-exposure-control cameras, set the lens opening as recommended in the film instruction sheet for the prevailing light conditions; or, use an exposure meter to determine the required *f*-stop in the following way:

1. Set the meter for the daylight speed of the film.
2. Take an incident-light reading at the subject position, with the meter pointed toward the camera position.

   Or, take a reflected-light reading from an 18 percent reflectance neutral gray card held at the subject position. Be careful not to cast a shadow on the card.

   Or, take a reflected-light reading of the subject from the camera position, with the meter tilted to exclude the sky.
3. Note the *f*-stop called for at a shutter speed of 1/30 sec. This is the shutter speed of most super 8 and 8 mm cameras operating at the standard 18 frames per second.
4. Set the lens to the *f*-stop indicated and proceed with the filming.

In any outdoor situation, beware of subjects moving from one area to a brighter or darker area. Only automatic-exposure cameras can adjust for the change, and they may lag a bit. If a subject moves into a dark area, but the light area still occupies about one-half the picture, the camera cannot make a sufficient exposure adjustment. It is best to stop filming and reposition the camera or subject (or change the exposure setting on manually controlled cameras) to achieve correct exposure under the new conditions.

Indoor Movies with a Movie Light

The weather is always fine for indoor movie-making. A movie light and type A color film are the only necessities for making movies of indoor activities at night or during the day, at any time of the year. It is usually easiest to use a movie light that is specially designed for the camera. With most super 8 cameras, attaching such a movie light automatically moves the built-in filter away from the lens, and the camera is ready for making indoor movies.

When using other movie lights with a super 8 camera, either insert the special filter key supplied with the camera, or set the filter switch for tungsten light, depending on the type of camera being used. For other cameras, make the adjustments recommended in the instruction manual.

When a movie light is attached to the camera, the illumination is aimed wherever the camera is aimed; therefore, when the camera moves, the light moves with it. Most of today's movie lights are com-

	DAYLIGHT EXPOSURE TABLE*			
Film	Bright or Hazy Sun on Light Sand or Snow	Bright or Hazy Sun (Distinct Shadows)†	Cloudy Bright (No Shadows)	Heavy Overcast or Open Shade‡
Kodachrome 40 movie film (type A)	f/16	f/11 − f/16	f/8	f/5.6
Kodak Ektachrome 160 movie film (type A)	f/32	f/22 − f/32	f/16	f/11
Kodak (type G) Ektachrome 160 movie film §	f/32 − f/45	f/32	f/16 − f/22	f/11 − f/16

*For type A movie films with a No. 85 filter in the light path, and for type G movie films without a filter. Settings for 8 mm *Kodachrome* 25 film (daylight) are the same as those for *Kodachrome* 40 film (type A).
†For backlighted close-up subjects, increase exposure by two *f*-stops.
‡Open shade occurs when the subject is shaded from the sun, but lighted by a large area of clear sky.
§For the correct method of using type G movie film in a camera with a built-in type A filter, refer to the instruction sheet packed with the film.
NOTE: Many cameras do not have lens openings of f/22 or smaller and are therefore unable to properly expose high-speed films.

INDOOR EXPOSURE TABLE

Kodachrome 40 Movie Film (Type A)

Lens Opening	650-Watt Tungsten-Halogen Movie Light*		2-Lamp Light Bar* with 300- or 375-Watt (BEP or EBR) Reflector Photolamps†	650-Watt Sealed-Beam DWA Movie Light*
	Flood	Spot		
f/8	6 ft.	6– 9 ft.	3½– 5 ft.	4–5½ ft.
f/5.6	6– 9 ft.	9–12 ft.	5– 7 ft.	5½– 8 ft.
f/4	9–12 ft.	12–17 ft.	7–10 ft.	8–11 ft.
f/2.8	12–17 ft.	17–24 ft.	10–14 ft.	11–16 ft.
f/1.9	17–24 ft.	24–35 ft.	14–21 ft.	16–24 ft.

*Read the manufacturer's instructions for the minimum distance at which you should use your movie light.

†For new lamps with beams superimposed. After they have burned for 1 hour, use a lens opening ½ stop larger; after 2 hours, use a lens opening 1 stop larger. With a four-lamp light bar, use a lens opening 1 stop smaller than the table indicates—for example, f/5.6 rather than f/4.

NOTE: Since Kodak movie films with a speed of ASA 160 are designed specifically for use in existing-light movie cameras without supplementary lighting, exposure information on these films is not included in this table.

pact, single-light units with a small, high-intensity lamp; they produce about the same amount of light as a three-lamp movie light bar. These units give a constant light throughout their life.

CAUTION: For the safety and comfort of the subjects being photographed, read the manufacturer's instructions carefully before using any movie light.

Exposure with Movie Lights. With a camera that has automatic-exposure control, simply aim and film the same as you would for daylight movies. Just be sure to photograph subjects within the distance range given either on the light itself or in the instruction manual for the light.

If the camera has manually adjustable lens openings, set the lens according to the distance from the light to the subject. The exposure chart on most movie lights tells what lens openings to use for various subject distances; or, use the accompanying table as a guide. The lens settings given on a movie light and those in the table are for *average,* light-colored rooms. Very large rooms and rooms with dark decor do not reflect much light back on the subject, so use a lens opening one-half stop larger than the table indicates.

Bounce Lighting. An excellent technique for making subjects more comfortable during filming is to bounce light off a white ceiling. This provides a soft, natural lighting effect by supplementing the existing lighting in the room. The bounce light fills in shadows, making them less harsh, and increases the amount of light for taking movies.

Another advantage of bounce lighting is that the light is reflected evenly over a large area; with a manually adjustable camera, no exposure change is generally required for different subject or camera positions.

Many movie lights will tilt up so that they can be aimed at the ceiling. Direct the light so that it illuminates the ceiling between the camera and the subject. Do not try this technique in a room with a colored ceiling, because the color will be reflected onto your subject. If the ceiling is colored or if it is not at conventional room height, it will be necessary to aim the light directly at the subject.

For bounce movie lighting, use type A film without the built-in camera filter. Bounce lighting, however, is not as bright as direct movie lighting. To obtain enough exposure with bounce lighting in medium or large rooms, it may be necessary to use high-speed movie film if the camera lens is not fast enough for proper exposure with slower-speed films. If high-speed film cannot be used in the camera and there is not enough light for proper exposure with bounce lighting, it will be necessary to use direct lighting.

With an automatic camera, take movies as long as the low-light signal indicates there is enough light for proper exposure. With a manually adjustable camera, use an exposure meter to determine the lens opening; or as a guide, use a lens opening two stops larger than would be used for direct lighting at the same distance.

Movies by Existing Light

The easiest and most natural way to make movies is by existing light, using only the lighting that exists at the scene. Technically, bright sunlight outdoors is existing light. But for purposes here, *existing light* refers to light that is not as bright as that found under most outdoor daylight conditions. This includes the light from table and floor lamps, lighting fixtures, fluorescent lamps, floodlights, spotlights, neon signs, candles, and fireplaces—even daylight from windows or skylights. In other words, it is any type of lighting encountered in homes, schools, churches, museums, restaurants, auditoriums, and outdoors at twilight or after dark.

Existing light gives movies a realistic quality and also enables subjects to relax and be themselves. It is also more fun to take movies this way, because movie lights are not necessary. With a high-speed film and a camera designed for existing-light movie-making, subjects can be filmed in all kinds of inter-

Light bounced off a white ceiling adds a soft, natural effect to the lighting already in the room. Shadows are softened and light level is increased without washing out colors.

esting situations, such as events at home—holidays, birthdays, and everyday happenings—and events away from home—sporting events, plays, stage shows, school activities, and weddings. And outdoors at night, existing-light movie-making opens up a whole new world of exciting subjects to be photographed.

Indoors. In order to film subjects in the greatest possible variety of existing-light situations, a high-speed film and a camera that takes full advantage of dim existing lighting are necessary. Existing-light movies can also be made with a conventional camera, but filming subjects in dim lighting situations, such as the existing lighting in home interiors at night, is not always possible.

When a type A film such as Ektachrome 160 movie film is used to make color movies of subjects in existing tungsten light (regular light bulbs) or candlelight, move the built-in filter away from the camera lens. To film subjects in existing daylight indoors under fluorescent illumination or under mercury-vapor lighting, or subjects lighted by carbon-arc spotlights, use the built-in filter.

With more than one kind of light in the scene, that is, a mixture of different light sources, position the built-in camera filter for the predominant light source. Under some conditions the use of the camera

filter is a matter of personal choice. Movies made through the filter will appear "warmer," or more yellow-red, than those made without the filter. If in doubt, use the camera filter.

A type G film such as Ektachrome 160 movie film is intended for use *without a filter* under all lighting conditions—daylight, incandescent light, fluorescent light, stage and sports lighting, color TV, candlelight, firelight, and any *mixture* of light sources. No matter what source of light is available, pleasing color balance in movies should be attained with type G film.

Color movies made under fluorescent lighting on most films have an overall greenish cast because the lamps are deficient in red. To improve the color rendition in movies made under this kind of illumination, use either type G film (no filter) or type A movie film with a No. 85 filter.

Movies made under mercury-vapor illumination with most color films usually have a bluish-green cast because mercury-vapor lamps are also deficient in red light. Some improvement in color rendition can usually be noticed when type G (no filter) or type A film with a No. 85 filter is used to make movies under this type of illumination.

If a high-speed film cannot be used in a particular super 8 camera, use a film such as Kodachrome

Existing daylight not only provides ample light for an indoor portrait, but seems a fitting element in this study of pre-factory simplicity when objects were crafted by hand.

SUGGESTED EXPOSURES FOR EXISTING-LIGHT MOVIES INDOORS*

Subject	Kodak Type G Ektachrome 160 Movie Film Kodak Ektachrome 160 Movie Film (Type A) Kodak Tri-X Reversal Film 7278	Kodachrome 40 Movie Film (Type A) Kodak Plus-X Reversal Film 7276	Kodachrome 25 Movie Film (Daylight)
Home interiors at night—areas with bright light	f/2	—	—
Circuses— floodlighted acts	f/2.8	—	—
spotlighted acts (carbon-arc)	f/4†	f/2†	f/2
Ice shows— floodlighted acts	f/4	f/2	—
spotlighted acts (carbon arc)	f/4†	f/2†	f/2
Stage shows— average lighting	f/2.8	—	—
bright lighting	f/5.6	f/2.8	—
Basketball, hockey, bowling	f/2.8	—	—
Boxing, wrestling	f/4	f/2	—
Interiors with bright fluorescent light	f/2, − f/2.8†	—	—

*Since lighting conditions vary, these exposures are approximate.
†Use a No. 85 filter with type A film.
NOTE: Exposures are for no filter unless the filter is indicated. The No. 85 or type A filter is built into most super 8 cameras and some 8 mm cameras.

40 movie film (type A) for color movies, or Kodak Plus-X reversal film 7276 for black-and-white movies. But since these films have moderate speed, you can take properly exposed movies in existing light of brightly lighted subjects only, such as spotlighted acts at an ice show or subjects in existing daylight. The rules for using the built-in, or No. 85, filter with the color films are the same as those for using the filter with type A film.

The existing lighting in homes at night is quite dim compared with other lighting, so a high-speed movie film and an existing-light camera will be necessary in order to make well-exposed movies. With cameras that do not transmit as much light to the film, a movie light will probably have to be used, or existing-light movies can be made indoors in the daytime. Excellent results can be obtained indoors under existing-daylight conditions because the lighting is generally flattering to people.

In home interiors, be sure to turn on all the lights in the room at night to make the lighting as bright and even as possible. In the daytime, open all the window drapes. If more light is required, film a subject near a lighted lamp, or near a window in the daytime. Avoid using camera angles that include a bright lamp or window behind the subject, because this could mislead the exposure meter in the camera and cause underexposure of the subject.

With an automatic movie camera, movies can be made as long as the camera's low-light signal does not indicate the lighting is too dim. However, with some brightly illuminated scenes, such as stage shows lighted by floodlights, acceptable results can be attained even though the low-light signal appears.

The exposure meter in the camera is probably being influenced by the large dark areas surrounding the brightly lighted subjects. When a scene is evenly lighted throughout and the low-light signal appears, it is probably too dim for proper exposure.

Spotlighted subjects photographed with an automatic movie camera will often be overexposed, with subsequent loss of detail and washed-out colors. This is because such subjects are usually far away and surrounded by large areas of darkness. The automatic-exposure control is influenced by the greater dark area and causes the lens diaphragm to open too much for proper exposure of the intensely lighted subject. Manually adjustable and semi-automatic cameras, and cameras in which you can override the automatic-exposure control can be used to obtain better exposure with spotlighted subjects.

Many movie cameras with through-the-lens viewing and metering do not let all the light pass through the lens to expose the film. Some of the light is diverted through the viewfinder, and some is used for the exposure control. This loss of light may make a difference in exposure of as much as one stop. An $f/1.9$ lens, for example, may have a maximum effective lens opening of $f/2.8$. As a result, it may not be possible to make movies in dim light with cameras that have these characteristics.

With a camera that has manually adjustable lens openings, use an exposure meter to find the correct exposure. If a meter is not available, use the exposures suggested in the table on the previous page. Lighting conditions vary, though, so the exposures are only approximate.

Outdoors at Night. After-dark movies add an unusual and colorful touch to movie showings, and they are easy to make. Existing-light movie-making allows the filming of a variety of interesting night subjects, such as city street scenes, lighted statues and fountains, lighted signs, Christmas displays, sporting events, amusement parks, and fireworks.

Movies filled with bright lights and color are not restricted to daylight hours or home interiors. High-speed film will prove invaluable in creating dazzling nighttime scenes such as this.

SUGGESTED EXPOSURES FOR OUTDOOR MOVIES AT NIGHT*†

Subject	*Kodak* Type G *Ektachrome* 160 Movie Film *Kodak* *Ektachrome* 160 Movie Film (Type A) *Kodak Tri-X* Reversal Film 7278	*Kodachrome* 40 Movie Film (Type A) *Kodak Plus-X* Reversal Film 7276
Brightly lighted downtown street scenes	*f*/2.8	—
Brightly lighted nightclub or theater districts— Las Vegas or Times Square	*f*/4	*f*/2
Neon signs and other lighted signs	*f*/5.6	*f*/2.8
Store windows	*f*/4	*f*/2
City skyline— 10 minutes after sunset	*f*/5.6	*f*/2.8
Fairs, amusement parks	*f*/2	—
Fireworks	*f*/4	*f*/2
Burning buildings, campfires, bonfires	*f*/4	*f*/2
Night football, baseball, racetracks‡	*f*/4	*f*/2

*Since lighting conditions vary, these exposures are approximate.

†No filter.

‡If the lighting at these events is provided by mercury-vapor lamps, which are slightly bluish-green in appearance, type G film (no filter) will produce better color rendition. Color rendition can be improved in type A color films by using the No. 85 filter that is built into most movie cameras. If you use the filter with a camera that has manual exposure control, use a lens opening one stop larger than indicated in the table—for example, *f*/2.8 instead of *f*/4.

Since the existing light outdoors at night is so much dimmer than daylight, it is best to use a high-speed film and a camera with an *f*/2.8 or faster lens.

For most night scenes, type A film produces more satisfactory results without a filter than it does with the built-in camera filter; colors look more natural and the film has a higher speed. Some subjects, such as outdoor sporting events, may have lighting provided by mercury-vapor lamps, which have a slightly bluish-green appearance. With this kind of lighting, colors will look better if the built-in, or No. 85, filter is used. Movies of such subjects will still probably have a blue-green cast, but without the filter they would look much too blue. The filter absorbs light and reduces the effective speed of the film, so using the filter is practical only when the low-light signal indicates that the light is bright enough for correct exposure with the filter.

Type G movie film is intended for use without a filter under all lighting conditions. If it is used to photograph scenes illuminated by mercury-vapor lamps or fluorescent lights, it will probably provide slightly better color rendition than that provided by type A films and the No. 85 filter.

With an automatic camera, aim and make movies as long as the low-light signal indicates there is enough light for proper exposure. Sometimes, because of the large areas of darkness surrounding some night subjects, the low-light signal may appear in the camera even though there is enough light on the principal subject for proper exposure. In this situation, the camera's exposure meter is being misled by the large dark areas. It is still possible to take movies successfully, although only part of a roll should be exposed. Looking at the results will help determine whether the exposure is acceptable.

With an adjustable camera, use an exposure meter. If one is not available, try the exposures suggested in the accompanying table. Since conditions vary, consider the recommendations as guides.

Christmas is a holiday as rich in sounds as in sights. Squeals of laughter and favorite carols add special warmth to holiday movies.

When filming very dimly lighted subjects and more exposure is needed, film at a slow camera speed of 9 frames per second (with cameras that have this feature) instead of the normal 18 frames per second. Filming at the slower speed gives twice as much exposure, but it also speeds up the action in projected movies, producing a fast-action, comedy effect. *Except when special effects are desired, use a slower-than-normal camera speed for stationary or slow-moving subjects only.*

Sound Movies

Some super 8 sound cameras such as Kodak Ektasound movie cameras have a built-in microphone as well as the ability to accept an accessory mike. Other cameras use only plug-in microphones, which make it easy to get a close-sound pick-up from a distant subject, but present the problem of concealing the microphone and its cord in the scene. When magnetically striped film is used, the sound is recorded at the same time the picture is exposed.

Audio Considerations. In addition to the features that make a good silent movie, a sound movie must have sound that is interesting, that is a pleasant or informative addition to the picture, and is of good quality.

Background noise is the greatest enemy of good sound. Noises from traffic, lawnmowers, nearby hammering or sawing, children playing, television and radio programs, telephones, and doorbells must be avoided if possible.

If unwanted background noise is unavoidable, there are two choices:

1. Place the microphone as close as possible to the desired source of sound, and try to control that sound so that it is the dominant sound within the scene and will be picked up by the automatic gain control (AGC) in the camera amplifier.
2. Leave the sound track blank and fill it in with suitable commentary and/or background music later. Some super 8 sound projectors permit post-recording onto sound-striped film.

Microphone Use. Early model sound movie cameras featured only an off-camera (or extension) microphone. An advantage of the off-camera mike is that it can be placed very precisely near the sound source to provide optimum sound recording under most conditions. However, it takes time, effort, and ingenuity to place the mike in a good location so that the cord will not get in the way and restrict freedom of movement while photographing the movie. In many situations an extra person is needed, just to handle the microphone.

Cameras equipped with an on-camera microphone *and* an off-camera extension mike provide added versatility. An on-camera microphone is practical for many movie-making situations and reduces the need for an extra helper.

Off-camera microphones will give best results when placed 1 to 5 feet from the sound source. If possible, keep the mike just outside the picture area; or try to conceal it or make it inconspicuous within the scene. Should it be impossible to do either of these things, forget the mike and let it show. If the camera is equipped with an on-camera mike, this would be a situation in which to put it to good use. On-camera microphones work best when the distance from the camera to the subject is not too great and when the amount of extraneous noise is minimal or at least controllable.

For indoor movie-making, try to avoid rooms with large, hard surfaces from which sound can reverberate, and avoid laying off-camera mikes on a hard surface. Providing padding under an off-camera mike wherever it is placed can be a help. The more soft or padded surfaces in a room, the better the chances are for good sound quality.

Outside, the same rules apply. Try to avoid hard surfaces nearby. Shoot out in the open as much as possible or with lots of surrounding bushes and trees. Wind noise can seriously degrade the quality of sound. This can be minimized by covering the microphone with a porous material, such as a mitten or a few layers of handkerchief.

Editing and Splicing

Editing refers to taking out the parts of a movie that keep it from looking its best, like the part that is too dark because there just wasn't enough light. Editing is also cutting apart some of the scenes, if necessary, and rearranging them to tell the story in the most interesting way. Editing also involves splicing movies together onto larger reels, such as 200- or 400-foot reels, so that an uninterrupted showing can be run for about 12 to 28 minutes rather than for about 3½ minutes.

Editing considerations and splicing techniques are covered in separate articles.

(Right) An off-camera microphone can prove an indispensable aid in the making of sound movies, because it travels as the sound moves. The photographer should try, however, to keep it out of camera range when shooting. Photo courtesy Ehrenreich Photo-Optical Industries, Inc.

(Left) While a built-in microphone does not require constant repositioning and has no cord to worry about, it does impose limits on subject-to-camera distances.

Showing your Movies

Here are a few tips that will make seeing good movies even more enjoyable:

Set up, thread, and focus the projector before the audience arrives. For sound movies, adjust the sound level beforehand.

If possible, fill the screen with the projected image.

To avoid a distorted image, line up the projector with the center of the screen so that the front of the projector does not have to be tipped upward.

Have the first few frames of the movie in the projector gate so that as soon as the projector is turned on, the audience will see the start of the movie, not a glaring white screen.

Make sure the room is dark enough for good viewing. Eliminate any stray light that illuminates the screen.

Add a pleasant touch to silent movies with appropriate background music from a record or tape.

Keep a spare projection lamp handy.

• *See also:* CLOSE-UP MOVIES; EDITING MOVIES; MAGNETIC SOUND FOR MOTION PICTURES; MOVIE FILMS, STORAGE AND CARE OF; PROJECTION, AUDIOVISUAL; SPLICING FILM.

Further Reading: Fellows, Malcolm Stuart. *Home Movies.* New York, NY: Drake Publishers, Inc., 1974; Ferguson, Robert. *How to Make Movies.* New York, NY: Penguin Books, 1972; Goodwin, Nancy and James Manilla. *How to Make Your Own Professional Movies.* New York, NY: Macmillan Publishing Co., 1971; Lidstone, John and Don McIntosh. *Children as Film Makers.* New York, NY: Van Nostrand Reinhold, Co., 1970; Linder, P. *Filmmaking: A Practical Guide.* Englewood Cliffs, NJ: Prentice-Hall, Inc., 1976; MacLoud, David and editors of *PhotoGraphic Magazine. Guide to Movie Making.* Los Angeles, CA: Petersen Publishers, Inc., 1973.

Hübl, Arthur von

(1852–1932)
Austrian military officer, photographer, photochemist

As director of the Military Geographical Institute of Vienna, Hübl made many innovations in the use of photography in surveying, mapping, and map printing, including contributions to the art of color photography and color printing. As early as 1882, he published a method of making an improved platinotype paper; in 1898 he invented multiple gum printing; in 1903 he offered improvements in the ozotype process. His formula for a highly concentrated glycin developer, known as Hübl Paste, was popular with pictorial photographers for many years.

Hunt, Robert

(1807–1887)
British scientist

During his lifetime Robert Hunt was one of the leading authorities on photography. His *Art of Photography,* published in 1841, was the first general work dealing with photography on metal, paper, and glass. *Researches on Light,* 1844, included one of the first historical accounts of the development of photography, as well as the results of research into the nature of light and its action on metallic compounds, organic substances, plant growth, and inorganic bodies. Much of this information laid the foundation for later scientific understanding of the principles of photographic reactions.

Hunt was a Fellow of the Royal Society, Keeper of the Museum of Practical Geology, and a founding member of the first photographic club in London, the Calotype Club. Although not an inventor of a major photographic process, he did invent at least three variant methods of producing images on paper. The *Chromatype* used paper sensitized with a solution of copper sulfate and potassium bichromate. It was not sensitive enough for camera use, but was suitable as a printing-out material for photogenic drawing—the term for contact printing in the 1840s. The *Energiatype* was a paper that produced a negative image after two to eight minutes of exposure in the camera, with development in ferrous sulfate. The *Fluorotype* was paper sensitized with a sodium fluoride solution. It required about 30 seconds camera exposure in bright sunlight to produce a negative image when developed in ferrous sulfate.

In 1841, Hunt suggested the use of hydrogen sulfide to intensify or tone photographic images. During the 1850s he attempted unsuccessfully to produce images in platinum, using ferric oxalate in combination with a platinum salt. During this same

decade, as the first "art" movement in photography emerged, Hunt was one of the few authorities to publicly express critical reservations about making photographs that imitated styles of painting.
• *See also:* CALOTYPE; CYANOTYPE; HISTORY OF PHOTOGRAPHY.

Hurter, Ferdinand

(1844–1898)
Swiss-born English chemist

Hurter and Vero C. Driffield established the modern science of photographic sensitometry. Hurter's work covered every aspect of the problem. He first devised an actinometer, so that light intensities could be accurately measured. Having done so, he and Driffield worked out a system for determining the sensitivity of photographic emulsions, involving measurement of exposure, control of development (and the establishment of a development factor that he called "gamma"), and the measurement and plotting of the resulting densities. His first publication was in 1890. In 1898, the Royal Photographic Society awarded Hurter and Driffield the Progress Medal of the Society. In 1918, the Royal Society established the Hurter and Driffield Memorial Lectures.

Many of the photographic measurement systems currently used, such as ASA film speeds, contrast-index, densitometry, process monitoring, and so forth, are based on the work of these pioneers.
• *See also:* CHARACTERISTIC CURVE; DENSITOMETRY; DRIFFIELD, VERO CHARLES; GAMMA; SENSITOMETRY.

Huygens, Christiaan

(1629–1695)
Dutch mathematician, astronomer, physicist

The research and discoveries of Christiaan Huygens in optics and light established principles of fundamental importance to photography.

In 1655, Huygens devised new ways of grinding telescope lenses. The resulting improved instruments were used for the first observations of a satellite of Saturn as well as the discovery of the rings of that planet. In the 1680s he made lenses for aerial telescopes. The lenses—from 122 to 210 feet in focal length—were mounted on poles high in the air; the image was viewed through an eyepiece near ground level. The Huygens eyepiece design, an almost perfect apochromat, is still used in some instruments.

Huygens invented the pendulum-regulated clockwork movement, which greatly increased the accuracy and reliability of time-measurement devices. Among the immediate benefits were more precise astronomical observations and predictions.

His research in physical optics led to the first convincing formulation of the wave theory of light, with which he was able to prove the fundamental laws of optics. It opposed and eventually supplanted the corpuscular, or particle, theory that had been advanced by Isaac Newton. Huygens also experimented with the nature of polarized light, and discovered the double polarizing action of calcite.
• *See also:* LIGHT; OPTICS; POLARIZED-LIGHT PHOTOGRAPHY.

Hydrochloric Acid

Chlorhydric acid, Muriatic acid, spirit of salt

Used in platinum-printing fixing baths, tray cleaners, bleach baths for toning, and intensifiers.
Formula: HCl
Molecular Weight: 36.47

Clear, colorless, or slightly yellowish liquid, giving off acrid, irritating vapor; poisonous, corrosive. Hydrochloric acid is soluble in water and mixes with alcohol. The pure form is a solution of hydrochloric acid in water, at a strength of 36 percent.
DANGER: Poisonous; corrosive; avoid breathing vapor.

Hydrogen Peroxide

Hydrogen dioxide, Dioxygen

Strong oxidizing agent used in hypo eliminators to oxidize residual thiosulfates to sulfates.
Formula: H_2O_2
Molecular Weight: 34.02

Clear, colorless liquid, consisting of a solution of H_2O_2 in water. The drugstore variety, known as U. S. P. XI grade, is a solution of from 2.5 to 3.5 percent of hydrogen peroxide. This is commercially specified as being "10-volume" hydrogen peroxide; then a "20-volume" solution would contain about 6 percent of hydrogen peroxide, and so on. The strongest commercial solution is "100 volume" or 30 percent hydrogen peroxide, sometimes called "Superoxol"; at this strength it is dangerously caustic and must be handled with care. In addition, evolution of oxygen from the solution may build up pressures sufficient to break the bottle.

Hydroquinone

Hydrochinon, Quinol, paradihydroxybenzene, 1, 4-benzenediol

Developing agent.
Formula: $C_6H_4(OH)_2$
Molecular Weight: 110.11

Shiny, white needle-shaped crystals, slightly soluble in cold water, very soluble in hot water, cold alcohol, and ether. Hydroquinone oxidizes readily in solution, and also in the crystalline form in the presence of moisture. Reduction potential is 1.0. Hydroquinone developers are capable of producing very high contrasts, but tend to lose shadow detail when used alone. For this reason, hydroquinone is almost always used in combination with another developing agent, mostly metol, but recently phenidone-hydroquinone combinations have become popular. Both combinations have a property called "superadditivity," in which the combination has a higher activity than the sum of the separate activities. At low alkalinity, hydroquinone has little developing power, its presence in developers like Kodak developer D-76 being mainly as a preservative for the metol, which does the actual developing.

When a lens is focused at infinity, the hyperfocal distance is the distance from the near limit of depth of field to the camera. The aperture on this 28 mm lens is set at f/8 and the focus scale at infinity; this makes the hyperfocal distance about 11 feet. Maximum depth of field can be had when the lens is set at its hyperfocal distance. Photo courtesy Vivitar Corp.

Hydroxide

Hydroxide is the generic term for compounds of a metal with the hydroxyl group (OH). Most hydroxides are strongly basic, with pH ranging to 13 and above. Hydroxides of alkali metals are called "caustic alkalis"; the term is mostly used to describe sodium hydroxide and potassium hydroxide. The latter are used in photography in high-contrast developers that require very high alkalinity. Old books sometimes refer to NaOH as "sodium hydrate," but this usage is archaic.

Hyperfocal Distance

When a lens is focused at infinity, the distance beyond which all objects are in acceptably sharp focus is the *hyperfocal distance.* For example, if a 35 mm lens is set at $f/11$ and focused at infinity, objects from 11 feet to infinity will look sharp. The hyperfocal distance for these conditions is therefore 11 feet.

If the lens is then refocused to the hyperfocal distance, 11 feet, objects from half the hyperfocal distance (5½ feet) to infinity will appear in sharp focus. This gives the maximum possible depth of field for that aperture.

Many photographers waste depth of field without realizing it. In the example given, if the camera lens were focused at 50 feet instead of the hyperfocal distance for the *f*-stop in use, the depth of field would be from 10 feet to infinity, instead of from 5½ feet to infinity. The result is a loss of about 4½ feet of foreground sharpness.

Depth-of-Field Scale

The hyperfocal distance is different for each *f*-stop setting of a given lens. The distance may easily be calculated for each aperture by using the formula given below. However, there is a quick way to focus at the hyperfocal distance for any *f*-stop if the lens barrel has a depth-of-field scale, as is the case with lenses for most 35 mm and medium-format cameras. Set the infinity mark (∞) on the lens distance scale opposite the index mark for the *f*-stop in use at one side of the depth-of-field scale. The index mark for that same *f*-stop at the other side of the scale will point to the distance at which the depth of field begins—that is, to half the hyperfocal distance. And the focusing index mark in the center of the scale will point to the hyperfocal distance itself. KODAK Professional PHOTOGUIDE, publication No. R-28, has depth-of-field dials for lenses used with medium- and large-format cameras, which can be used to find the hyperfocal distance in the same way.

Figuring Hyperfocal Distance

Depth-of-field scales and tables, and hyperfocal distances are somewhat arbitrary since they are based on an acceptable "circle of confusion." (*See:* DEPTH OF FIELD.) Any point in a scene that is closer or farther away than the distance focused upon will register on the film as a small, blurred circle rather than as a point. This blurred circle is called the circle of confusion. When these circles are small enough to appear as points, the subject looks sharp. But the farther a point in the scene is from the plane the camera is focused upon, the larger the circle of confusion becomes. When the circles become so large that the subject no longer appears sharp, it is no longer within the depth of field.

In using the following formula to determine hyperfocal distance, you may use the values for circle of confusion in this table, or a value of the lens focal length (F) divided by 1000 (0.001F). To have the depth of field consistent for a series of lenses on a single format, use this formula for the normal focal length, and use the same diameter for all the lenses in the series. For example, for a 2¼" × 2¼" camera, the normal focal length is 80 mm; thus, 80 ÷ 1000 = 0.08 mm. Use this value for all the wide-angle and telephoto lenses for this camera, no matter what their focal length is. In using the following table, select the value in millimetres or inches to match the unit in which the focal length is measured. The formula for hyperfocal distance (near limit of depth of field when lens is set at infinity) is:

$$H = \frac{F^2}{f \times d}$$

where:

H = hyperfocal distance
F = focal length of lens
f = *f*-number setting
d = diameter of circle of confusion.

Format Size	Diameter Circle of Confusion	
	mm	inches
35 mm or 126	0.05	0.002
Roll films	0.12	0.005
4" × 5"	0.15	0.006
5" × 7"	0.20	0.008
8" × 10"	0.30	0.012

• *See also:* DEPTH OF FIELD; FOCUSING SYSTEMS; OPTICS.

Hypo

Commonly used term for fixing baths or the fixing agent in fixing baths. The term is an abbreviation of "hyposulfite of soda," an obsolete name for sodium thiosulfate, which is the principal ingredient in most fixing baths. The discovery of hypo by Sir John Herschel in the late 1830s and its use as a fixing agent for photographic images, including daguerreotypes, made photography feasible by making permanent images possible.

Formula: $Na_2S_2O_3 \cdot 5H_2O$
Molecular Weight: 248.19
• *See also:* FIXERS AND FIXING; SODIUM THIOSULFATE.

Identification Cards

Photographs are highly effective as personal identification on drivers' licenses, student activity cards, industrial and governmental security passes, bank credit cards, passports, and other documents. The mechanics of producing the photograph are practically the same for the various forms of personal identification. However, some details, such as the lamination of security passes, vary with the desired end result.

Planning

In addition to deciding where and how laboratory production will be done, one should consider several other factors before making color ID cards. These factors include location of the camera, scheduling of the photography, the number of prints that are needed from each negative (some can be used for personnel files, medical files, and department rosters), the length of time the cards are to be used, the desirability of lamination, the accommodation of personnel turnover, and the replacement of lost or damaged ID cards.

Design

Because security requirements vary widely and have considerable influence on ID card design, specific recommendations will not be given in this article. On the other hand, the ID card illustrated may serve as a practical example. The original has a picture $1\frac{1}{2}'' \times 2\frac{3}{8}''$ in size, with a $2\frac{1}{16}'' \times 2\frac{3}{8}''$

This identification card, reproduced original size, has a black panel to allow overprinting of the photograph, thereby avoiding a white line between photo and panel. The company's name, logo, and address appear in the panel on the front of the card, along with the employee's number. Fingerprint, signature, and physical description appear on a safety paper insert on the back of the print.

AMPHOTO
750 Zeckendorf Blvd.
Garden City, N.Y.

ID no. 1225

signature panel on the side. (Notice that the background of the signature panel is black. This allows overprinting of the signature panel, which prevents a white line from showing between the picture and the panel. If the panel were light in color, the overprinted picture would be visible. Although a black background is not necessary, a dark color should be used.) An insert of safety paper (such as that used for checks) is attached to the back of the print. It contains detailed identification such as fingerprints, signature, and vital statistics. The ID pass becomes tamper-resistant when it is laminated in plastic.

Photography

A color negative is required for the production of multiple identification photographs. This negative can be used to make both black-and-white and color prints.

Cameras and Film. Any camera having a color-corrected lens, an accurate shutter, and the ability to accommodate available color-film sizes can be used for exposing identification photographs. Excellent results are obtained when a 35 mm single-lens reflex camera with a medium telephoto lens is used. The 20- or 36-exposure magazines of film are convenient and easily handled. They are well-suited to operations where relatively few exposures are involved; however, when large-volume production is involved, it is desirable to use a camera that has been designed specifically for ID photography. Cameras of this type are available from professional photographic dealers. Although such cameras have different features, each of them accepts film in 100-foot rolls (sometimes longer). The potential production rate of these cameras is many times greater than that possible with cameras intended primarily for amateur photography, professional portraiture, or commercial use. At least one color negative film is available in 100-foot rolls in 35 mm, 46 mm, and 70 mm widths. Complete instructions for use are included with the film. It should be pointed out, however, that exposed film should not be kept in the camera longer than 48 hours (to avoid changes in the latent image). Therefore, if a 100-foot roll of film has not been exposed within 48 hours, the exposed portion should be removed and processed.

Kodak Vericolor ID Film. This film is designed to record high-contrast copy in addition to produc-

ing pleasing portraits. It is balanced for electronic flash without a filter, and has a speed of ASA 80.

Two exposures—one of the subject and one of the legend or insignia—are made simultaneously on a single film frame in a camera designed for ID photography. The negative is printed with a single exposure on conventional printing equipment. This system affords a simple method for making identification cards.

All negatives should be exposed under the same conditions. This eliminates the need for the printer operator to judge the negatives individually, and makes it possible to produce identically exposed prints because only one set of print exposure conditions is used.

Location. The area in which the ID photographs are taken should be selected carefully. It should be easily accessible and yet secluded enough to prevent distraction of the subject during photography; large enough to accommodate the operating personnel, their equipment, and those waiting their turn to be photographed; and near a room that can be made totally dark (for reloading the camera). A mirror should be provided in the waiting area for the subject's use.

Permanent Installation. Whether or not a single location is practical depends on the number of people to be processed and on the layout of the plant or office. There are many advantages to having a permanent installation. First, the camera and lights can be made immovable; this eliminates readjusting the equipment for each new group of subjects. Second, operating personnel (photographic and stenographic) perform more efficiently in a permanent installation than they would if moved from one location to another. Next, adequate privacy can be assured in permanent facilities so that production personnel are not disturbed. Finally, problems resulting from variations in room lighting and inadequate or inaccessible power supply can be avoided in a permanent location.

Portable System. The primary advantage of a portable system, where the equipment is taken to different areas in the plant, is that lost time of personnel is greatly reduced. Such losses can be a major factor when large groups of personnel come in from widely scattered work areas to be photographed. In the event that your personnel are distributed in this manner, you should consider setting up the equipment in centrally located buildings throughout the grounds. After the employees in one area have been photographed, the equipment can be moved.

Identify the Negatives. Some means should be used to record the subject's name on the negative so that the finishing personnel and stenographers can be sure that the photograph is that of the person described on the insert sheet. After the picture and descriptions are matched, the name is cut off the print. This identification should not be removed from the negative because it will be needed if reprints are ordered at a future date. A small card with the name and identification number of the subject (printed by hand) can be placed near the subject at the time the negative is exposed.

If you intend to use this method of identification, be sure to determine the depth of field covered by the camera lens, because under some conditions the name on the card may be out of focus. Also, be sure that the card will not be visible when the negative is printed.

Lighting

Correct lighting for color identification photographs is similar to that used for professional portraits. Electronic flash is recommended because of its exposure repeatability, action-stopping speed, and uniformity of color temperature. If this light source is not available, however, photoflood or photoflash lamps can be used. For color photography, the intensity of the fill light on the subject should be approximately one-half that of the main light—a lighting ratio of 3:1. The correct lamp-to-subject distance for this lighting ratio can be determined with an exposure meter by temporarily using the modeling lamps of the flash units, or by substituting photoflood lamps in place of the electronic flash lamps.

In identification photography, the lighting arrangement should not be changed. Therefore, the setup used must provide good modeling for all types of faces. (*See:* LIGHTING; PORTRAITURE.)

For uniformity, all subjects must be in the same position relative to the camera and lights. This can be accomplished either by elevating or lowering the camera and lights for each subject or by placing the subject on a seat that can be raised or lowered. A chair such as those used by dentists or barbers should be considered. If the camera has no range-finder, marks can be placed on the background, outside the range of the camera, to assist in placing the subjects in the same position.

Film Processing

A simple method of processing small quantities of 35 mm color film is to use either a daylight-loading processing tank or stainless steel processing reels for 20-exposure magazines of 135 film. Use the tank if you need to process only one magazine of film at a time. With the stainless steel reels, it is possible to process a number of magazines of film simultaneously in specially designed tanks. Follow the instructions furnished with the chemicals recommended for the type of film you are using.

Process monitoring is extremely important in the production of color negatives and prints used for identification photos. All negatives must be processed correctly to produce prints that are uniform in color balance and density. It is nearly impossible to use picture negatives to judge the condition of the processing solutions or to determine whether the recommended processing procedures are being followed. For this reason, sensitometric control strips should be used. Kodak control strips for the various types of processing are available for this purpose.

Negative for Legend

The printing step in the production of ID passes sometimes involves the combination of projection and contact printing. Projection printing is used for the portrait (where enlargement is necessary), while the legend and insignia are contact printed.

Once the film has been processed, no further preparation is needed for the picture negatives. The negative for the legend and insignia, however, does require some preparation. All of the words that are used on the card must be set in type, and must then be photographed to produce a black-and-white negative on a high-contrast negative material, such as Kodalith ortho film or Kodalith pan film. One way to do this is to send the information for a group of cards to a printer and have the type set and the negatives made with graphic arts photographic equipment. Remember that the name and the address of the company need be set up and photographed only once, regardless of how many different cards are to be prepared. The alternative to having the printer make the negative is, of course, to have the type set and the proofs given to you. The proofs can then be photographed with any copy or view camera, and the high-contrast negative material processed in your own darkroom. Using these negatives, you can print the legend on the card in black letters or, by printing through appropriate filters, you can produce the letters in color.

Mounting and Printing

The final step before the printing operation is to mount sections of the negative material—namely, the person's name, title, and division, and the company's name and address—on an opaque mask (which will cover the top of the contact-printing attachment box). Arrange the various elements to provide the desired format and to locate them correctly in relation to the color portrait. (*See:* CONTACT PRINTING.)

Finishing

Cutting. The final operation is to cut and laminate the processed and dried paper to the correct card size. For small-volume production, the cutting can be done with a hand trimmer. If the volume of production is high, an automatic print cutter, such as the Kodak roll paper cutter, model 5RD-K, should be considered.

Laminating. ID cards can be protected from tampering and wear by laminating them in plastic. The successful lamination of a color photograph requires strict adherence to recommended procedures. No change should be made in such procedures unless extensive experimentation proves that such a change will have no adverse effect on the ID card. Failure to investigate a new procedure thoroughly may result in poor lamination or loss of color in the print, either of which could reduce the security value of a card and spoil its appearance.

• *See also:* CONTACT PRINTING; LAMINATING; LIGHTING; PORTRAITURE.

Image Effects

The image recorded on a photographic plate or film is the end product of many complex events. Inevitably, some variables may occur during exposure and development of the latent image that affect the image, either in the amount of silver that forms it, or in the way the silver records details of the subject. Exposure effects and development effects are inseparably linked because an invisible latent image cannot be evaluated until the exposed silver halide is reduced to metallic silver during development. For convenience of discussion, however, the effects relating to exposure have been separated from those resulting from the chemical processing procedures.

Exposure Effects

When a photographic emulsion is exposed to actinic radiation, a variety of end results are possible, depending on the quality of radiation and the manner in which it acts on the silver-halide grains. It is also possible to obtain the same photographic response, as measured by the optical density produced, from a variety of exposure conditions.

Reciprocity Effects. In 1862, Bunsen and Roscoe proposed a general law for photochemical reactions that stated that the product of a photochemical reaction is dependent on the total energy employed. In photography, this means that the density of the image formed is dependent upon the energy (E) of the exposure, which is equal to the product of the intensity of exposure (I) and the time of exposure (t). Most photographic materials show some loss of sensitivity (decreased image density) when exposed to very low or very high illuminance levels, even though the total energy of exposure remains constant by adjustment of exposure time. This loss in sensitivity is known as the "reciprocity effect" or "failure of the reciprocity law." The failure of the law means that the image density is indeed dependent upon both intensity and time of exposure. Since photographic work is done at very low or very high levels of illumination, reciprocity effects may become significant. They are, therefore, an important factor in the choice of materials.

Reciprocity Determination. The usual method of studying reciprocity effects is to measure the amounts of exposure required to produce a constant density at different levels of illuminance. A typical curve illustrating reciprocity effects is shown in the accompanying illustration. The 45-degree lines on such a diagram are lines of constant time, whereas the vertical lines represent constant illuminance. From left to right on the diagram, the illuminance increases and the duration of exposure decreases. If

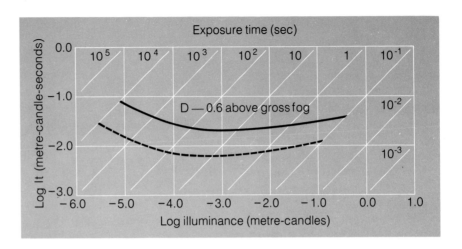

the curve generated for a particular emulsion were parallel to the log illuminance axis, it would indicate that there was no departure from the reciprocity law; that is, constant total exposure ($I \times t$) was required to produce the desired density, regardless of the illuminance level. The reciprocity curves for most materials, however, turn upward at the left, showing that for very low levels of illumination and exposures of long duration, the effective sensitivity of the material is decreased, so that more total exposure (either more light or longer exposure times) is needed in order to produce the desired density. As shown in the illustration, the curves also turn upward at the right, indicating a loss in effective sensitivity when the material is exposed to high levels of illumination for short periods of time.

Reciprocity curves differ in shape from product to product. Some curves are less concave than the ones shown, but each has a low point or low region at which the emulsion is most responsive to light. Both the shape of the reciprocity curve and the region of greatest photographic response can be controlled within limits during manufacture in order to fit the intended use of the product. Generally, a product that is designed to perform best when exposed to low levels of illumination for extended periods of time is not an equally effective recorder for high levels of illumination at short exposure times, and vice versa.

Factors Affecting Reciprocity Characteristics. The temperature of an emulsion and the environment in which it is exposed are the major factors that can alter the reciprocity characteristics of a photographic plate or film. Early work on the temperature dependence of sensitivity of photographic emulsions revealed that in some instances emulsion sensitivity, or the *effective speed* of the emulsion, can be increased by lowering the temperature of the emulsion during long exposures to low-intensity radiation. Conversely, lowering the temperature had the affect of decreasing sensitivity for exposures made at high-intensity levels.

While temperature and exposure environment are important factors to be considered in reciprocity behavior in scientific photography, reciprocity effects do not vary importantly with wavelength of the radiation to which materials respond. The range of temperatures usually encountered in ordinary photography does not affect reciprocity to the extent that a correction must be made for it.

Intermittency Effect. Related somewhat to reciprocity effect is the *intermittency effect.* A continuous exposure may not produce the same density as another exposure in which the same total energy is applied to the material in a number of separate installments. Since intermittent exposures are often used in absorption spectrophotometry, the intermittency effect is of considerable importance. Fortunately, however, it has been shown that a continuous and an intermittent exposure of the same average intensity and the same total exposure time become equal in their effects when the frequency of interruption is above a certain critical level. Although this critical level of frequency varies with intensity, a good practical rule to follow is to divide the intermittent exposure into at least 100 installments, regardless of the overall exposure time. This effect is not usually encountered in regular picture taking.

Clayden Effect. If a photographic emulsion receives a very short first exposure to very high-intensity radiation and then a second exposure to radiation of moderate intensity, the two do not add in the normal fashion, but actually subtract exposure. The first, very high-intensity exposure *desensitizes* the emulsion to the second exposure. If the first exposure has affected only a part of the emulsion, and the second exposure is uniform over all the emulsion, the image of the first often appears reversed upon development; that is, a positive instead of a negative is formed. This phenomenon is known as the *Clayden effect*. It has been observed frequently in the photography of lightning flashes, where it gives rise to so-called "black lightning."

Villard Effect. The *Villard effect* results from exposing conditions similar to those responsible for the Clayden effect—a high-intensity first exposure followed by a moderate-intensity second exposure. This similarity has been responsible for creating some confusion in differentiating between the two effects. It is generally agreed now that the term Villard effect is reserved for describing a *latent-image reversal* in which there is a loss of developability, not merely a desensitization as with the Clayden effect. The net result is the formation of a positive image accompanied by a decrease in developed density.

Solarization. The shoulder region in the characteristic curve of an emulsion's response usually shows that, with further increases in exposure, the curve becomes horizontal and no additional increase in density results. If exposure is increased far beyond the point at which D-max is first obtained, some photographic materials show a decrease in density. This effect is known as *solarization* and amounts to a whole or partial reversal of the image.

Some films, such as black-and-white duplicating films, make use of this principle. They are uniformly exposed by the manufacturer to the point just short of where the maximum shoulder density starts to lower. The additional exposure given by the photographer produces a positive image with normal development. No reversal processing is required.

Herschel Effect. If an emulsion that has not been sensitized to red or infrared radiation is exposed to blue or white light, a latent image will be formed in the normal way. In some cases when the emulsion is subsequently exposed to red or infrared radiation before it is developed, some of the effect of the original exposure will be erased. Thus, the long-wavelength radiation is capable of destroying, to some extent, the latent image formed by the blue light. This is the *Herschel effect*. It is not subject to reciprocity-law failure so far as is known. However, the energy required to destroy a latent image by the Herschel effect is several orders of magnitude higher than that required to form the initial latent image.

Sabattier Effect. The *Sabattier effect* (sometimes erroneously called solarization) is achieved by interrupting the normal processing procedure in order to make a second fogging exposure. This effect may be deliberately produced for artistic effects, but it may also be produced unintentionally if development is carried out under safelight illumination that is not "safe" or when there is undetected light entering the darkroom. The result is a reversal image that may be partial or complete, depending on the relative intensities of the first and second exposures.

Processing Effects

In addition to the effects that are characteristic of either the photographic material itself or the manner in which it is exposed, adjacency effects, otherwise known as *development effects* or *neighborhood effects,* may arise during development. These effects refer to phenomena that alter the density-exposure relationship, usually with respect to small details as opposed to large uniform areas of a plate or film. The exhaustion of the developer with use and the manner in which agitation affects the diffusion of developing agents and reaction by-products within the emulsion layer can cause these localized changes in density, which may jeopardize the accuracy of results. Among these localized effects are *edge effects,* the *Eberhard effect,* and the *Kostinsky effect.*

Edge Effects. At the boundary of a dark image and a light background, the reaction products diffuse from the dark image into the region of light density and restrain development in this region near the dark image. At the dark edge, developer is less exhausted because fresh developer from the light region diffuses into the dark image at a location well within the dark area. Thus, the image density is lower inside the image than at the extreme edge. The

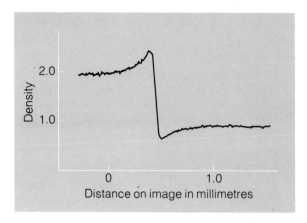

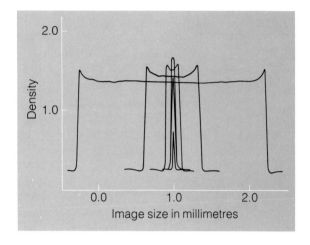

(Left) Microdensitometer tracing showing border effect at the edge of a dark image. (Below) Microdensitometer tracings showing the Eberhard effect on densities of narrow images. (Bottom) Relation between density and width of narrow images.

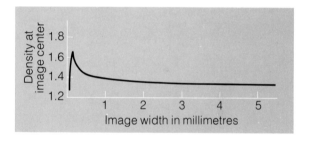

resulting density pattern across such an image edge gives a curve similar to that shown in the accompanying illustration. The high-density rim is known as the *border effect,* and the low-density halo outside a dense image is called the *fringe effect.* Edge effects vary from product to product and are influenced by development conditions. Very dilute film developers give greater edge sharpness because of this effect.

The modulation transfer function curves of many films show a response greater than 100 percent at low frequencies. This apparent "getting something for nothing" is a direct result of edge effects.

Eberhard Effect. When two small areas of unequal size are given equal exposure and development, the density of the smaller area will, in general, be higher than that of the larger area, as a result of the border effect. This phenomenon is known as the *Eberhard effect.* It is shown graphically in one of the accompanying illustrations by microdensitometer traces across a series of slit images of decreasing width and in the other illustration by the plotting of density at the centers of these images as a function of image width. For this particular emulsion-developer combination, the maximum density is reached with slit images about 0.1 mm in width. Narrower images show a reduced density that can be explained by a loss of exposure with very small images, caused by the scattering of light away from the image with no compensating scattering of light within the image, as in the case with large images. Flare light in the microdensitometer may also cause an apparent reduction in the density of fine lines.

A major consequence of this effect is that fine lines on a clear background may have a different characteristic curve from ordinary sensitometric areas; the microsensitometry shows a higher contrast than the macrosensitometry. Thus, it is necessary to calibrate a system properly when doing photographic photometry of fine lines that vary in dimension. This effect is of importance in astronomical photography.

Kostinsky Effect. When two small images, such as those formed by double stars or double emission lines, lie close together, a form of development inhibition known as the *Kostinsky effect* may take place. In the region between the two images, the developer is exhausted and the reaction products accumulate to a much greater extent than at other points around the image. As a result, development is inhibited where the images nearly touch, but proceeds normally elsewhere. The result of this asymmetrical inhibition is a warped shape that exaggerates the separation of the two images. In determining the exact location of stars, this effect must be considered.

Other Considerations. The preceding paragraphs describe several development effects that can occur at the sharp boundaries between image areas of different density—effects that are attributable largely to the unequal distribution of the developer and the reaction products of development. The magnitude of these processing effects is influenced by several factors: the density difference between adjacent areas, the degree of development, developer composition, and efficiency of agitation. The first three factors are interrelated in that a particular plate or film is usually selected on the basis of its capability to record an image under certain conditions. It is then exposed and processed according to recommendations in order to yield the desired results. The importance of the remaining factor—agitation—cannot be overemphasized with respect to its influence on minimizing edge effects and also in achieving uniform and efficient development of the recorded image.

Individual tests using your own processing technique should be run to determine which conditions give minimum adjacency effects. Although improved agitation will usually reduce the magnitude of the effects, even the most vigorous agitation may not eliminate the effects encountered with some emulsion-developer combinations. Under some conditions, when certain effects such as increasing sharpness using edge effects are desirable, the opposite approach is used.

• *See also:* AGITATION; CHARACTERISTIC CURVE; INFRARED; RECIPROCITY EFFECT; SABATTIER EFFECT.

Incandescent Lamps

An incandescent lamp consists primarily of a tungsten filament enclosed in a protective, gas-filled envelope that is commonly globular or tubular in shape. The envelope may be clear, frosted, or opal, and may be neutral or colored. The filament has a relatively high electrical resistance that causes it to glow as heat is generated by the passage of an electric current through it. The filament must be raised to a temperature of more than 2000 C (3632 F) to obtain a useful amount of light for most purposes. Tungsten is used as a filament material because it has the required high resistance and the highest melting point of all the metallic elements. Further, it has the required strength, even at high temperatures, to withstand the jars of reasonable handling.

In spite of its high melting point, the filament material slowly evaporates as the lamp is operated; even in a vacuum, the rate of evaporation is high enough that the evaporated material gradually forms a dark deposit on the inner walls of the glass envelope. This deposit progressively lowers the transmission of the glass, hence lowering the output of the lamp, and changes the color of the light as the bulb ages with use. To minimize these effects, the lamp is filled with an inert gas such as argon. This inert gas prevents combustion of the filament material, and because it is kept at a higher pressure than the vapor pressure of the filament, it greatly reduces evaporation. This has the practical effect of keeping the lamp clear for a much longer time. More importantly, it permits the filament to operate at a higher temperature, thereby producing a whiter (higher color temperature) light and increasing the light output in proportion to the current consumption. That is, the efficiency of the lamp is increased.

The other important parts of an incandescent lamp are the base, which provides support for the lamp and electrical contact with the source of electricity; the leads, which are low-resistance wires that conduct the electricity to the ends of the filament; and the filament supports, which are non-conductors that hold the filament in place in the globe.

Lamp Efficiency

The efficiency of a tungsten-filament lamp varies with the temperature of the filament. It is not easy to measure this temperature directly, but it can be ascertained from the color temperature of the emitted light. The physical temperature of a radiant body in degrees Celsius is equal to the color temperature of the radiated energy in Kelvin degrees, minus 273. This is strictly true only for a perfect radiator, such as a black body, but it is sufficiently accurate with regard to tungsten filaments to be useful.

Image Effects

Light output efficiency can be increased by operating a tungsten-filament lamp at a high color temperature. To obtain the largest possible light output, with the least power consumption, the filament should operate at the highest possible color temperature, thereby increasing the number of lumens per watt.

Light output is measured in lumens. A tungsten filament lamp of the typical home-illumination type operates at about 2650 K color temperature and emits about 10 lumens per watt. Thus, a 100-watt lamp working at this color temperature would emit 1000 lumens.

Efficiency can be increased by operating the lamp at a higher color temperature. Since the voltage remains approximately the same under normal conditions, this is achieved by changing the thickness and design of the filament and the composition and pressure of the gas in the bulb. A lamp operating at about 2950 K produces about 19 lumens per watt, so a 100-watt lamp at this color temperature would emit 1900 lumens, or almost twice as much light as the lower-temperature lamp, for exactly the same power consumption.

This leads to an obvious conclusion: To obtain the largest possible light output, with the least power consumption, the filament should operate at the highest possible color temperature. This is practical up to a point. Photographic lamps for studio use and for use in projectors usually operate at about 3200 K. Their efficiency is roughly 28 lumens per watt; thus a 100-watt lamp of this type emits about 2800 lumens.

Where maximum light output is required, as with certain projection lamps and photolamps, raising the color temperature to 3400 K achieves an efficiency level of about 34 lumens per watt, or 3400 lumens for a 100-watt lamp.

Obviously, this cannot be continued indefinitely. At 3400 K color temperature, a tungsten filament is at a physical temperature of about 3027 C (5481 F). The melting point of tungsten is 3380 C (about 6100 F). Raising the filament temperature any closer to this limit would gain, at best, only 50 K in color temperature and would greatly shorten lamp life through filament failure.

Even at 3400 K, lamp life is very short, due to evaporation of the filament. The first No. 1 photoflood lamps (3400 K) had a life of only about 2 hours. Current models use heavier filaments and higher gas pressure to achieve an average life of 4 hours, but this is still very short. Inescapably, lamp efficiency is a trade-off against lamp life.

These color temperatures refer to the output of the filament, and of a clear bulb. Another way that the color temperature can be raised without actually increasing the temperature of the filament is to filter the light. Blue photolamps are made of blue filter glass that raises the color of the 3400 K filament to about 4900–5000 K, closely approximating daylight. However, the amount of light is decreased by the filtering action.

Lamp Life

The life of an incandescent lamp, barring accident, is dependent upon the temperature at which the filament operates. This can be controlled within limits by changing the voltage supplied to it. For instance, if a lamp has a life of 1000 hours at its rated operating voltage, increasing the voltage will shorten the life by raising the filament temperature; lowering the voltage will lengthen the life of the lamp.

The effect is not proportional, but super-proportional, and follows a percentage rate for lamps of any size. Typically, raising the voltage by only 4 percent will cut the life of the lamp in half; lowering the voltage by about 5 percent will double the life. Greater changes produce even more drastic results. Reducing the voltage by 10 percent will increase the life of the lamp 400 percent, but will reduce the light output by only 15 percent. If greater output is required, raising the voltage by 10 percent will reduce the life to only 20 percent (one-fifth, or for example, 200 hours for a normal 1000-hour lamp), but will increase the light output by a full 40 percent.

This applies to any type of lamp. A photoflood lamp, for instance, is simply an incandescent lamp working at well above its rated filament voltage. (The British term for such lamps—"overrun"—is highly descriptive.) The expected life is shortened by nearly 99.6 percent—from 1000 hours to 4 hours—but the light output for a consumption of 250 watts is nearly equal to a 750-watt lamp under normal operation. However, whenever the operating voltage changes, the color temperature of the light also changes.

A voltage-control transformer can be used to raise the output and color temperature of light from standard lamps. For example, the original Colortran unit was a simple step-up transformer used with ordinary 150-watt PAR-type reflector-flood bulbs. The transformer had two taps that raised the voltage about 25 and 45 volts, respectively. These changes elevated the color temperature to 3200 K and 3400 K with greatly increased light output, but considerably shortened lamp life. Arrangement of the lights and focusing was done at the lower voltage; it was raised just to take the picture, so that the overall life of the bulbs was not shortened greatly.

A continuously variable voltage transformer of sufficient capacity can be used similarly. In general, the color temperature of an incandescent lamp increases by 10 K for each volt the input is raised above normal, and decreases by 10 K for each volt the input is lowered. This holds true, however, only for a narrow range around the normal operating voltage of the lamp. The exact voltage change required for a given change in color temperature can be determined with a color-temperature meter, or by exposure tests on color film with standard color-reference patches.

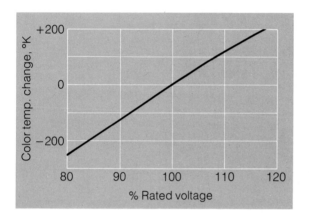

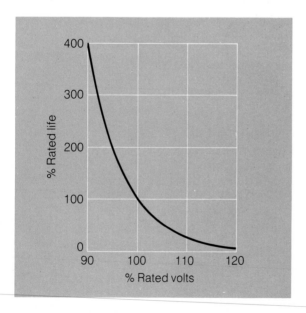

(Above) Typical color-temperature variations for incandescent lamps. Whenever the operating voltage of an incandescent lamp changes, the color temperature of the light also changes. (Below) Typical life variations for incandescent lamps. Increasing the voltage from the rated operating voltage will shorten the life of an incandescent lamp by raising the filament temperature; lowering the voltage will lengthen the life of the lamp.

Incandescent Lamps

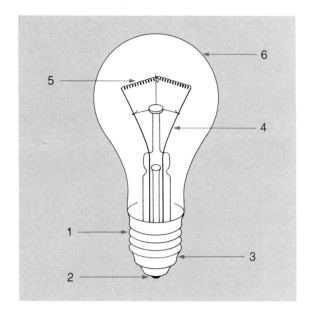

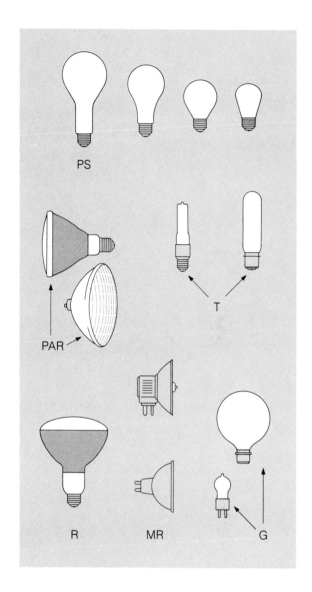

(Above) Parts of an incandescent lamp: (1) one contact, (2) other contact, (3) base threads, (4) filament supports with leads, (5) filament, and (6) envelope or bulb. (Right) Common incandescent bulb shapes (not to scale): (PS) pear shape, (T) tubular, (G) globe, (R) reflector, (MR) mirror reflector, (PAR) parabolic reflector.

Tungsten-Halogen Lamps

The most recent improvement in incandescent lamps is the so-called "quartz-iodine" or "tungsten-halogen" lamp. These lamps use halogen vapor in place of argon or other gases, and have a very small outer envelope of fused-quartz or high-silica glass. They produce much greater output of virtually unchanging color temperature throughout their lives, without increased power consumption. They are considerably smaller than equivalent tungsten-filament lamps, and operate at much higher temperatures. For additional information, see the article TUNGSTEN-HALOGEN LAMP.

Lamp Designation and Description

Most incandescent lamps for photographic use are designated by a three-letter ANSI code: for example, BEP or DDB. The letters are not abbreviations, but are chosen arbitrarily; the code for a given type of lamp applies to corresponding lamps of all manufacturers. Some lamps have a double code such as CVS/CVX to indicate that they can be used to replace either of the designated types. This is done where the two lamps differ only in some unimportant detail, for example having a black or a clear glass top.

Older lamp designations usually consisted of wattage indication, letters for bulb shape, and a number for bulb size. For example, a common lamp used in portable projectors and spotlights was designated 500-T20, indicating that it was a 500-watt,

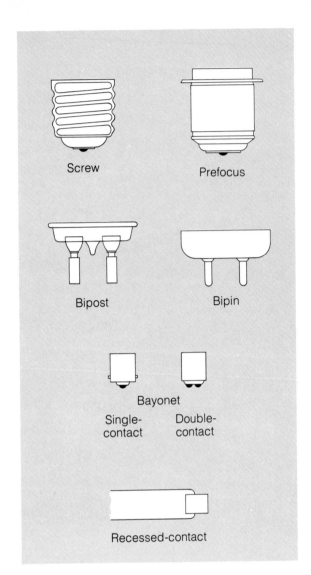

Screw

Prefocus

Bipost

Bipin

Bayonet

Single-
contact

Double-
contact

Recessed-contact

Industrial Photography

The field of industrial photography probably encompasses more different uses of photography, and calls for a greater range of photographic techniques, than any other kind of professional photography.

As the chart on the following page shows, there are four major kinds of pictures commonly required: service, promotional, photoreproduction, and scientific and technical. The chart lists many applications for each kind of picture. The table on photography in industry in this article gives some idea of how many different kinds of photography are required to carry out these applications—and the list of topics could easily be expanded.

It is obvious that no single photographer can master more than a small portion of this vast range. As a result, the photography department or section of an industrial organization tends to grow from a nucleus of specialists whose initial task is to meet the technical photographic needs of the organization. This is so because it is easier to find a freelance photographer who can take portraits of the members of the board or feature pictures for the annual report than one who can photograph the impact of sandblasting on super-chilled glass, for example.

Although there are freelance specialists and photographic consultants in the field, the great bulk of industrial photography is carried out by organization employees. The person who makes the most valuable kind of staff industrial photographer is one who has a variety of photographic skills coupled with training or education in the particular industrial field—one who has studied to be an engineer, designer, chemist, physicist, or other kind of special-

tubular bulb, ²⁰⁄₈ of an inch (2½ inches) in diameter. The ANSI code for this lamp is now DMS (screw base) or DMX (prefocus base). The earlier designations are often retained in listing the specifications of an ANSI-coded lamp. Lamp catalogs describe lamps in tables by the use of a variety of abbreviations for lamp shape and size, filament structure, and base style and size. The accompanying illustrations show the most common bulb shapes and bases.
• *See also:* BLACK BODY; COLOR TEMPERATURE; LIGHTING; LIGHT UNITS; TUNGSTEN-HALOGEN LAMP.

PHOTOGRAPHY IN INDUSTRY

Picture-Making		Specialized Applications	
Service Pictures	**Promotional Pictures**	**Photoreproduction**	**Scientific and Technical Pictures**
Industrial engineering	Advertising	Engineering drawing-reproduction	Instrument trace recordings
Production control	Products	Microfilming	Photomicrography
Inspection	Services	Photocopy	Photomacrography
Purchasing and procurement	Catalogues	Phototemplate	Electron micrography
Inventory	Sales albums		X-ray diffraction
Construction progress	Public Relations		Microradiography
Maintenance	Newspaper releases		Autoradiography
Safety education	Stockholders' reports		Nuclear photography, etc.
Construction planning	Contract promotion		
Training	Executive portraits		
Employee identification			
Basic and applied research			

Biomedical engineering is a very specialized field best photographed by someone with an understanding of the technologies involved. Many industrial photographers are specialists in a particular field who also happen to be skilled photographers. Photo by Vic Luke.

ist, either before or after learning to be a skilled photographer.

Once a photographic capability is established within an organization, it inevitably is called upon for an ever-widening range of tasks. One after another, various departments request such things as record pictures and assistance in preparing slide programs and visual displays. Thus, at least one member of the photographic staff becomes more and more of a generalist, meeting the non-technical service requests within the organization. Eventually, if the company is large enough, some of these activities

The promotional aspect of industrial photography includes advertising and public relations. Executive photographs and "corporate pictorials" are used in annual reports, house organs, and other publications issued by corporations either to stockholders, employees, or the general public. This is the phase of industrial photography in which freelance photographers are most frequently employed. Photo by William Rivelli.

Industrial Photography

(Right) The ability to present a purely functional object in a dramatic or pleasing manner is one of the prime functions of the industrial photographer. Photo by James Karl. (Below) The infernos of heavy industry like Youngstown Steel have been photographed many times. They have their own peculiar beauty and fascination, and photographs such as this will always be in demand for service, educational, and promotional purposes.

may be taken over by the departments concerned. An automatic camera setup enables the personnel or security department to carry out identification card photography, for instance. The in-company magazine staff employs its own photographer; the audiovisual staff expands to take over slide production; the design and drafting department acquires photoreproduction facilities. Such developments are usually all to the good, for they allow the photographic department to concentrate on its primary functions.

As photography in industry has grown, photographers have found use for virtually every technique and every kind of equipment invented in photography. They have come to use motion pictures and video recording with as much ease as they use still photography. Time and again they have found themselves at the frontier of photographic techniques, and have pressed manufacturers to produce new materials and equipment to solve their problems—or have gone on to invent their own. The great diversity of the field of industrial photography offers the opportunity to be a scientific or technical specialist, a broad general-service photographer, or the administrator of a small or a large photographic organization. And there is even the opportunity to encompass all of these in the course of a career.

Industrial Photography Topics

Many of the articles and entries in this encyclopedia are either directly or indirectly related to industrial photography. Consult the index to determine where a given technique is discussed.

Infrared

Wavelengths in the visible portion of the electromagnetic energy spectrum range from about 400 nanometres (nm) at the violet end, to about 700 nm at the red end. A large band of wavelengths longer than the most extreme visible red comprises the infrared, or "below the red," region of the spectrum.

As the infrared region extends far beyond the end of the visible region, the wavelength increases. The radiation merges into heat waves, and finally into radar and radio waves. Even though the infrared extends far out, it is only the region quite near the visible red that is photographically actinic. The longest wavelength of radiation recorded by photography is about 1350 nm, but the most common applications of infrared photography deal with the region between 700 nm and 900 nm. The accompanying diagram shows the relationship of the infrared to the visible region of the spectrum, and the limits of the actinic infrared range. The techniques of recording images by means of this energy are covered in the article INFRARED PHOTOGRAPHY.

It can be seen from the diagram that photographic emulsions are especially sensitized to record only the near infrared spectrum. Beyond this range, storage and use of a specialized film would be impractical because of radiated heat. Even warmth at about body temperature, in the camera and the surroundings, would fog the film. For some applications now served by thermal recording, such specialized film, even if it could be made, would have to be

The photographically actinic regions of the electromagnetic spectrum.

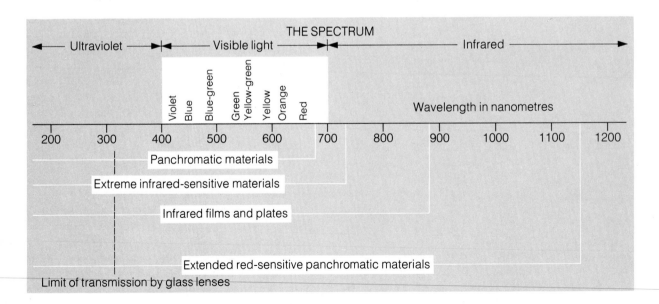

stored and used at the low temperature of liquid nitrogen.

Infrared radiation can be separated into four broad ranges of increasingly longer wavelengths:

1. The actinic range, which comprises the near-red part of the radiation produced by incandescent objects, like the sun or a lamp filament. Such radiation can be reflected, or emitted through luminescence, by subjects that are not hot themselves.
2. The hot-object range. This radiation comes from nonincandescent subjects, such as heated flatirons or electrical components, having temperatures around 400 C (752 F).
3. The calorific range. This radiation is produced by objects with temperatures around those of boiling water and steam pipes (below about 200 C [392 F]); it is nonactinic.
4. The warm range. The human body and warm ground radiate in this range; it also is nonactinic. The wavelength of radiation in this category is around 9000 nm, almost 13 times longer than the longest visible wavelength; it will be appreciated why recording such radiation on film is impossible.

- *See also:* INFRARED PHOTOGRAPHY; LIGHT; SPECTRUM; THERMAL PHOTOGRAPHY; WAVELENGTH.

Infrared Photography

Photography with infrared radiation as the principal source of exposing energy can be accomplished with conventional cameras in the wavelength region from 700 to about 1200 nanometres (nm) by using specially sensitized films. In addition, the camera lens is usually fitted with a filter that excludes the near ultraviolet and all or part of the visible spectrum.

This capability for recording infrared radiation photographically is achieved in the same manner by which more conventional films acquire sensitivity beyond the blue, into the green and red portions, of the visible spectrum; that is, sensitizing dyes are incorporated in the emulsion that absorb in selected wavelength regions and transfer the exposing energy to the silver-halide crystals.

Infrared-sensitive materials with practical photographic properties have a useful upper limit in spectral sensitivity at about 900 nm. The balance of the photographic infrared can be served by highly specialized materials such as Kodak spectroscopic plate and film, type I-Z. The latter products have relatively poor keeping qualities, necessitating special handling in shipping and deep-freeze storage until shortly before use. In most applications, they must be hypersensitized by chemical treatment prior to exposure.

Fortunately, a broad range of technical and illustrative applications of infrared photography can be accomplished in the 700–900 nm range. By using conventional cameras and techniques, reflected and transmitted infrared radiation can be imaged directly on film. Similarly, it is possible to record infrared luminescence from certain materials that respond to excitation by green, blue, or ultraviolet radiation. The same procedures can be used to record the self-radiance of objects that have been heated to at least 250 C (about 480 F). Objects that have been heated to more than 500 C (about 930 F) emit visible light and therefore can be photographed with films having panchromatic or extended-red panchromatic sensitivity. However, such heated objects also emit strongly in the infrared, so there may be special situations where it would be appropriate to record marginally incandescent objects with infrared films.

Thus, infrared photography has grown in usefulness and significance because it provides a means for recording in visual terms (tonal or color differences) information about objects or scenes as they create or affect radiation beyond the upper limit of visible light. While the photographic infrared is but a small part of the total infrared region, it is important to remember that it is nearly as broad as the visible region and that it is capable of yielding much information.

Recording Infrared Radiation

As explained in the article INFRARED, the portion of the infrared range closest to the visible wave-

DISTINCTIONS BETWEEN METHODS OF RECORDING INFRARED RADIATION

Infrared Photography	Thermography
1. Directly records reflected radiation up to about 1200 nanometres.	1. Indirectly records radiation from 700 to at least 14,000 nanometres.
2. Uses ordinary cameras and lenses with special filters.	2. Uses sophisticated opto-electronic imaging equipment with infrared detectors.
3. Uses ordinary photographic light sources to record reflected or transmitted infrared radiation.	3. Does not always require an external energy source when emitted radiation (heat) is being recorded.
4. Records infrared radiation emitted by objects that have been heated to at least 250 C (about 480 F) but not above 500 C (about 930 F). In this range, the object itself is the energy source. Above 500 C, conventional photographic techniques can be employed.	4. Responds to emitted infrared energy from objects, such as living things, at relatively low temperatures.
5. Records infrared luminescence from certain materials that respond to excitation by green, blue, or ultraviolet radiation.	

lengths is actinic—it can be recorded by *infrared photography,* using suitably sensitized film and a conventional camera and lens. Thermal infrared radiation does not expose photographic materials; it can be recorded by *thermography,* using specialized non-photographic materials or complex auxiliary equipment that translates the infrared radiation into a visible form; which can then be photographed with conventional films. For more information on this second method of infrared recording, see the article THERMAL PHOTOGRAPHY. The accompanying table lists some of the major distinctions between infrared photography and thermography.

Types of Infrared Photography

Black-and-White. Regular infrared photography can be defined as the technique of using a camera lens to focus an infrared image on an emulsion sensitized to infrared radiation in order to obtain a black-and-white negative record from which a positive print can be made with conventional photographic materials.

The subject producing the image reflects or transmits varying amounts of the infrared radiation falling on it, or emits luminescence in the infrared region when illuminated with energy of suitable wavelengths. Most forms of infrared photography require an external source of infrared; in the case of IR luminescence, the external source is visible or ultraviolet radiation.

The lights commonly used for ordinary photography can supply or excite the infrared radiation in indoor reflection, transmission, or emission techniques. Electronic flash units are best for use with many living subjects. Sometimes, however, the subject is hot enough to radiate actinic infrared itself. Outdoors, sunlight furnishes adequate infrared, but the intensity is somewhat variable because of haze and cloud cover.

Infrared emulsions are sensitive to violet, blue, and red light, as well as to infrared. Therefore, a filter has to be used over the camera lens (or sometimes, the light source) to block unwanted visible light rays. This filter passes the infrared radiation reflected or transmitted by the subject and excludes visible light and ultraviolet.

To remove reflected infrared from a luminescing specimen, it is necessary to hold back infrared from the light source with a blue-green, infrared-absorbing filter. Then, any infrared radiation arising from the subject can only be due to luminescence. It is also necessary to place an infrared filter over the lens to bar the reflected visible light coming from the exciting source. Similar attention to the use of filters is required in infrared photography of self-radiant objects.

Color. Infrared color photography originally had its beginnings with the development of a film for aerial camouflage detection. Since that time, many ground and laboratory uses and other aerial applications have been found for infrared color photography. Infrared color photography is accomplished with a daylight color film sensitized to infrared: Kodak Ektachrome infrared film. Unlike the usual color film, the three emulsion layers of this infrared film are sensitized to green, red, and infrared, rather than to blue, green, and red. A yellow filter is used on the camera to withhold blue, to which these layers are also sensitive. When processed, a yellow positive image records in the green-sensitive layer, a positive magenta image appears in the red-sensitive layer, and a cyan positive image appears in the infrared-sensitive layer (see accompanying diagram).

Blue can be formed in the transparency even though blue has been excluded from the image by the yellow filter. When the yellow image in the green-sensitized layer is bright, magenta and cyan will predominate and will combine to form blue. Numerous other colors can be formed, depending on the proportions of green, red, and infrared reflected or transmitted by the subject. As an example,

healthy leaves record red because they are "bright" in infrared; this produces a light-toned cyan image of the subject that allows red from the other layers to predominate.

In infrared color photography, the visible light component is, of course, added to the infrared record. As a result, this film does produce characteristic colors in photographs of many animal and botanical substances. It is the infrared component, however, that produces the modified color renditions. As an example, a red rose with healthy green leaves will record as yellow with red leaves. This translation of the color of objects is the basis of infrared color photography, and is a valuable asset to the study of the infrared phenomenon.

Because infrared photography formerly has been done with black-and-white films, the infrared-

Color formation with infrared color film. The three emulsion layers of the film are sensitized to green, red, and infrared. When the film is processed, a yellow positive image appears in the green-sensitive layer, a positive magenta image appears in the red-sensitive layer, and a cyan positive image appears in the infrared-sensitive layer.

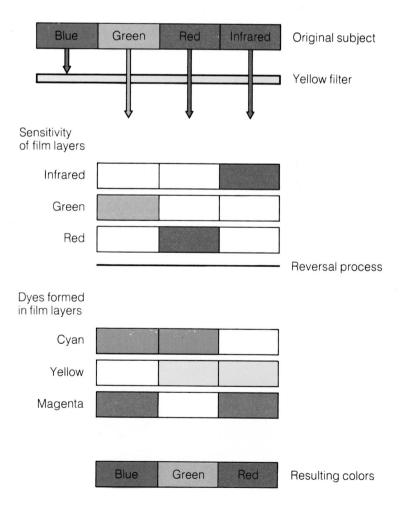

reflection characteristics of substances have not been appreciated. In the visible-light region, such variations in characteristics appear as colors. The actinic infrared band is fully as wide as that from green to red, so several infrared "colors" exist potentially. It is only when the infrared radiations are translated by intricate photographic procedures into visible color differences that distinctions can be observed in a color photograph. Infrared color film provides a simple means for making a partial translation of this nature; it converts an infrared image into a color one and combines it with visible-light components.

(Right) Color (non-infrared) and (below) infrared modified-color renditions. The dramatic change in the rendition of human skin and veining demonstrates the usefulness of infrared color in medical photography.

The piece of camouflage material under the flower pot had not been treated to reflect infrared, as the helmet cover had been. Note the differences in the colors of the fruits.

Infrared Photography

Equipment

Cameras. Any type of view camera regularly used for ordinary photography can be used for infrared photography. Because much infrared work deals with small specimens, the camera should be adaptable for close-up photography.

The most useful 35 mm equipment is a single-lens reflex camera with an automatic diaphragm. It is well suited to hand-held operation with infrared color film. Also, when opaque, infrared-transmitting filters are placed over the lights instead of over the lens, this camera can be hand-held for black-and-white infrared photography. But when such filters have to be placed over the lens, a camera with a separate viewfinder is needed.

If the camera has a through-the-lens exposure meter, the meter should be turned off when an opaque filter is employed. Some work can be done, especially outdoors, with a red filter and with the meter in operation. The camera should be set for the film speed rating without a filter. However, a red filter will affect the spectral response of the meter and may indicate an incorrect exposure for automatic operation. Tests will indicate the need for setting an adjusted exposure index.

Checking the Camera. About the only precaution to take with a camera is to be alert to a possible radiation leak through a leather bellows or the camera body, or through a plastic lens board. Should obscure streaks show up on negatives, such a defect is a probable cause. A camera can be checked by placing unexposed infrared-sensitive film in it and then moving a strong tungsten light around in front of it for about a minute. Any density that occurs on the film is due to an unsafe bellows, lens board, or camera body—provided the shutter and film holder are safe.

To rule out the shutter, cover the lens with a metal cap when you do the test. For sheet-film cameras, load the film into the holder in the dark and insert the holder into the camera in the dark, too. The dark slide of the holder is thus taken out of consideration. If the camera has a focal-plane shutter, be alert to the possibility that a rubberized fabric curtain may transmit some infrared—evidenced by curtain streaks. The same precaution may be needed with a thin, soft rubber lens cap.

Checking Film Holders. To check a dark slide for leaks, leave it in position over a loaded sheet of infrared film. Then place a large coin upon the outside of the slide and hold the light over the holder for about a minute. If neither streaks nor a shadow image of the coin appear after development of the film, the slide is safe. (Streaks coming in at the edges of the negative would indicate, in the absence of a coin shadow, that the holder may not be safe for panchromatic photography either.) Wooden slides and some hard-rubber slides transmit infrared rays readily and should not be used. Formica, metal, and most special-composition slides are "safe" for use with infrared-sensitive films.

Loading 35 mm Film in Total Darkness. The Kodak high speed infrared films must be loaded and unloaded in total darkness because the felt-lined slots of the magazines are not "lighttight" to infrared. Since darkroom loading is not required for most other films, this procedure may require a bit of practice to obtain proficiency. The camera must be returned to total darkness to unload an exposed roll.

Film removed from a refrigerator should be allowed about 1 hour to reach room temperature and about 1½ hours if it is removed from a freezer. Exposed and unexposed film can be safely stored in the sealed film can.

Most changing bags are not fully opaque to infrared radiation. When loading and unloading infrared film in a changing bag, a location with subdued lighting is advisable. It is best, however, to first test the opacity of the changing bag with a sheet of film or a piece of 35 mm film that can be pulled from a magazine in the darkroom and put into a bag. A reliable test should be conducted under work conditions for about twice the amount of time required for loading and unloading film.

Lenses. Most good camera lenses serve for infrared photography. Unless a lens has been especially achromatized for infrared photography, however, there will be a difference between the infrared-focus position and the visual-focus position. Usually, this will give rise to no serious problems, yet it ought to be investigated. Some lenses have a red dot on the focusing scale to indicate an average correction for infrared photography.

In the field of document copying, a lens of high quality is advisable, because of the fine detail often involved. And even though such subjects do not present depth-of-field problems, the lens should be stopped down to about $f/11$ in order to offset the differences between visible-light and infrared performance.

Focusing. In general, if the focusing is done on the near side of the region of interest, no correction need be made. To explain: In focusing, it is customary to shift back and forth across the sharp-focus position. This action can be stopped just when the image of the plane focused upon goes slightly out of focus as the motion is *increasing* the lens-film distance toward what would be a nearer visual focus.

Sometimes a specific correction may have to be made. As a general rule, an average correction of 0.25 percent of the focal length should be added to the lens-film extension for infinity focus. It is often difficult to judge whether or not the best definition has been obtained. This can frequently be ascertained by examining details in the negative instead of the sharpness of the area of major interest, which may not itself have fine structure.

For most subjects the lens will have to be stopped down to at least $f/11$ so that sufficient depth of field will be provided. This procedure also helps offset differences between visual and infrared focus.

Even when the lens is focused correctly, the infrared image is not as sharp as a panchromatic one. Since lens aberrations have been corrected for panchromatic photography, the anastigmatism is not as perfect in the infrared. Another aspect to consider is subject sharpness. Many biological infrared images are formed from details not on the outside of the subject. Details have a translucent, scattering medium interposed between their outlines and the lens. This accounts for the misty appearance of many infrared reflection records; lateral scattering produces a similar effect in emission photographs.

The camera is focused in the usual way when infrared color film is used, because the visual component of the image predominates.

Lights. Photographic lights of all kinds have high emission in the infrared region of the spectrum.

In most lighting setups, the visible-light intensity does not have to be greater for infrared photography than it does for regular photography. Photographic exposure-meter readings for various setups with photoflood and similar lamps can be directly related. However, the fundamental exposure has to be based on exposure tests in order to obtain negatives of a desired quality.

Tungsten Lamps. Infrared heat lamps are not more efficient to use than photographic ones; the converse is true. The infrared lamps are designed for therapeutic use; their radiation is predominantly in the hot-object region of the spectrum. However, the actinic radiation for infrared photography ranges from 700–900 nm. The photoflood lamp is the most efficient incandescent source there is for such radiation. For a given intensity of actinic infrared, the photoflood proportionately emits less visible light than either a household service bulb or a heat lamp that is not filtered. The photoflood lamp also is much cooler (for a given exposure level of infrared) than either of the other lamps. This is an important factor when lamphouses with infrared-filter windows are used or when heat can be harmful to the subject. Balanced against this efficiency is the relatively short burning life of photofloods.

It is practical to use 3200 K photographic lamps in place of photofloods. They are about as efficient as photoflood lamps and have a somewhat longer life. They are available in most photographic departments. Tungsten-halogen (quartz-halogen or iodine) lamps are also suitable for many phases of infrared photography, provided infrared has not been filtered out.

Flashbulbs. It is practical to coat a dark-red, infrared-transmitting envelope over photoflash lamps in manufacture, because they are used only once. Other sources are usually too hot for such treatment. Flashbulbs of this kind are designated "R."

They are valuable when bright visible light has to be withheld from living subjects, as well as from the emulsion. For instance, they may be used for photographing eye responses or the actions of an animal in the dark. The use of the "R" flashbulbs would eliminate the need for special lamphouses with windows covered by large sheets of filter material. The practicality of changing bulbs for each exposure must be considered. Guide numbers published for these bulbs apply to photography indoors. For outdoor work it is necessary to open up the lens an additional f-stop.

Clear photoflash lamps can be used for routine studio work with live subjects. The filtering is then done at the lens or over the lamp reflector.

Electronic Flash. Electronic flash units have many advantages in the photography of living subjects. Their benefits of coolness and short exposure time are extendible to infrared photography. The amount of infrared radiation emitted in electronic flashtube setups is comparable to the intensities in photoflash setups that would be employed for photographing the same subjects. Another advantage of these units is that they are more readily obtainable with compact reflectors than is tungsten flood equipment. Low-voltage flash units have a higher proportion of infrared radiation than high-voltage units.

Special-Purpose Light Setups. To photograph in the dark, simply cut a sheet of gelatin filter to fit tightly over electronic flashtube reflectors. The size of the window can be drawn on a sheet of wrapping paper; then the gelatin filter can be placed between this and another sheet of paper for cutting.

When a lamphouse is constructed to hold tungsten lamps, adequate ventilation must be provided to prevent overheating. The vents must be lightlocked to minimize stray illumination.

Provided short or synchronized exposures are given and the lamps are filtered, no infrared filter is needed over the lens when (1) photography is done in the dark or under dim light; (2) photographs are made in the dark of responses to non-stimulating red light; or (3) low-level red illumination only is used for observation. (*See:* SURVEILLANCE PHOTOGRAPHY.)

In addition to tungsten lamps, white fluorescent tubes can be utilized in the photography of infrared luminescence. Fluorescent lights such as those commonly found in greenhouses do not supply infrared for reflection photography. Luminescence is an emission technique and thus can benefit from the use of cool-burning fluorescent tubes. (*See:* ULTRAVIOLET AND FLUORESCENCE PHOTOGRAPHY.)

Lamps for Infrared Color Photography. Electronic flash illumination is best for indoor infrared color photography. Photoflash bulbs are not suitable. Photoflood and quartz-halogen lamps should only be used when circumstances demand, and then only with special filtering, discussed in the section on filters. It is necessary to employ heat-absorbing glass or a gelatin cyan filter.

It is worthwhile to make every effort to utilize electronic flash illumination in this technique. Not only can simpler filtering be achieved, but also the advantages of coolness and quick exposure times can be gained.

Filters. Since infrared emulsions are sensitive to the blue region of the spectrum as well as to part of the red and to the near infrared region, filters are needed for infrared records. Filter factors are given in the accompanying diagram.

In an emergency, black-and-white photographs can be made with infrared-sensitive materials with-

Transmission ranges of Kodak Wratten filters for black-and-white infrared photography. Multiplication factors (×) are shown for modifying exposures calculated on the basis of the No. 87 filter.

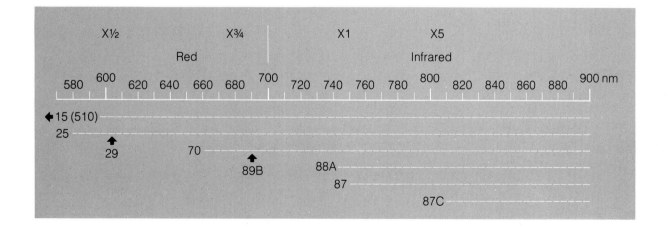

Successive sky-darkening and haze penetration effects obtainable with filters. Panchromatic filters are shown at left, infrared renditions at right. The numbers of the Kodak Wratten filters used appear beneath each record. Use of a polarizing filter is also indicated.

Panchromatic—No filter

Infrared—No. 25 filter

Panchromatic—Polarizing filter

Infrared—No. 87 filter

Panchromatic—No. 25 filter and polarizing filter

Infrared—No. 87 filter and polarizing filter

Infrared Photography

out a filter, but the rendering will be more like that of a blue-sensitive film. The quality will usually be less satisfactory than that produced by either an orthochromatic or a panchromatic film. Reds, greens, and yellows will be reproduced darker than normal; blues, lighter.

Infrared color photography calls for particular filtering methods. In some black-and-white and color techniques, absorption filters are needed for the illumination. Camera filters for photographing infrared luminescence are covered in the section on that topic.

Filters for Black-and-White Infrared Photography. Several considerations govern the choice of filters. The following Kodak Wratten filters will absorb violet and blue for black-and-white infrared photography: No. 15—orange; No. 25—red; No. 29, No. 70—deep red; and No. 87, No. 88A, No. 87C —infrared, visually opaque. The transmissions of these filters are indicated in the accompanying diagram. The red filters can be used when the camera has to be hand-held or when circumstances, like activity on the part of a live subject, make the adding of an opaque filter after focusing impractical. However, critical focusing through the red filter is somewhat difficult.

Kodak Wratten filter No. 89B has been designed for aerial photography. It produces records quite similar to the No. 25 filter. However, it affords additional penetration of haze with only a slight increase in exposure time. For aerial photography, filters should be mounted in glass of optical quality; unmounted gelatin filters are likely to result in poor definition.

When photographing in the dark, most individuals can detect a slight red glow through a No. 87 filter if they happen to be looking directly at the source during an exposure. Bouncing the radiation off a low ceiling, a reflector, or a wall is often helpful, when a subject might see a tell-tale glow as photographs are made in the dark. Alternatively, a No. 87C filter should be considered. The filter coating on the "R" infrared flashbulb cuts just beyond the visible region. Since the cut is not sharp, a glow can be detected. Still, such bulbs do away with the need for an infrared filter over the lens when the scene is in darkness or when ambient illumination or observation illumination is so low as not to affect a synchronized exposure.

Filters for Infrared Color Photography. While Kodak Ektachrome infrared film does not call for the use of an opaque filter for the infrared color photographic technique, a Kodak Wratten filter No. 12—minus blue—should be used over the camera lens. This filter absorbs the violet and blue to which the emulsion is sensitive. The color balance of the film is such that no other filter is normally needed in biological work with illumination of daylight quality.

For outdoor use, a Kodak Wratten filter No. 12 ought to be used, although a No. 8, 15, or 21 filter can be utilized for special effects. However, for scientific photography, the No. 12 filter must be used for consistent results.

Kodak Ektachrome infrared films are somewhat sensitive to aging. Also, slight differences in emulsion batch, processing, and working conditions are unavoidable. For a given project it may be necessary to trim the balance with Kodak color compensating filters—CC05 or CC10 filters will usually suffice. The following data provide a guide to making such adjustments.

FILTERS FOR COLOR BALANCE IN INFRARED COLOR PHOTOGRAPHY

Kodak Color Compensating Filters*	Desired Color Shift
Cyan	From green .... to .... more magenta
Cyan-2	From yellow .... to .... more blue
Blue	From cyan .... to .... more red
Magenta	From blue .... to .... more yellow

*Yellow, red, and green color compensating filters are of no particular value and are not used, except sometimes in photomicrography.

Any filter placed in an intense light beam should be examined periodically for fading from light and heat. When fading happens too frequently, it is necessary to find a cooler, usually broader, location in the beam.

When a light source, such as tungsten, has slightly too great a proportion of infrared radiation in its balance, or when a fresh batch of film is encountered that has a somewhat high infrared sensitivity, results are yellowish brown. Cyan filters that have some infrared absorption will compensate for this. These are the Kodak color compensating filters, cyan-2 series.

It ought to be noted that strong filtration is usually only required when tungsten illumination has to be used. Such compensation necessitates some exposure increase: for instance, for blue or cyan filters of 50 density, or for a cyan-2 filter of 50 density, about 1 stop additional exposure is needed.

Film Use

Black-and-White. As a general rule, a black-and-white infrared negative should look fairly dense. Grass and trees, particularly, appear much darker than they do in a panchromatic negative. The main features of the subject and areas that photograph dark (light on the negative) should be recorded on the straight-line portion of the characteristic curve. Small black shadows, of course, will have to be

A black-and-white infrared negative must be more dense than a typical panchromatic negative.

Print "softness" shows that visual and infrared cannot be brought to identical focus.

blank, because serious overexposure should be avoided. A shadow density of about 0.3 above fog for sheet film, and 0.5 above fog for roll film, yields good separation.

Color. Infrared color photography, often referred to as modified-color or false-color photography, is accomplished using Kodak Ektachrome infrared film and a Kodak Wratten filter No. 12. This film is ideally suited to photography with hand-held single-lens reflex cameras since it has a speed of ASA 100 and does not require the visibly opaque infrared filter used in black-and-white photography.

Storage. Storage of infrared-sensitive films in high temperatures or high humidity may produce undesirable changes in the films. To lessen the risk of losing sensitivity and of increasing fog, keep unexposed film in a refrigerator or freezer.

Unexposed Kodak high speed infrared film should be kept at 13 C (55 F), or colder, in the original sealed container. If the film is stored in a refrigerator, remove it 1 hour (1½ hours for sheets) before opening the package or can; if stored in a freezer, remove it about 1½ hours (2 hours for sheets) before opening. Films in long rolls or aerial films will require longer warm-up times (as much as 6 to 8 hours). This will prevent condensation of atmospheric moisture on the cold film. Keep exposed film cool and dry. Process the film as soon as possible after exposure to avoid undesirable changes in the latent image. If it is necessary to hold exposed but unprocessed film for several days (such as over a weekend), it should be refrigerated below 4 C (40 F) and allowed to warm up before processing. For critical uses and for extended periods of time (6 months or more), film in sealed packages should be stored at −18 to −23 C (0 to −10 F).

Processing. Machine- or hand-development of black-and-white and color infrared film must be done in the dark. *No safelighting* or infrared inspection equipment can be used in the darkroom during processing. Any custom processing laboratory should be advised of this restriction.

Infrared films are carried through the processing procedure like any other films. Developers and average processing times are shown in the instruction sheets packaged with the films. Development contrast can be varied within certain limits to provide negatives of more, or less, contrast. For records of faint patterns, films can be developed for a 30 percent increase over the average time, if moderate developers are used. The additional fog is negligible and the resultant pattern is strengthened. Consistent development contrast is imperative in making comparable serial records.

Some applications call for negatives of the highest practical contrast; they can be obtained with very active developers. The use of such developers causes some increase in graininess and requires a reduction in exposure.

Kodak Ektachrome infrared film in the 35 mm format is processed in Process E-4 chemicals or Process EA-5 chemicals. Consistent processing is essential for comparable results.

Infrared Photography Outdoors

Outdoor infrared photography is relatively simple because it does not call for the specialized lighting and filtering techniques of indoor work. There are two main purposes for infrared photography outdoors. The first is for obtaining technical and scientific information. The second is for providing unusual pictorial effects.

Technical Photography. The success of outdoor photography by infrared lies in the fact that infrared radiation and visible radiation often are reflected and transmitted quite differently by common natural and man-made objects. For example, chlorophyll in live, green foliage and grass absorbs a large percentage of the visible radiation that falls upon it, but transmits most of the infrared. This radiation is reflected by the leaf and blade structure, and therefore is recorded light in tone by means of a black-and-white infrared photograph.

Because of the special properties of infrared color film, healthy foliage records red, whereas verdure under stress photographs in other distinctive colors. Painted materials that match chlorophyll in color, but which have not been treated to reflect strongly in the infrared, will appear dark in an infrared photograph. Some buildings and many types of soil, rocks, and sand also have high infrared reflectivity, which accounts for their lighter appearance or characteristic colors in infrared photographs.

Most photographic materials render blue sky relatively light, but, since little infrared radiation is present in the blue sky, the infrared materials render it dark. This property is often utilized in black-and-white infrared photography to emphasize clouds.

Photo taken using infrared color film and a No. 15 Kodak Wratten filter provides best color distinction in foliage studies for scientific and agricultural purposes.

The degree of darkening varies with sunlight and haze conditions. Many dyes that appear brightly colored to the eye do not absorb infrared, and therefore record as white. Infrared color photography depicts blue sky in an almost natural color. The sky reflected specularly from water, or from wet leaves, also records blue. The recorded colors of pigments depend on their reflectance characteristics and are quite unpredictable.

When a distant scene is photographed on the usual photographic material, object detail is often obscured by smoky haze even when a red filter is

Infrared photo taken with a No. 21 Kodak Wratten filter gives interesting effects which can be used expressively in pictorial photography.

used. The same objects may be well defined in an infrared photograph for these reasons: (1) the longer-wavelength infrared is scattered somewhat less than is visible red light; (2) the infrared reflectivity and absorption characteristics of natural objects usually enhance the subject contrast; and (3) the ratio of object brightness to atmospheric brightness is usually increased by higher reflectivity of scene details to infrared radiation. The last of these three factors probably contributes the most toward the minimizing of the haze effect. On the other hand, infrared photographs of subjects in a heavy fog are

Infrared Photography

not usually satisfactory because of the large particle size of the water droplets.

Pictorial Photography. Many dramatic pictorial infrared photographs are obtainable in black-and-white or color. Travel photographs can often be enhanced by the haze penetration afforded by black-and-white infrared photography.

Infrared landscape photographs in black-and-white are characterized as follows: the sky is depicted almost black; clouds and snow are white; shadows and the shaded side of trees are dark, but

A black-and-white infrared photograph in effect lightens the foliage and darkens the sky of a landscape.

usually show more detail than a panchromatic rendition; grass and leaves appear very light as though covered by snow; distant details are rendered with remarkable clarity. Infrared color photography records foliage in a striking red, flowers in modified colors, and some types of stone in quite natural shades—all backed by a pleasing blue sky with white clouds in good contrast.

Fashion photography with infrared color film produces striking results. Fabrics appear in modified colors, whereas skin tones, though somewhat "cold," are almost normal. Accessories may change

Infrared photography has been used here to penetrate haze for a pictorial record of Mt. Hood as seen from Lost Lake. Note that although the trees on the far shore are in shade because of back lighting, they have not been recorded as a black strip, as would be the case with panchromatic photography.

Infrared Photography

Infrared Photography

◄ *(Left) Infrared color film can produce stunning effects for fashion photographs. Fabrics and accessories may change color dramatically. In actuality, the model's hair was ash blonde, her dress beige-gray, and the background was green. The area of eye makeup which appears green in this photo was red; the purple area, green.*

Dramatic impact can often be introduced into architectural photographs by means of infrared photography. The infrared picture at left was made with a Kodak Wratten filter No. 87. The panchromatic comparison at right shows that even with a No. 15 orange filter, the results are neither as striking nor as three-dimensional.

dramatically; in one instance, a black hairpiece recorded red.

The photographic illustrator can often dramatize his subjects by making infrared pictures of them. This type of photography gives a good separation of the planes of buildings and darkens the sky to provide a contrasting background. Lightening the tones of trees often avoids "black holes" in the composition. A comparison between panchromatic and infrared rendering of architecture is shown in the accompanying illustrations.

Infrared photographs taken outdoors in sunlight and then printed slightly darker than normal strongly suggest that they were taken by moonlight. As a matter of fact, some of the "night" scenes in professional motion pictures are made in sunlight on infrared-sensitive film. Basically, well-exposed negatives are made and these are printed somewhat dark. Through this means, sunlight appears to be moonlight. The technique has limited use for fully realistic

effects, because foliage is rendered somewhat light in tone.

Aerial Photography. While infrared aerial photography is primarily useful in enhancing the contrast of the terrain, there are other distinct advantages. For example, bodies of water are rendered very dark in sharp contrast to land, assuming that the day is clear. Fields and wooded areas are rendered very light. Coniferous and deciduous growth is differentiated, the former appearing darker than the latter. Cities are rendered darker than fields. For this reason, in infrared pictures taken at very high altitudes, urban areas appear as dark patches surrounded by lighter countryside. Aerial infrared photography has had many important applications in agriculture, archaeology, ecology, forestry, geology, and hydrology.

For aerial photography with conventional cameras, the lens should be set at a focus setting of 15–25 metres (about 50–80 feet) so that infrared radiation

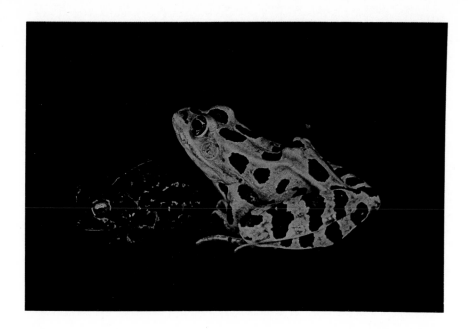

The skin of the frog has high infra-red reflectivity, while that of the barely visible toad does not.

at infinity distance will be recorded in sharp focus. Some lenses provide an infrared focus position, a red dot, to simplify this focus adjustment.

Modified Black-and-White Technique. A specific phase of aerial infrared photography in sunlight uses a modification of the more common technique. Most infrared aerial photography is done through red (No. 25) or infrared (No. 89B) filters, but certain phases of aerial (and, most likely, ground) photography are better accomplished by making the infrared record through an orange filter (No. 15). Use of the orange filter has been called the "modified black-and-white infrared technique," as opposed to the "true infrared technique."

The shadows of trees are sometimes so dense in a true infrared record that the excessive contrast of the print makes interpretation difficult. The modified technique results in more luminous shadow detail. The presence of grass or moss adds to this luminosity.

Indoor Lighting

The types of lamps that are suitable for various lighting methods have been discussed in a previous section. Regardless of the kind, the arrangement is the same for each kind of lamp, with a given subject.

Probably the greatest single factor for success in infrared photography of any type of subject is flat lighting. For comparable serial records the lighting must be consistent. A single flash holder at the side of a camera is not suitable, except sometimes for small specimens.

Direct Lighting. In this method of lighting, the lamps are aimed directly at the subject; no reflectors or diffusing media are employed. One light on each side is sufficient for lighting small subjects. Four lights, two on each side, should be employed for those presenting areas larger than about 20 inches square. When pairs of lights are used in any application, they must all be of the same wattage, and in most instances, must be placed at equal distances from the subject.

Lighting for Copying. The same basic lighting can be used for all flat two-dimensional subjects. These include documents, paintings, flat mineral and fossil surfaces, cloth, wood sections, and flattened leaves. One lamp on either side of the subject-lens axis usually suffices. The diameter of the reflectors should be about 20 to 30 centimetres (about 8 to 12 inches). Reflector photofloods are well suited to this application. In order to preclude specular

Infrared Photography

reflections in the direction of the lens, the inside rim of each reflector should be on a line 45 degrees from the surface of the subject. The reason for this is that the reflectors themselves are essentially part of the light source.

Lighting for Specimens. It is vital to avoid, as much as possible, surface shadows from contrasty lighting, edge shadows, and reflections from improper placement of the lights. Thus, there are two requirements for the illumination employed—evenness and the correct lighting angles. A large percentage of the faults seen in unsuccessful infrared photographs can be traced to neglect of these principles.

Flat, even lighting calls for an adequate number of lights, an equal amount of illumination on both sides of the camera-subject axis, and proper distribution of the lighting over the subject.

Diffuse Lighting. For irradiating complex shapes, or even for obtaining simple and consistent illumination for regular specimens, indirect, diffuse lighting by means of a tent or cubicle is strongly recommended.

The cubicle is particularly useful for providing diffuse, even lighting for all kinds of infrared color photography. It is also advantageous for many black-and-white programs, especially when animals are photographed. The lighting is so diffuse that a restless subject is suitably illuminated in spite of any minor changes in position that it may make. In addi-

Visually, these two brilliant caterpillars had the same color as the green leaf on which they were photographed.

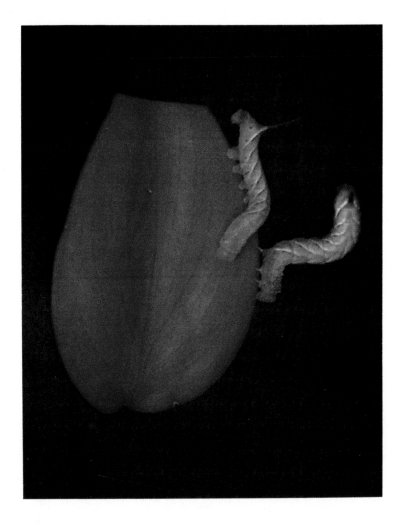

Simple and complex botanical specimens (bell pepper and pea) photographed to compare types of illumination. This photo was made with direct lighting from two reflector photofloods.

tion, because the lighting is so diffuse, an assistant can remain inside to perform manipulations during photography if the cubicle is large enough. In order to have room and to disturb the light distribution the least, the assistant should stand back from the subject as much as possible, and behind a background card placed on the table.

Transmission Lighting. Thin sections of various types can be examined by the differential amount of infrared transmitted by them. The basic setup comprises an enclosure for the light and a masked window, or opening in a partition, over which the specimen is placed. For example, a thin, ¼-inch piece of wood was photographed in this way: A 300-watt reflector photoflood bulb was placed into a ventilated but lighttight box. Opal glass in the top provided a window and a support for the specimen. The lamp was 15 centimetres (about

Infrared Photography

6 inches) below the glass. An opening just smaller than the specimen was cut in black film-separator paper to mask off stray light. The paper did transmit some infrared radiation but not enough to cause flare. Exposure had to be found by trial because there was not enough visual light transmission through the wood to activate the exposure meter needle. Focusing was done by reflected light in order to prevent overheating.

Paintings. Paintings can be photographed with transmitted infrared by directing illumination through them from behind. If the work is to be done routinely, a large lighttight box or tunnel can be utilized. In the back of the tunnel there should be an adjustable opening large enough to present the area to be examined. The front of the box should have a hinged door to provide access to the camera, which is mounted inside. When the camera has been focused, the door is closed. The shutter can be operated by means of a long cable release extending through a small hole in the tunnel.

When only an occasional painting is checked in this fashion, it might not be worthwhile to rig a tunnel. It would be practical to place the camera in one room and the lamp in the next, with the painting supported in the doorway between. Opaque curtains would serve to minimize the amount of illumination spilling over into the room having the camera. The painting could be transirradiated through the back of the canvas. A 500-watt reflector photoflood, 2 metres (about 6 feet) from the picture, would serve. An electric fan should be used to keep the picture cool, because it is vital not to overheat the painting. Whenever there is the least possible danger of this, a method based on a flash technique must be worked out. This would be especially necessary if the painting were lined by means of a wax adhesive.

Using this setup with Kodak high speed infrared films, an exposure of 15 seconds at $f/5.6$ can be tried, but correct exposure will vary with the subject.

Experiments with electronic flash units indicate that a studio-type lamp at 1 metre (about 3 feet), and having a 225 watt-second rating, would have to be fired 1 or 2 times. When the multiple flash method is employed, care must be taken not to jar the painting or the camera.

• *See also:* AERIAL PHOTOGRAPHY; CRIME PHOTOGRAPHY; DOCUMENT EXAMINATION BY PHOTOGRAPHY; EVIDENCE PHOTOGRAPHY; INFRARED; PHOTOINTERPRETATION; SCIENTIFIC PHOTOGRAPHY; SURVEILLANCE PHOTOGRAPHY; THERMAL PHOTOGRAPHY; ULTRAVIOLET AND FLUORESCENCE PHOTOGRAPHY.

Further Reading: Bernard, Burton. *ABC's of Infrared.* Indianapolis, IN: Sams, Howard W. & Co., 1970; Conn, G.K. *Infrared Methods: Principles and Applications.* New York, NY: Academic Press, 1960; Eastman Kodak Co. *Applied Infrared Photography,* pub. No. M-28. Rochester, NY: Eastman Kodak Co., 1977; ———. *Medical Infrared Photography,* 3rd ed., pub. No. N1. Rochester, NY: Eastman Kodak Co., 1973.

Insect Photography

To photograph insects successfully, you will need a knowledge of close-up photography and, as with other aspects of nature photography, some information about your subjects. Knowing the basic functions and habitats of insects will help you to locate and photograph them. For example, it is much easier to get a picture of an emerging annual cicada if you know the approximate time of year this event occurs in your area. Also, if you know that dragonflies usually live along the edges of ponds, you will not spend time looking for them above the timberline. Local entomologists or botanists, or your state conservation office, can usually give you information about insects in your area. Almost any public or school library will have some books on entomology.

There are two major aspects of the photography of insects:

1. Field photography—photography done outdoors under whatever situations prevail.
2. Indoor photography—work done in the studio or the home, where you can be in total control of the situation.

Excellent pictures are possible in both environments. However, the percentage of good pictures is usually higher when you have control over the subject, the lighting, and the background. Some picture subjects, such as mating damselflies, can be photographed only in the natural surroundings of the field. Other subjects, like moths or butterflies, can be photographed more easily in controlled situations than in the field.

Equipment

Whether you work indoors or outdoors, you can use almost any camera for photographing insects.

Not only is the flight of insects erratic and completely unpredictable, but they move through the air at speeds of up to almost 50 feet per second and beat their wings up to 1,000 times per second. Consequently, specialized equipment and sophisticated techniques are required to photograph them on the wing. For this photograph, the wasp was persuaded to fly through a narrow beam of light focused onto a photoelectric cell which then triggered a rapid-opening shutter. To freeze the wings, a flash speed of 1/25,000 sec. was used. Photo by Stephen Dalton, FIIP, FRPS. ▶

While certain subjects, such as moths and butterflies, can be photographed in the field under whatever conditions may prevail, they are equally, if not more easily photographed indoors under more controlled conditions. Photo by Norm Kerr and Lee Howick.

However, a single-lens reflex camera makes the work easier and more precise. With an SLR you view the subject through the camera lens; consequently, parallax is eliminated. Also, if the subject appears in sharp focus in the viewfinder of this camera, it will be in sharp focus in your picture. With a non-reflex camera, you can use a focal frame or another kind of measuring and framing tool, but these items will often disturb your subject. With either type of camera you will also need close-up equipment (like a close-up lens or a lens-extension device) so that you can take pictures at the very close subject distances necessary for insect photography.

For lighting, electronic flash is almost essential even for daylight photography. The extremely brief burst of light from electronic flash offers the advantage of "stopping" action, and at the close flash-to-subject distances used in insect photography, the light on the subject is so bright that you can use a small lens opening for maximum depth of field. Almost all of the light for the exposure comes from the flash, and almost none from the daylight. This causes the background to go quite dark and the insect to stand out in contrast. (In other situations you may want to use a black cloth or paper backdrop to assure a dark background.)

In addition to the above-mentioned equipment, a small reflector made by gluing crumpled aluminum foil to a piece of cardboard about 1 foot square in size can be useful. The only other equipment you

Basic lighting setup for insect photography. The distance from the fill light to the subject should be about 1.7 times the distance from the main light to the subject. The fill light is at about camera height, and the main light about a foot above camera height.

need is a tripod, a cable release, and film. While insects make excellent subjects for either black-and-white or color film, the colorful nature of many of the subjects will almost dictate that color film be used.

Lighting

The basic lighting setup shown in the accompanying illustration represents only a starting place. Individual situations almost invariably require some

Even such common insects as these ladybugs make interesting picture subjects. The colorful nature of many insects will almost always require the use of color film for best results. Photo by John Brandow.

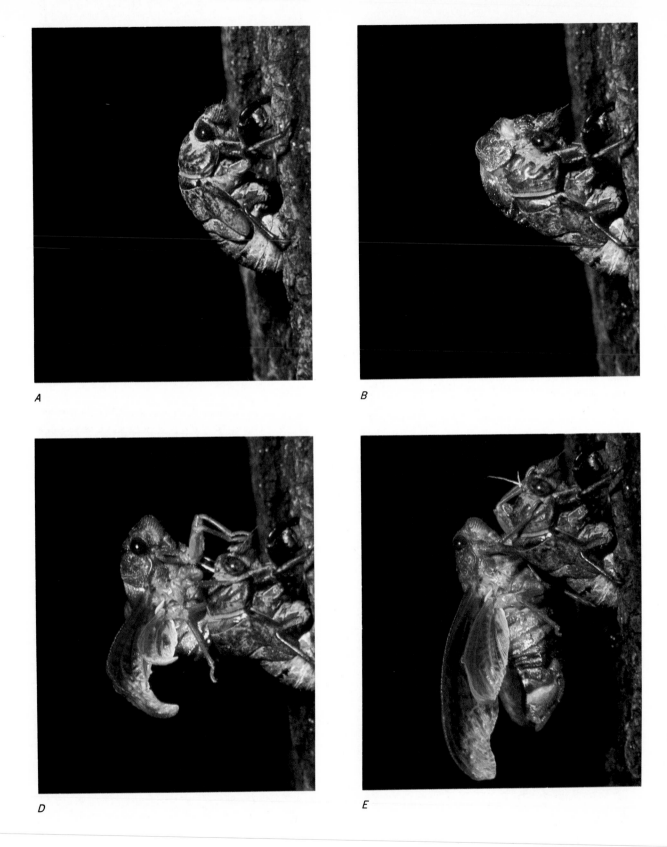

A

B

D

E

This sequential picture series shows the emergence of an annual cicada. (A) Cicada nymph on tree; nymph has just emerged from ground. (B) Nymph case begins to split. (C) Immature wings still held by nymph case. (D) Insect halfway out of case. (E) Blood is pumped into wings to fully form them. (F) Wings are full and dry; cicada is ready to ascend tree. Photos by John Brandow.

C

F

shifting of the lights. Exposure is based on the distance from the *main* light to the subject.

A reflector is indispensable for filling in the shadows when you use only one flash or when you are shooting with the sun as your only light source. Even with two electronic flash units, it can be useful for brightening shadow detail.

In the Field

Whenever possible, try to photograph insects on warm, sunny, and preferably windless days. That is when insects are most active and when you are likely to find more of them.

Bright, colorful clothing and sweet aromas, such as those provided by colognes and perfumes, help attract insects like butterflies and bees. In the field, pleasant aromas are a definite lure to insects. Of course, some stinging insects can be a nuisance. Should a wasp or bee start flying around you, try to ignore it (do not swing at it), and chances are it will go away.

In the early mornings of the hot summer months, watch for the nymph stage of the annual cicada. During these months the full-grown nymph emerges from the ground and crawls up on rough-barked trees. Then the skin splits and the winged adult insect emerges. This is a fine opportunity for you to shoot a sequential picture series. Fortunately, the insect will be easy to approach in this stage of metamorphosis. It is important to remain calm and patient, since total emergence of the insect may take from 20 minutes to more than an hour.

Insects are also rather easy to approach when they are mating. This usually occurs in spring and early summer. An interesting phenomenon to photograph is the mating of damselflies. These insects pair to mate and lay their eggs. In pairing, the male fastens the pincers located on his posterior around the neck of the female. Mating often occurs on reed

Insect Photography

The mating of damselflies is an interesting phenomenon to photograph. (Below) Paired damselflies. (Bottom) Mating damselflies. (Right) In a rare situation, involving an already paired male (center) and female (bottom), a second male (top) mistakes the male in the center for a female. Photos by John Brandow.

stalks near the edge of a pond. Be cautious as you set up to take your pictures—one bump, and your subjects may make a quick exit. Since the eggs are laid almost immediately after fertilization, you may also be able to photograph the eggs as they appear.

As you walk through the fields and the forest, and along the water's edge, keep alert for insects. Take a close look under stones, leaves, and logs. Also, you will find that many specific plants attract insects. The more you know about your subjects the easier it will be to locate and photograph them.

Indoors

Insect photography indoors is a bit easier than it is in the field because you can completely control the lighting and background. Since breezes are eliminated, the problems of shaky leaves, branches, and flowers is somewhat lessened.

Moths and butterflies are good indoor subjects. You may find a cocoon, or chrysalis, in the field and bring it indoors to be photographed. If you do not find one, you can also purchase cocoons from biological-supply companies.

To photograph the emerging animal, first fasten the cocoon to a branch. Be sure you do not use glue that contains solvents or other chemicals that may kill or malform the pupa in the cocoon. White liquid glue or a bit of very fine thread can be used. Position the cocoon against an appropriate background of branches or shrubbery.

Cocoons can be stored in the refrigerator until you want to photograph them. Emergence will not occur until after the cocoons are taken out of cold storage. The time between removal from the refrigerator and emergence will vary from one week to several, depending on the species. Emerging insects frequently begin leaving their cocoons between about 8 A.M. and 10 A.M. One way to forecast an approaching emergence is to shake the cocoon gently. If you can not hear any movement of the pupa, emergence is probably imminent.

Emergence *may* be preceded by a moist condition on the end of the cocoon. However, the precise moment of emergence is impossible to predict, and

Certain types of locations attract specific insects. Dragonflies, such as this red-bodied specimen, are generally found near bodies of water.

Moths and butterflies are good indoor subjects as the emergence of the larva and the moth itself may be controlled by refrigerating the cocoon until the photographer is ready to photograph it. (Left) Cecropia larvae; (above) female cecropia moth. Photos by John Brandow.

unless you are able to keep a rather constant watch over the cocoon, it is wise to have several cocoons of the same species on hand. When one butterfly emerges, you will know that the others will not be far behind.

Subduing Specimens

It is often useful to slow up other specimens. The food compartment of a refrigerator provides the most practical means for slowing up cold-blooded creatures. Insects, as well as reptiles, amphibians, and mammals that hibernate, become very easy to work with upon chilling.

Technique

In insect photography it is very difficult to follow around even the slowest-moving specimens. Even with the simplest of equipment, following an insect, focusing on it, arranging lights, and releasing the shutter—all before the subject moves—are almost impossible.

One of the most effective methods of getting good photos of insects involves setting up camera and lights in a more or less permanent position, and then confining the action of the subject insect to the area in front of the lens. The area will be defined by the field of view of the lens, the prefocused distance, and the depth of field.

For example, if an insect is to be photographed on a branch, set up the camera and focus on the branch, arrange the lights, and then introduce the insect to one end of the branch. As it traverses the branch, a number of exposures can be made.

The moth in the accompanying photo was photographed at 1:1. It was fluttering around on the twig at the time the synchronized electronic flash exposure was made. To confine the action to a small area, a hole (slightly larger than the field of view of the camera) was cut in a carton. The box was lined with black paper on the inside, and a mirror was taped in place to provide some backlighting.

The camera was first aimed and focused on a dead moth attached to the twig. The living moth was then allowed to crawl freely on the twig, and the photographer manipulated the stick so as to keep the moth within the confines of the action field. When

Even slow-moving insects like this moth caterpillar are difficult to follow around. It is easier to set up the camera and lights, and then induce the insect to enter and remain in the confined area in front of the lens. Photo by Editorial Photocolor Archives.

This moth was photographed by confining its action to a small, black-lined box (described in the text). The camera was first aimed and focused on a dead moth; when the live specimen approached the same spot, the exposure was made.

Insect Photography

the specimen was oriented so that it was heading toward the light, the exposure was made.

The spider in the accompanying illustration was photographed as it was dropping on its drag line. In this case the area of action was outlined by two horizontal sticks, one at the top of the camera field and one at the bottom. The sticks were in the same plane as a nail, from which the spider was to be pushed. The camera was focused on a cotton thread temporarily hung from the nail. The night sky served as a background.

The spider was placed on the nail and induced to drop. The flash exposure (1/10,000 sec.) was made just as the creature passed the top stick. By means of such photographs, it was possible to demonstrate that a spider does not hang from its spinnerets—it cannot, because the thread is a liquid there. Instead, with comb-like claws on its hindmost feet, it snubs the line where it has set solid.

Butterflies in the open present a photographic challenge because it is difficult to predict where they will land. But the probability of a landing can be increased by removing the flowers surrounding the one on which the camera is focused. When the plants are protected ones, cheesecloth can be used to temporarily drape adjacent blooms.

Creating a Set

Building a set on which to photograph insects not only confines the action of the animal to a defined area, but also adds a natural background. Remember when creating a set to include only those items associated with the particular insect being photographed. It would be wrong to photograph an insect on a plant where it is never found.

It was found practically impossible to make the accompanying photo of the water strider in the field. For one thing, the water had to be not more than two inches deep in order to keep the shadow small and near the specimen. Also, the creature was too wary in the wild. And, of course, it was not possible

This spider was photographed while dropping on its drag line in an action field outlined with a stick at the top and bottom of the camera field. Note how the spider snubs the line with its tarsal claws.

Insect Photography

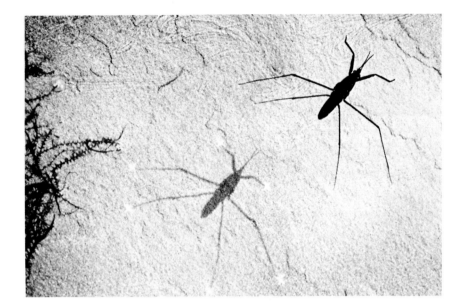

To simulate a running stream, the water strider's natural habitat, a set had to be built that could be placed in the sun to obtain the sharp shadow. Note, in the shadow, the star-shaped images of the sun produced by air bubbles held in the insect's tarsal claws.

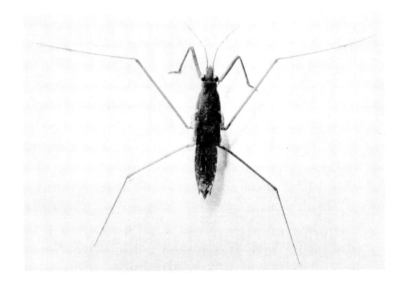

When the water strider was photographed in the laboratory on water in a petri dish, details of its structure were recorded, but not the phenomena produced by the direct rays of the sun.

to make surface-tension experiments in the running stream. The set was made in a 14″ × 17″ photographic tray. It comprised a few thin, flat stones and a water plant. The whole set could easily be placed in the sun when the sharp shadow was needed.

Photography was simplified by taming the specimen. To do this, four panes of window glass were placed vertically around the tray to prevent escape. For two days the photographer periodically walked around the set and bent over it. The second day he dropped small insects onto the water for food. By the third day, the glass could be removed; the creature made no attempt to escape and would take food from the hand. It was not alarmed in the least by the photographic procedures.

The difference between a photograph made of the strider in a set and one made in a petri dish can be appreciated when the two are compared.

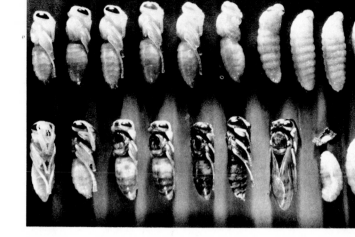

(Right) A photographic series showing the development of a hornet was made by opening a nest and removing the different stages of grubs and pupae. These were then arranged chronologically on a card and photographed with copying lighting. The egg, and intermediate and terminal stages of the grub, appear at the right of the lower row. Reading upwards and counterclockwise, the many stages of pupation are shown. The last specimen is the imago.

Illustrating an Insect's Natural History

The best photographs of insects not only show the animal clearly, but also illustrate some particular aspect of its life cycle or show it exhibiting a characteristic trait. Of course, this is always possible to do, especially if specific photos are needed for documentation or comparison.

The accompanying series portrays the development of a hornet. The individual stages were easy to find because the female laid four or five eggs in rapid succession and then rested. By opening the spiral of cells in the nest, distinctly different stages were found periodically arranged. The grubs and pupae were extracted and arrayed on a card for photography. Copying lighting was utilized, with lamps directed from both the top and the bottom of the photograph.

Quite often it is desirable to mount insects in specific attitudes. Before they dry out, legs, antennae, and wings can be positioned and allowed to set. The fireflies in the accompanying photos were arranged in the manner shown so that all the identification keys to the species were visible. An impro-

(Above left) The male (left) and female (right) of the firefly were photographed to associate the large eyes of the male and the small eyes of the female and the large lantern of the male. (Left) The method of setting the fireflies prior to photographing them is illustrated here.

vised setting board for the fireflies was made with paper matches taped to a card to provide racks upon which the insects' appendages were affixed with rubber cement. Note how the head of the center insect was propped up.

In 30 to 60 hours, the insects are set, depending on their size. The cement can be softened with thinner and the insects can then be removed. Any structures upon which cement remains should be washed with the thinner.

A Kodak Wratten filter No. 56 (green) was placed over the camera lens for the purpose of lightening the tone of the firefly lanterns. A contrasty print was made in order to further emphasize these light organs by revealing their shape.

Insects can be killed for mounting by placing them inside a dark-toned cardboard box. This is irradiated with an infrared lamp for a short while. The specimen is quite relaxed for posing. For quicker results, killing jars can also be employed by those experienced in their use. Dried insects must be humidified for two or three days before they can be manipulated. A sealed container, with moistened cotton inside, can serve as a humidifier.

• *See also:* CLOSE-UP PHOTOGRAPHY; NATURE PHOTOGRAPHY; PHOTOMACROGRAPHY.

Further Reading: Brevoort, Harry F. and Eleanor Fanning. *Insects from Close Up.* New York, NY: T.Y. Crowell, Inc., 1965; Dalton, Stephen. *Borne on the Wind: The Extraordinary World of Insects and 100 Photographs.* New York, NY: Readers Digest Press, 1975.

Instant Photography

Instant photography, or as Dr. Edwin H. Land describes it, "one-step photography," is the process of taking a picture and activating the light-sensitive material for automatic self-processing so that a finished print is available for viewing in seconds or minutes. Instant photography requires special materials and cameras (or camera backs). This field was pioneered by the Polaroid Corporation, starting with the introduction of a viable black-and-white process in the late 1940's.

The rapid access to finished prints makes the various camera and film systems available from Polaroid Corporation and Eastman Kodak Company attractive to amateur photographers, professional photographers, scientists, engineers, and others. Depending on the application, the user can choose from a variety of black-and-white and color materials. For the amateur photographer, the integral-pack color films that self-develop when expelled from the camera, such as that used with the Polaroid SX-70 system, or Kodak instant print film PR10, which is used with Kodak instant cameras, have become popular. Professionals, for the most part, use peel-apart films in special holders or adapters with professional studio cameras and with a vast range of scientific instruments such as microscopes and oscilloscopes.

Integral-pack films have the advantage of processing to completion without the user timing and with no waste products to discard. Peel-apart films yield a flat print without extra backing so that they are easily mounted. Black-and-white materials are available only as peel-apart films. One version of the peel-apart films provides a usable black-and-white negative as well as a positive print; in this case, the film negative requires aftertreatment to preserve it.

In addition to still-camera films, an instant-movie-film camera and viewer have been introduced by Polaroid Corporation. The details of instant-print materials and how they work are given in the article DIFFUSION TRANSFER PROCESS.

Insurance Photography

Many people feel secure in the belief that their valuable possessions will be replaced in case of fire or theft because they have insurance. But insurance companies can only pay for items that can be documented after the damage has been done. It is often very hard to remember and prove what possessions were in a house or studio that has been completely destroyed by fire or broken into by thieves.

Try to visualize everything in your kitchen, dining room, attic, or garage. What is in the drawers, in cupboards, in boxes, and on shelves? What is in the darkroom, in the equipment cabinets, in the studio shooting space? If you have a hobby collection such as coins, stamps, or antiques, or if your hobby involves tools or special equipment, can you list everything from memory?

If a "memory inventory" is difficult now, it would be virtually impossible to compile when it became necessary to file an insurance claim after suffering loss. Although insurance might be in force, you could still lose money unless a complete inventory could be produced to substantiate your claim.

The Insurance Information Institute and major insurance companies agree that the best way to document possessions is to make a room-by-room photographic inventory, and then to record the cost of the items and the purchase date on the back of each photograph.

A photo inventory is more valuable than a written inventory, especially in the case of things such as antiques and jewelry that can increase in value. Pictures give a graphic presentation surpassing any written description; they can record details, shapes and configurations, and colors that cannot be put into words.

Photographs can also be used to show evidence of damage, break-in, fire, or other factors. Photographic records taken before as well as after the fact will help the insured and the insurance company to determine the current or replacement value of lost or damaged items.

Insurance photographs are not only valuable to photographers; anyone who has possessions can benefit from having a photo inventory, in case of damage or loss. A photographer can often make a good income by offering that service to others. But whoever the pictures are made for, the most important thing is not to delay in making the record.

Equipment and Films

Flash illumination is by far the easiest way to take insurance pictures indoors, so any camera that permits the use of flash can be used. Close-ups of small items will be required; therefore, interchangeable lenses, or perhaps lens attachments or extensions, will be helpful. Negative film should be used in order to obtain prints. This will permit enlarging pictures of small objects or selected portions of a group of items as required. Prints also provide space on the back to record data about the items pictured. Whether color or black-and-white film is to be used is determined by the subject matter. Color prints make the most accurate photo inventory because they show all the details of an item in color. For example, the color of the wood and upholstery on an antique chair might be a major factor in determining the correct market value of the chair.

Taking the Pictures

Outdoor Views. An insurance inventory should start with the house or studio building itself. Photograph the exterior from the front, back, and each side. Also photograph any additional buildings on the property such as a tool shed, a children's playhouse, or a separate garage, and any backyard development such as a swimming pool with unusual landscaping. Then take a view of the house and the neighborhood to the right of it, and another view of the house and the neighborhood to the left of it.

Photographs are invaluable records for proof of damage or loss through fire, burglary, or natural disasters. This photograph of a burning house will help illustrate the extent of the fire and the ensuing loss.

Take the pictures on an overcast day when the lighting is even, so that all the details will show in the finished picture. Sunshine creates heavy shadows that can hide detail. Use a tripod and a small *f*-stop to get sharp details in all areas of the picture.

While taking pictures outdoors, do not forget to photograph such things as a car, a motorbike, snowmobile, or boat on a trailer. A photograph of a vehicle will not only help document a claim with the insurance company, but it will help the police in looking for the vehicle if it is stolen.

Overall Views of Rooms Indoors. The easiest way to take pictures indoors is with flash. Be sure to keep within the recommended distance range for the camera or flash. The distance range is given in the camera manual or on the back of some flash units.

Start with one wall of the room, and take as many pictures as necessary to record everything along that wall—overlapping each picture slightly. Include as much as possible in each picture. To avoid reflections from shiny walls, mirrors, or windows, stand at a 45-degree angle to the reflective surface. Move around the room in a clockwise direction until everything has been photographed. Be sure to open closet doors and photograph the items inside. Repeat this process with every room, including the attic, basement, and garage.

Close-Ups of Valuable Items. Take a close-up picture of any valuable item, or anything that might increase in value such as antiques, jewelry, paintings, and sculpture. Move in as close as the camera will allow, or until the subject fills the picture area.

Take the picture with flash, but check to make sure that the unit is not closer than the recommended flash range. If it is necessary to get closer than the recommended range, put one layer of white handkerchief over the flash to reduce light output.

For small objects such as china, silver, and jewelry, group similar items together on a plain-colored rug to photograph them. When arranging sets of china, turn one of the plates over so that the brand name shows.

(Below) Silverware is difficult to photograph indoors with flash because of glare. Either photograph it outdoors or reduce glare by putting one layer of handkerchief over the flash; alternatively, use a fast film that does not require flash. (Left) Use plain backgrounds for photographing small, intricate objects.

The fine features of this antique figurine show better when photographed against a plain wall. If it is impossible to show the hallmark on the bottom, tag the photograph with this information.

Insurance Photography

When photographing anything with a shiny surface or something covered with glass, take the picture at a 45-degree angle to avoid glare spots.

(Above) Open all containers to exhibit their contents. A carved wooden chess set was stored inside this antique owl, making the owl even more valuable than it appears from the outside. (Left) Fine handiwork may someday become heirlooms. This handmade quilt may someday have a high money value.

While taking close-up views, open the drawers of any dressers or chests and photograph the contents. Also open containers, such as tool boxes, and photograph the contents.

Do not forget to photograph that valuable item being used to take these pictures—the camera. A borrowed camera or a friend will do the job.

Organizing and Storing a Photo Inventory

After the prints are finished, write any pertinent information about the photographed items on the back of the picture, using a ball-point or felt-tip pen; or type the information on self-sticking labels and put them on the back of the prints. For example, write the purchase date and the price of the items, if they are known. For pictures of closets and dresser drawers, count the number of dresses, suits, shoes, and other items; and list them on the back of each print. Also write the inventory date on the back of each print; color prints processed by Kodak will have a date printed on the back.

Before storing the photo inventory, take a few minutes to estimate the present value of the property by using the photos as a reference. Then check your insurance policy to make sure there is enough insurance to cover the total value of your possessions. Store the inventory, along with any receipts you may have for major items, in a safe-deposit box or any other *locked place away from your home.*

Be sure to keep the photo inventory up to date by photographing any new items acquired and adding the prints to the inventory.

Losses not Covered by Insurance

Photographs can be especially valuable when there is a loss not covered by insurance. The repairs for most losses not covered by insurance are tax deductible after the first $100.*

If it became necessary to replace the trees in your yard due to damage by an ice storm, and it cost $1000 to replace them, $900 could be added to your income tax deductions. "Before and after" pictures, along with the receipt for the work, would substantiate the claim if the Internal Revenue Service ques-

---

*Rules governing losses not covered by insurance (including acceptance of photographic proof) are specified in IRS publication No. 547, *Tax Information on Disasters, Casualty Losses, and Thefts,* which is available at any district tax office.

tioned it. Even if the trees were not replaced, the deduction may be valid because the loss would decrease the value of your property.

If collision damage to your car is incurred and it is not covered by insurance, you are probably entitled to a tax deduction. A picture of the damage, along with the repair bill, is likely to satisfy any tax investigator.

Use pictures to record any damage done to you or your property. They will be valuable evidence if damages must be collected from someone else.

Here is how one man collected by having pictures for evidence. Contractors for the local gas company were digging a trench in his front yard near a huge oak tree. The digging removed almost half of the tree's roots. While the trench was open, he took pictures to show the damage, just in case the tree died—and it did. So he sent the pictures, along with a letter explaining the facts, to the president of the company. On the basis of this evidence, the utility company volunteered to take down the dead tree, cut it into fireplace lengths, and plant two other trees in its place. This cost the gas company $460, and it cost the homeowner a roll of film, processing, and a postage stamp.

Photographing Automobile Collision Damage

Some people carry a camera in their car so that they can photograph any damage from an accident right on the scene. Pictures taken on the scene are more valuable than those taken later because they show the conditions under which the accident occurred. On a modern expressway, it is often necessary to move the damaged cars to the side of the road before a policeman arrives to make out a report, and several pictures taken *before* the cars are moved can be valuable evidence later. These photographs can be used when filing a claim with an insurance company, or to substantiate a case in court.

Cameras that take flash pictures without batteries are practical to carry in a car, since there is no worry that the batteries might be dead when a flash picture is required. Load the camera with color film and wrap it in a plastic bag to keep out the dust. Store the camera out of sight under the seat, where it will be out of the heat of the sun. Keep an extra roll of film in the bag to avoid running out at a crucial time.

Loss through so-called acts of God—floods, hurricanes, ice storms, and other natural disasters—may not be covered by insurance. However, such losses may be taken as income-tax deductions and should definitely be recorded.

For complete photo coverage of an accident, take the following pictures:

1. An overall view of the scene, including the cars involved.
2. A close-up of the license plates of any cars involved.
3. Overall views of each car, and close-ups of the damage, including close-ups of any paint marks.
4. The contact point between the cars, if possible.
5. General views that include the first witnesses on the scene.
6. A long shot of the cars on the street, relative to the center line, to show the lane each car was in.
7. Skid marks on the pavement. If it has been raining, skid marks will not show up very well in a picture, so ask someone to put his foot at the beginning of the skid mark. Take a picture of the skid mark, including the person, to show how far the car skidded.
8. A general picture showing the weather conditions. Include snow alongside the road, or puddles of water from rain.
9. Through the windshield from the driver's position to show any signs, such as stop signs, that may have been hidden from view by overgrown foliage.
10. Close-ups of stopped clocks and speedometers, if the cars are a complete loss.
11. The people in the other car or cars standing around the scene of the accident, which may help prove later that they were not injured, in case they try to bring suit.
12. Close-ups of any physical damage suffered to the people in your car, such as broken teeth or bruises.

People who have taken pictures of an accident have found that their opponents often lose interest in filing a claim against them when there are pictures to prove what actually happened.

Substantiating Consumer Complaints with Pictures

Have you ever been annoyed because an appliance stopped working soon after it was purchased, or because a household item turned out to be defective after it was used for a short time? A letter of explanation to the manufacturer of the product con-

Insuring Photographic Equipment

Photographic equipment is seldom insurable in and of itself, but equipment is readily insurable as a part of several kinds of the broader coverage available for private homes, cooperative apartments, condominiums, and rental homes or apartments. Under certain circumstances even mobile homes are insurable under a homeowner's policy.

There are other options: Lloyds of London will for a price insure almost anything imaginable. And, there are photographers who deposit an amount equal to their insurance premium in a savings bank; they claim that in ten or twenty years they are ahead of the game. But in the early years of this kind of self-insurance, of course, coverage is minimal.

Coverage

For most owners of photographic equipment, professional insurance counsel is suggested. You will need the services of a good general insurance agent or broker. The recommendation of a fellow photographer may help you find the best person. By and large, the broker's fees are paid by the insurance companies. Your only cost is the premiums.

The umbrella "multiple-peril" insurance is most often sold under the names "Basic," "Broad," and "Comprehensive." Your insurance agent can explain exactly what is covered by this overall insurance. Generally speaking, you are insured against fire, theft, explosions, vandalism, and similar perils.

The Floater. Your photographic equipment is then insurable by what is known as a Personal Articles Floater. This extra insurance usually applies to all of your personal property.

Photographic equipment eligible for coverage under the Personal Articles Floater includes: cameras, lenses, projection equipment, ancillary equipment such as audiovisual programmers and dissolvers, portable recording and playback systems, and miscellaneous articles such as films, binoculars, tele-

cerning the problem will help, but the explanation will be much more effective if it is documented with pictures. For example, take some close-up pictures of that broken toy or of the rust appearing on a new washing machine. Send the pictures with a letter of complaint to the manufacturer of the product.

Manufacturers are impressed with complaints documented with pictures, and sometimes they offer to do even more than you would expect in repairing the damage. For example, a man who had an appliance with a defective motor took pictures of a defective fan blade that had broken off and caused damage inside the motor. He also used pictures to document some other complaints he had about the attachments that fit this appliance, and offered suggestions about how these attachments could be improved in future models. He sent the pictures and a letter to the manufacturer. In return, he received a replacement motor, free of charge, and a complete new set of attachments for the appliance—also free. Pictures can help tell the story of a consumer complaint, and they may bring exceptional results.

• *See also:* CRIME PHOTOGRAPHY; EVIDENCE PHOTOGRAPHY; TRAFFIC ACCIDENT PHOTOGRAPHY.

scopes, microscopes, and similar equipment used *in conjunction* with photographic equipment. In other words, you can insure your $1000 telescope only if you can show that it is compatible with one of your cameras.

Each piece of equipment must be individually valued and fully described. For example, if a camera and light meter are to be insured, there must be a specific amount of insurance for the camera and for the light meter. It is an excellent idea to document the cost and the replacement value of each item of photographic equipment you own. And the insurance company will need to know the following: make, model, serial number, date of purchase, and whether you are listing a lens, a camera body, or whatever.

Insurance companies permit writing blanket coverage on miscellaneous small items: filters, holders, carrying cases. This coverage is customarily limited to 10 percent of the total amount you have chosen to insure. Blanket coverage in excess of 10 percent may be allowed if you can show that it is impractical to list articles individually.

Note that this form of protection is not available for photographic dealers. And, oddly enough, it does not cover television cameras or television recorders. Both these categories can be protected by a different tactic; again, your broker or agent is the best guide.

Keep Records

It is a good idea to do most of your buying from a single camera store. While it is tempting to "shop around" for the best buys in camera equipment, there are potential disadvantages to this procedure. A store that knows you as a good customer will be more willing and able to supply you with a list of make, model, serial number, date of purchase—and, of course, value of your equipment. Records will be all in one place; and this information is necessary when you buy insurance.

The camera store where you have been a fairly steady customer will be willing, in most cases, to give you a full inventory of the equipment you have purchased from the store, and, as a courtesy, appraise other equipment you may have bought elsewhere. Many stores make no appraisal charge for good customers; other shops will ask 5 percent of the appraised value for their trouble.

Insurance coverage for equipment valued at more than $50,000 will require some negotiating, but it can be done.

Rates

Rates for Personal Article Floaters appear to be fairly uniform in the United States—however, the umbrella multiple-peril cost may be higher in what are thought of as inner-city, high-crime areas. The following table is approximate.

PERSONAL ARTICLES FLOATERS—PHOTOGRAPHIC EQUIPMENT

	Non-Commercial	Commercial* (Except Motion-Picture Producers)	Motion-Picture Producers
Annual Rates per $100 of Insurance—excluding North Carolina & Texas			
First $5000	$1.50	$2.40	$3.25
Next $10,000	$1.25	$1.95	$2.60
Over $15,000	$1.05	$1.55	$2.10
Annual Rates per $100 of Insurance—North Carolina			
First $5000	$1.45	$2.35	$3.25
Next $10,000	$1.20	$1.90	$2.60
Over $15,000	$1.00	$1.50	$2.10
Annual Rates per $100 of Insurance—Texas			
First $5000	$1.80	$2.25	$3.25
Next $10,000	$1.40	$1.80	$2.60
Over $15,000	$1.00	$1.45	$2.10

*Insurance companies use "commercial" as applying to any individual engaged in any branch of photography for remuneration.

The prices reflect Personal Articles Floater costs for photographic equipment as reported by commercial insurers. Similar protection is available, by the way, for jewelry, furs, fine arts, sporting goods, musical instruments, silverware, and stamp and coin collections.

All valuable possessions covered by the floater will be protected against theft, loss, or damage caused by just about anything, with the obvious exceptions of wear and tear, inherent defects in the valuables, and harm caused by animals, insects, and nuclear attack.

Your coverage should be designed to protect you anywhere in the world—at home, in Abruzzi, or in Anaheim.

It is also general practice for your floater to cover additionally acquired equipment *not* listed on the policy for 30 days. Before the end of that time, new equipment must be described, assigned a value, and the company informed that you wish this equipment insured. Of course, the premium may be raised.

If your insurance is for the *replacement* value of your equipment, you will want to have a photo dealer re-appraise the replacement value of what you own, probably on an annual basis.

When you report to the insurance company that your equipment, or equivalent equipment, now costs more, your premium will probably increase, but your coverage will increase as well.

All of the above applies to insurance underwriters in what has come to be known as the private sector. If you encounter difficulties in buying photographic equipment insurance, there are other avenues to explore.

Federal Crime Insurance

The Federal Crime Insurance Program is authorized to sell federal crime insurance in states where the administration has concluded that commercial insurance is essentially unavailable to those who want it.

This insurance is only available for burglary and robbery and the limit is, for individuals, $10,000. Both crimes are theft: Burglary implies forced entry and you will have to prove it; and the federal program has certain requirements about locking devices on your premises. Robbery, of course, implies force or the threat of force. The states currently covered by federal crime insurance are:

Alabama	Arkansas	Colorado
Connecticut	Delaware	Florida
Georgia	Illinois	Iowa
Massachusetts	Minnesota	Missouri
New Jersey	New York	Ohio
Pennsylvania	Rhode Island	Tennessee
Virginia	District of Columbia	

Your insurance broker should be willing to help you with this kind of insurance since it does pay a commission; and policies are sold through licensed property insurance brokers and agents.

Federal Crime Insurance applications can be obtained from any licensed property insurance agent or broker in any eligible state. In addition, Federal Crime Insurance applications and information concerning the program can be obtained by calling the toll-free number 800–638–8780 or by writing:

Federal Crime Insurance
P.O. Box 41033
Washington, DC 20014

FAIR

Some states operate Fair Access to Insurance Requirements (FAIR) Plans. These include the District of Columbia and Puerto Rico. State coverage is basically the same as federal coverage, and financial backup is provided by federal resale of reinsurance to private insurance companies.

Crimes against property, as reported by the FBI, vary somewhat from year to year. Over the last ten years, the numbers, rounded out, look something like this:

Robbery: 400,000 offenses; property loss $140 million.
Burglary: 3,000,000 offenses; property loss $1.5 billion.
Larceny/theft: 6,000,000 offenses; property loss $1.2 billion.

Photographic equipment is expensive, easily portable, and readily resold. Ample coverage against loss is available and advisable.

Intensification

Intensification consists of adding density to a developed and fixed silver image to increase its density, contrast, or both.

The majority of intensifiers work by adding silver or some other metal, such as mercury or chromium, to the silver in the image. A few intensifiers add a stain that increases image opacity to printing light. However it is created, additional density is deposited only where some silver image already exists and, with few exceptions, in proportion to the amount of silver already present. Thus, the effect is to add the most density to highlights in a negative, and the least to the shadows. This action increases the contrast of the image in much the same way as continued development would have done. Intensification, therefore, is primarily useful in improving an underdeveloped negative; it does little to underexposed images, because if no detail is present in the shadows, none can be added by an intensifier.

Intensifiers that add significantly more density to the highlights than to the middletones and shadow areas are considered super-proportional. They function to increase negative contrast to a high degree, and are useful mainly in line work in photomechanical processes. The best-known intensifier of this type is the Monckhoven formula; see Kodak formula In-1 and the alternative blackener for it later in this article.

No single intensifier is known that will work subproportionately; that is, adding density to the shadows without greatly intensifying the highlights. A two-step procedure called Harmonizing, discovered by Joseph Maria Eder, has been recommended. Essentially it consists first in bleaching the image in Kodak intensifier In-1 or Kodak intensifier In-4, then redeveloping it partially in a moderately strong developer, and fixing out the remaining silver. In this case, the shadows redevelop rapidly, and density is added in those areas. The highlights, on the other hand, are incompletely redeveloped, and gain only little density; in fact, they may actually be reduced. The procedure requires considerable skill and judgment and is not recommended as a routine matter. An alternate method is to use a single solution intensifier, such as Kodak intensifier In-6, and to locally intensify the shadow areas, increasing the densities and contrast.

Intensifying Prints

A small degree of intensification of a black-and-white print can be achieved by treating the fixed image in a very dilute solution of Kodak rapid selenium toner. Selenium is deposited on the silver in the image, deepening tones and increasing local contrast in shadow areas; the effectiveness of this treatment is not the same for all emulsions. One part toner should be diluted with from 9 to 30 parts water; or alternatively, it may be added to a washing aid such as Kodak hypo clearing agent at the same dilution. If the toner is used in water, the following procedure should be used. The print should be treated with a washing aid after fixing, then washed, and treated with the selenium solution. After a 2- to 3-minute toning, the print should be rinsed and treated again with fresh washing aid, and then given a final wash. The usual time of effective treatment in the toner is two to three minutes; longer times or careless handling may produce pinkish tones or spots. Cold image-tone papers intensify with no noticeable change in color, while warm image-tone papers may be toned slightly brown.

This process also improves the keeping properties of a silver image by providing an overcoating of selenium, which is less susceptible to attack from atmospheric contamination than the regular silver image. It is sometimes used as one of the final steps in archival processing.

Various other toning processes also add a measure of intensification to a print image, but are usually accompanied by a definite change in image color.

Intensifying Negatives

With modern negative materials and printing papers, and modern control techniques for exposure and development, reduction or intensification operations are seldom needed, but they may occasionally be used to salvage a mistake when it is not possible to remake the negative.

In general, some increase in graininess may occur with intensifiers, especially in the treatment of coarse-grained emulsions.

Precautions. Intensification always involves some danger of ruining the image. Therefore, the best possible print should be made before attempting such treatments. In addition, to reduce the likelihood of staining or other damage, the following precautions should be observed:

1. The negative should be fixed and washed thoroughly before treatment and be free of scum or stain.
2. It should be hardened in the formalin hardener, Kodak prehardener SH-1, before intensification. (*See:* HARDENING BATHS.)
3. Only one negative should be handled at a time, and it should be agitated thoroughly during the treatment.

Following the treatment, the negative should be washed thoroughly and wiped off carefully before drying.

Formulas. The mercury intensifier and the quinone-thiosulfate intensifier, In-6, are recommended where extreme intensification is desired but where permanence of the resulting image is not essential. If permanence is essential, either the chromium or the silver intensifier should be used.

Kodak mercury intensifier In-1

Bleach the negative in the following solution until it is white; *then wash it thoroughly.*

Potassium bromide (anhydrous)	22.5 g
Mercuric chloride	22.5 g
Water to make	1.0 litre

Following the bleach and wash, the negatives can be intensified in any of the following solutions. Each solution, as listed, gives greater density than the one preceding it.

1. A 10% sulfite solution.
2. A developing solution, such as Kodak developer D-72 diluted 1:2.
3. Dilute ammonia (1 part of concentrated ammonia [28%] to 9 parts of water).
4. For greatly increased contrast, the following solutions, used as directed:

Solution A

Water	500.0 ml
Sodium cyanide	15.0 g

Solution B

Water	500.0 ml
Silver nitrate, crystals	22.5 g

DANGER: Mercuric chloride and sodium cyanide are poisonous materials and may be fatal if swallowed. Sodium cyanide reacts with acids to form the poisonous gas, hydrogen cyanide. Cyanide salts and solutions must never be used except in adequately ventilated areas. Mercuric chloride and sodium cyanide must not be allowed to contact the skin. Use impervious rubber gloves while handling these chemicals or their solutions. The outer surface of.the gloves and the hands should be washed thoroughly after each use. Containers of mercury intensifier solutions should be adequately labeled as poisonous. If they are used in the home, they should be stored in a locked cabinet out of the reach of children. Read carefully any directions on the manufacturer's label for these substances. Follow regulations of local health authorities regarding disposal of waste solutions.

To prepare the intensifier, add the silver nitrate, Solution B, to the cyanide, Solution A, until a permanent precipitate is just produced; allow the mixture to stand a short time; then filter. The resultant solution is called Monckhoven's intensifier.

Redevelopment cannot be controlled as with the chromium intensifier, Kodak chromium intensifier In-4, but must go to completion.

Kodak chromium intensifier In-4

Use the following formula:

Stock Solution

Potassium dichromate (anhydrous)	90.0 g
Hydrochloric acid (concentrated)	64.0 ml
Water to make	1.0 litre

NOTE: See precautions on handling negatives given previously.

To use, take 1 part of stock solution to 10 parts of water.

Harden the negative first in Kodak special hardener SH-1. Bleach thoroughly at 18 to 21 C (65 to 70 F), then wash 5 minutes and redevelop fully in artificial light or daylight (not sunlight) in any quick-acting, nonstaining developer that does not contain an excess of sulfite. Then rinse, fix for 5 minutes, and wash thoroughly. Greater intensification can be secured by repeating the process.

WARNING: Slow-working developers, such as Kodak developer D-76, Kodak Microdol-X developer, and Kodak developer DK-20, should not be used, since they tend to dissolve the bleached image before the developing agents are able to act on it.

Negatives intensified with chromium are more permanent than those intensified with mercury.

Kodak silver intensifier In-5

The following formula is the only intensifier known that will not change the color of the image on positive film on projection. It gives proportional intensification and is easily controlled by varying the time of treatment. In-5 acts more rapidly on fine-grain materials and produces greater intensification than on coarse-grain materials. The formula is equally suitable for positive and negative film.

Stock Solution No. 1
(store in a brown bottle)

Silver nitrate, crystals	60.0 g
Distilled water to make	1.0 litre

Stock Solution No. 2

Sodium sulfite (anhydrous)..	60.0 g
Water to make	1.0 litre

Stock Solution No. 3

Sodium thiosulfate (pentahydrated)	105.0 g
Water to make	1.0 litre

Stock Solution No. 4

Sodium sulfite (anhydrous)..	15.0 g
Kodak Elon developing agent	25.0 g
Water to make	3.0 litres

NOTE: See precautions on handling negatives given previously.

To use, prepare the intensifier solution as follows: Slowly add 1 part of Solution No. 2 to 1 part of Solution No. 1, shaking or stirring to mix the solutions thoroughly. A white precipitate will appear. This is then dissolved by adding 1 part of Solution No. 3. Allow the resulting solution to stand for a few minutes, until it clears. Then add, stirring constantly, 3 parts of Solution No. 4.

When the mixing procedure is completed, treat the film immediately. The intensifier solution will remain stable for approximately 30 minutes at 20 C (68 F).

The degree of intensification can be regulated by varying the time of treatment according to the density desired, but the time used should not exceed 25 minutes. When intensification is sufficient, immerse the film for 2 minutes, with agitation, in a 30 percent sodium thiosulfate solution. Then wash the film thoroughly.

The stability of the mixed intensifier, and the rate of intensification, are easily changed by varying the thiosulfate concentration. To obtain a more active, but less stable, working solution than the one above, use 90 grams of sodium thiosulfate (instead of 105 grams) in Stock Solution No. 3. Mix the working solution according to the procedure given above. This intensifier will keep for only 20 minutes at 20 C (68 F).

Whenever possible, use the intensifier in artificial light. The solution tends to form a precipitate of silver quite rapidly when it is exposed directly to sunlight.

Kodak intensifier In-6

This type of intensifier produces the greatest degree of intensification of any known single-solution formula when used with high-speed negative materials. The intensified image is of a brownish hue, and is not completely permanent; however, under normal storage conditions it will remain in satisfactory condition for several years. The intensified image is destroyed by acid hypo; under no circumstances whatsoever should the intensified negatives be placed either in fixing baths or in wash water that is contaminated with fixing bath.

Kodak intensifier In-6 is not suitable for fine-grain materials or for use when only moderate intensification is desired.

Solution A

Water, about 21 C (70 F) ..	750.0 ml
Sulfuric acid (concentrated) .	30.0 ml
Potassium dichromate	
(anhydrous)	22.5 g
Water to make	1.0 litre

Solution B

Water, about 21 C (70 F) ..	750.0 ml
Sodium bisulfite (anhydrous)	3.8 g
Hydroquinone	15.0 g
Kodak Photo-Flo 200 solution	
(undiluted)	3.8 ml
Water to make	1.0 litre

Solution C

Water, about 21 C (70 F) ..	750.0 ml
Sodium thiosulfate	
(pentahydrated)	22.5 g
Water to make	1.0 litre

The water used for mixing the above solutions for the intensifier should not have a chloride content greater than about 15 parts per million (equivalent to about 25 parts of sodium chloride per million); otherwise the intensification will be impaired. If you are in doubt as to chloride content, use distilled water.

CAUTION: Always add the sulfuric acid to the water slowly, stirring constantly, and never the water to the acid; otherwise the solution may boil and spatter the acid on the hands or face, causing serious burns.

To use, to 1 part of Solution A, add, stirring constantly, 2 parts of Solution B. Still stirring, add 2 parts of Solution C, and finally 1 part of Solution A. The prescribed order of mixing is important and should be followed.

The stock solutions will keep in stoppered bottles for several months; the mixed intensifier is stable for two or three hours without use. After using it once, discard the working solution, or it may leave a silvery scum on subsequent negatives.

To intensify negatives, first wash the negatives to be treated for 5 or 10 minutes. Harden them for 5 minutes in Kodak special hardener SH-1, and wash them again for 5 minutes.

The greatest possible degree of intensification is achieved by treating the negatives for approximately 10 minutes at 20 C (68 F). If a lesser degree of intensification is desired, treat the negatives for shorter times. Agitate them frequently during treatment to prevent streaking. Treat only one negative at a time when processing in a tray.

When a satisfactory degree of intensification is reached, wash the negative for 10 to 20 minutes and dry as usual. Because this is a single-solution intensifier, it can be used locally. Apply to small areas with a sable brush; apply to larger areas with a cotton swab or a ball of cotton, depending on the size of the area. Place in water to stop the action in one area before proceeding to another. Wipe off the surface water before applying.

• *See also:* ARCHIVAL PROCESSING; CONTRAST; FORMULAS FOR BLACK-AND-WHITE PROCESSING; HARDENING BATHS; REDUCTION; TONING.

Intermittency Effect

The intermittency effect is a loss in density in a sensitized material that can result when the exposure is not continuous, but broken into time segments. It is related to reciprocity effect.

An exposure that is given in a number of installments may not produce the same density as another exposure in which the same total energy is applied to the material in a continuous exposure. This effect is primarily of interest in scientific photography, but may also apply where photographs are taken with a repeating stroboscopic light source.

Fortunately, however, continuous and intermittent exposures of the same average intensity and same total exposure time become equal in their effects when the frequency of interruption goes above a certain critical level that varies with the intensity of the light or other form of energy. A good practical rule to follow to be sure that the intermittent exposure has exceeded the critical level is to make sure that at least 100 intermittent exposures are given, regardless of the overall exposure time.

• *See also:* IMAGE EFFECTS; RECIPROCITY EFFECT; STROBOSCOPIC PHOTOGRAPHY.

Internegatives, Color

While it is usually simpler to make color prints directly from color transparencies using a reversal color paper such as Kodak Ektachrome RC paper, there are times when it is desirable to make a color internegative from the transparency and to print the internegative on a color negative working paper.

Color internegative films have specially shaped characteristic curves with two slopes. An exposure that results in the transparency highlights falling on the upper slope adds to the highlight contrast being increased, which compensates for the loss of highlight contrast in the transparency and for the further loss in highlight contrast that occurs when the internegative is printed on paper. This compensation does not happen with prints on a direct reversal paper.

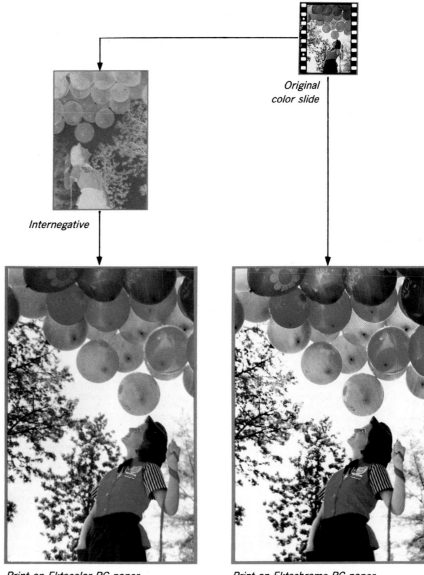

Original color slide

Internegative

As illustrated here, there are two ways of making color prints from color slides. One way is to print positive color transparencies directly onto Kodak Ektachrome RC paper. Alternatively, an internegative may be made from a positive transparency, and then printed onto Kodak Ektacolor paper in the same manner as an original negative made on color negative film.

Print on Ektacolor RC paper

Print on Ektachrome RC paper

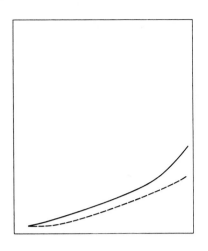

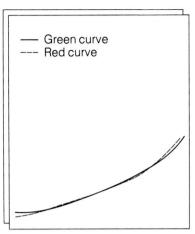

— Green curve
--- Red curve

(Left) The solid line is a typical curve showing correct exposure of an internegative. The dashed line is a curve showing inadequate exposure. Note that there is not enough of the high-contrast portion (AB) in the dashed curve. (Right) The overall contrast of an internegative can be controlled by exposure. Sheet bearing the green curve (solid line) is 0.05 log E to the right of the sheet bearing the red curve (dashed line). Determine the amount of horizontal shift required to make the curves match and adjust the filter pack. In this case, add 05M to the filter pack to eliminate the horizontal shift. Ignore the vertical shift.

Because of the specially shaped characteristic curves, the overall contrast of the internegative can be controlled by exposure. Increasing the exposure increases the negative density range, while decreasing the exposure lowers the density range. The contrast of the individual layers can be controlled by the use of color compensating filters. For example, increasing yellow filtration decreases the contrast of the blue-sensitive, yellow dye layers, in comparison to the contrast of the other two layers, while decreasing the yellow filtration increases the yellow layer contrast.

Internegatives can be exposed by contact, by enlargement, or with a camera. If enlargements are to be made from an internegative made from a small-size transparency, preferred practice is to make an enlarged internegative. Because of the special color reproduction requirements of a color internegative film, it may have as many as twenty-one total layers of emulsion, overcoat, dichroic filters, subbing, and antihalation backing. For this and other reasons, the sharpness of the film is somewhat lower than, and the graininess somewhat grainier than, transparency films. This is why enlarged internegatives are usually made when enlarged prints are needed. Kodak offers a service in which Kodak color negatives (internegatives) are made from transparencies on 2¼-inch wide film. For example, 35 mm slides are enlarged to 2¼″ × 3¼″ on color internegative film. Professional photo labs often will make internegatives in sizes up to 8″ × 10″.

Because it is almost impossible to judge internegatives by eye, color densitometry is almost a necessity. Control of the process is established by reproducing black-and-white film step scales on the internegative film, measuring the steps in red, green, and blue densitometry, and plotting three curves.

Where the break in curve shape comes on each of the three curves indicates any exposure or filtration changes necessary to make a properly exposed, balanced internegative.

Inverse-Square Law

The illumination received in a given plane varies not according to its distance from the source, but according to the *square* of the distance. The variation is inverse; that is, as the distance increases, the illumination diminishes. Thus, if a surface at a given distance from a source receives a certain amount of illumination, then a surface twice as far from the source will receive one-quarter of that illumination. As shown by the diagram on the next page, that is because the same amount of illumination is spread over four times as much area.

Application of Inverse-Square Law

The inverse-square law applies precisely only to a point source of light, and only segments of spheres are equidistant from a point. However, it may be practically applied to determine exposure adjustments for flat planes and most types of subject surfaces, and for small light sources that meet the following conditions:

1. The light is not obstructed by diffusing material or by barn doors, goboes, or other restrictive devices.
2. The light is not focused by a lens, as in a spotlight, or concentrated in a narrow beam by a deep reflector.
3. The largest dimension of the light source is one-tenth or less the width of the subject or the area being illuminated.

Most electronic flash units small enough to be hand-held or mounted on a camera meet these conditions, as does bare-bulb flash (except in small rooms with light-colored walls and ceilings that act as large, area reflectors).

Exposure Adjustment

The practical photographic problem that the inverse-square law solves is: What exposure adjustment is required when the light-to-subject distance is changed? The answer is obtained as follows:

$$\frac{\text{Exposure}}{\text{adjustment}} = \frac{\text{New distance}^2}{\text{Old distance}^2}$$

For example, if a light source 4 feet from the subject is moved to a position 16 feet from the subject, then:

$$\frac{16^2}{4^2} = \frac{256}{16} = 16$$

Because the distance/intensity relationship is *inverse,* the answer indicates that the light on the subject is $\frac{1}{16}$ of its former intensity, so 16 times more exposure is required. That can be obtained by multiplying the previous exposure time by 16, or by opening the lens aperture 4 *f*-stops.

Similarly, if a light is moved closer to a subject, say from 9 feet to 3 feet, the solution is:

$$\frac{3^2}{9^2} = \frac{9}{81} = \frac{1}{9}$$

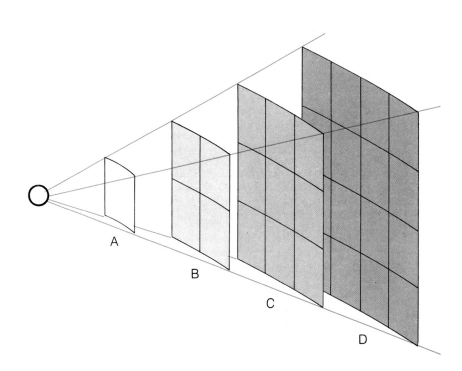

A surface 1 foot from a light source (A) receives a certain amount of light and has a corresponding brightness. A surface twice as far from the source (B) is ¼ as bright because the same amount of light is spread over 2² = 4 times the area. Similarly, at 3 times the distance (C), the light is spread over 3² = 9 times the area and so is ⅑ as bright. At 4 times the distance (D), the area covered is 4² = 16 times the area, and the surface brightness is 1/16 that of the closest surface (A).

That is, ⅑ the previous exposure is required because, from the closer position, the light falling on the subject is now 9 times brighter.

• *See also:* DIAPHRAGM; ELECTRONIC FLASH; EXPOSURE TECHNIQUES; FLASH PHOTOGRAPHY; LIGHT; LIGHTING.

Iodine

Element, forming iodides of various metals. It is used in photography in reducers and bleach baths, also as a constituent of some mordants used in dye toning. It is one of the halogens.

Formula: I_2

Molecular Weight: 253.84 (atomic weight 126.92)

Violet crystals, slightly soluble in water, very soluble in alcohol, ether, or chloroform. A water solution of iodine can be made by first dissolving potassium iodide in water, then dissolving the iodine crystals in the solution. Tincture of iodine, sold by pharmacists as an antiseptic, is a two-percent solution of iodine in alcohol; it is used in this form by print retouchers as a strong bleach to remove black spots. Silver iodide is a light-sensitive salt, but is rarely used alone, as it is "slow" compared to the other silver halides. It is commonly used in trace amounts to form imperfections in silver bromide crystals that serve as nucleating centers in the formation of latent images by exposure to light. Gaseous iodine is commonly used in quartz-iodine (halogen) lamps.

Iris Diaphragm

A device for producing a continuously variable aperture of approximately circular shape, the term "iris diaphragm" is derived from its resemblance to the iris of the human eye. An iris diaphragm consists of a set of semi-circular leaves connected to an operating ring so that, as the ring is turned all the leaves move to or from the center, varying the size of the opening.

The iris diaphragm is most commonly used in a lens to adjust the aperture; a calibrated series of

settings is marked with *f*-numbers, and the settings themselves are called *f*-stops. Iris diaphragms are also used to adjust the circle of illumination in certain spotlights, the cone of light in microscopes, and as a fade-in, fade-out device in motion-picture cameras. This last use requires a special form of iris in which one leaf has an extension that closes the aperture completely.

Pre-set diaphragms in single-lens reflex cameras have a stop ring that is set by the photographer at the *f*-number he or she plans to use in exposing the picture. The subject can then be viewed with the lens wide open, and just before the picture is taken, the diaphragm can be closed to the appropriate stop without taking the eye away from the finder to see the markings on the diaphragm ring. Automatic diaphragms on SLR cameras are made so that they stay fully open throughout the viewing, and automatically stop down to the correct *f*-number for the exposure, opening up again for viewing. They usually have a preview control to let the photographer stop down to the desired *f*-number to judge depth of field. Automatic diaphragms on non-reflex cameras are automatically set to the right *f*-number, but do not require the wide open viewing. Motion-picture cameras may have automatic diaphragms that continuously change aperture size, even while the camera is running, to adjust for changes in light. These may not be iris diaphragms, however, but may have a different form of construction.

At one time, an iris lens mount was made for use with large cameras. This unit had a set of heavy, tempered steel blades, and a geared knob to open and close them. The iris mount was attached to the front of a view camera; lenses of various sizes could be attached to the camera by inserting them into the iris and closing it down until it clamped the lens in place.

• *See also:* DIAPHRAGM; *f*-NUMBER; *f*-STOP.

Irradiation

When a beam of light strikes an emulsion, part of its energy is absorbed by silver halide crystals directly in its path, and part is reflected and refracted by those crystals to neighboring crystals; this phenomenon is known as irradiation. As the accompanying

(Right) Light striking an emulsion is deflected by reflection and refraction toward adjacent crystals. The degree of spread depends on crystal size and sensitivity, emulsion thickness, and light intensity. (Below) The effect of irradiation on acutance is measured by masking part of an emulsion with a knife edge. (A) Ideal resulting densities would show an abrupt change between unexposed and exposed portions of the emulsion. (B) Irradiation reduces sharp definition of the edge by spreading exposure into the masked area. (Right Bottom) (A) Light irradiated between two bright image details can reduce contrast by creating density in the space between them. Clarity of edges and tonal difference from background are both reduced. (B) When details are closely spaced or light intensity is extreme, density caused by irradiation may be great enough so that details can no longer be distinguished from the background or from one another. The result is degraded or completely lost resolving power.

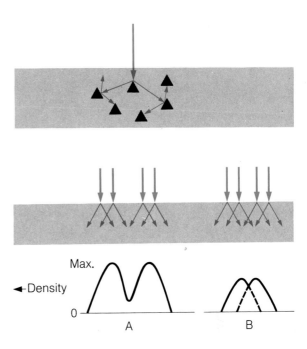

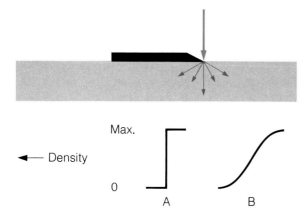

diagrams show, the spread of exposure by irradiation can reduce acutance (edge sharpness) and the resolution of fine detail in an image.

Irradiation is an inherent characteristic of an emulsion; it cannot be controlled by the photographer. Irradiation effects are greater in high-speed, thick-emulsion films that have a high percentage of large halide crystals with great light sensitivity, than they are in slower, small-crystal emulsions. The larger crystals seem to cause a greater amount of irradiation, and at the same time the thicker emulsion gives more distance for the irradiated light to spread. Further, the thicker emulsion provides a greater number of crystals that can potentially be affected by irradiated light. Both these factors increase the image spreading due to irradiation. Because of the greater light sensitivity of large crystals, only a small amount of irradiated light is required

to expose nearby crystals sufficiently for measurable density to be produced by development. In comparison, thin-emulsion films have tiny, tightly-spaced halide crystals of relatively low light sensitivity; all these factors tend to minimize irradiation.

If light causing halation is strong enough, irradiation at the points where the reflected light reenters the emulsion may emphasize the halation effect.

• *See also:* HALATION; IMAGE EFFECTS.

Ives, Frederick Eugene

(1856–1937)
American printer and photoscientist

F.E. Ives did much early work with halftone printing, using the cross-line screen. His interest in color photography led to the invention of a variety of devices for three-color separation and for additive viewing; these include the Photochromoscope camera, the Kromskop viewer, and various kinds of three-color projectors. He was also concerned with stereoscopic photography and did much research into the full-color parallax stereogram.

Jena Glass

Jena glass is a name for optical glass made by the Schott works in Jena, Germany. Schott and Abbe invented a number of glasses valuable in the manufacture of lenses in the late 1800's. Often the Jena glass terminology refers specifically to the barium crown glasses which, for the time, had high indices of refraction with relatively low dispersions. Use of these glasses made possible lens designs with improved chromatic aberration, including the first apochromatic (corrected for three wavelengths) lenses.

Jenkins, C. Francis

(1867–1934)
American engineer and inventor

With Francis Armat, Jenkins designed the first practical motion-picture projector, marketed as the Edison Projecting Kinetoscope. Later, Jenkins became interested in television, and devised several systems as early as the 1920's. He was the first president of the Society of Motion Picture Engineers.

Jet-Spray Processing

In the conventional developing machine used for both black-and-white and color processing of motion-picture films, there is a series of deep tanks, each containing a number of pairs of power-driven rollers over which the film travels. The time of processing depends upon the length of film travel in the tank and the speed with which the film travels. For example, if there are 80 feet of film in the developer tank, and the drive is running at 20 feet per minute, then the developing time is 4 minutes. Thus, the time in each bath is determined by the amount of film immersed in that bath and the speed of travel.

For commercial plants, where processing speeds of 100 feet per minute and more are desired, a great deal of film must be immersed in each tank, and necessarily, the tank must be very large and contain a great deal of solution. For this reason, it is not possible to replace solutions at frequent intervals, and a fairly complex continuous-replenishment system must be used in machines of this type. Some years ago, a different system was tried for black-and-white film, both for economy of chemicals and for certain other advantages.

In the new type of developing machine, the roller drive remained the same, but the tanks were empty. In each tank, a series of spray heads were placed so that the solution required impinged directly upon the moving film at a carefully metered rate. As the solution did its work, it ran off the film and down a drain at the bottom of the tank. No solution remained in the tank, and no recirculation pumps were used; the spent solution simply ran off to the waste line. Thus, no replenishment was needed. All film was processed in fresh developer. Careful metering of the developer and fixer flow made possible the same economy of solution as was attained by replenishment in the older system.

Further development of the jet-spray processing machine led to the design of much smaller machines, made possible by the use of very active solutions used at high temperatures—sometimes in the vicinity of 38 C to 46 C (100 F to 115 F). Thus, a much smaller amount of film had to be in the transport at any time, and the size and bulk of the machine could be greatly reduced.

A side benefit of the use of high-temperature processing was a useful increase in film speed. Actually, the true speed of the film was not changed, but the effect was much the same as "push-processing" of still films. With given types of subject matter, it was often possible to expose films at two to three times their rated exposure index, and secure usable quality. This was beneficial for newsreels, and occasionally for night exteriors in feature films, where the loss of detail in the shadows was not only tolerable but even desirable.

Jet-spray processing is one type of rapid-access processing used when there is a need to see the pictures immediately. There have been many military applications for rapid-access processing equipment.

This type of processing is not used in color development; the aerial oxidation of the developer seems to prevent its use. There is a similar system, using a thick, viscous form of processing bath applied to the film surface by rollers. This technology was introduced in the mid 1960s, but it has not become widely used.

Spray Processing of Paper

The same jet-spray principles can be used in the processing of paper. The Kodak Royalprint processor (Model 417) makes use of this type of high-turbulence, fountain-jet agitation in the fixing and washing steps. Because water-resistant, developer-incorporated paper is used in this processor, the developer and stop baths develop and stop the image in 9 and 5 seconds, respectively, by immersion above. However, adequate fixation and washing cannot be achieved in these relatively short times, so a jet-spray application of fixer and wash water at a temperature of 43 C (109.4 F) is needed in order to keep the times at 10 seconds or less. The entire process time in the Royalprint processor for an 8″ × 10″ dry print is 55 seconds, and prints are processed to the optimum stability level.

• *See also:* RAPID PROCESSING.

Joly, John

(1857–1933)
Irish professor and pioneer in color photography

Joly devised what was probably the first line-ruled screen plate color process, in 1893. This process was the forerunner of a number of other linear screen

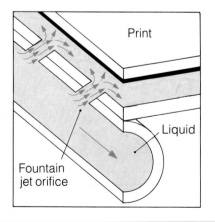

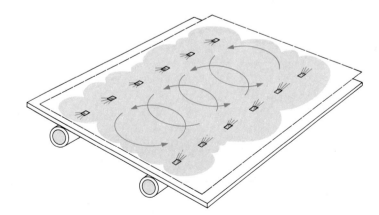

High-turbulence, fountain-jet agitation in the fixer and wash stages of the Kodak Royalprint processor, model 417. A jet-spray application of fixer and wash water at elevated temperatures (43 C) keeps the fixing and wash times at 10 seconds or less.

plates and color films, including the Paget, the Thames, and the Finlay processes, in which the color screen and the negative emulsion were on separate plates. The idea was later taken up by Dufay, who produced a color plate, and later a film, in which the ruled screen was directly beneath the emulsion and not separable from it.

• *See also:* DUFAYCOLOR; LINE SCREEN SYSTEMS.

Jones, Henry Chapman

(1855–1932)
English chemist and photographer

Jones was president of the Royal Photographic Society from 1912 to 1914. He was an instructor in and a writer of books on photography. He is best known for his introduction of a simple and practical sensitometer in the form of a calibrated step tablet. This was known as the Chapman Jones Plate Tester, and was widely used in England by manufacturers of plates and films. A small version of this device, about $3\frac{1}{4}'' \times 4\frac{1}{4}''$ in size, was also sold to amateurs who desired to carry out their own tests of emulsion speed.

Jones, Lloyd A.

(1884–1954)
American physicist and electrical engineer

Lloyd Jones was a member of the Kodak Research Laboratories from its inception in 1912, and he worked there until his retirement. Jones specialized in sensitometry and the measurement of the properties of photographic emulsions, establishing a fundamental theory of tone reproduction, which he outlined in graphic form with the now well-known quadrant diagram. With the addition of a flare curve, the method is still in use today and is found useful in predicting the behavior of a photographic system under practical conditions.

• *See also:* TONE REPRODUCTION.

This bleak photograph of a dilapidated and derelict old farm-house won Third Prize in the 1977 Kodak International Newspaper Snapshot Awards. Photo by Lincoln Steffens.

Joule

A joule is a basic unit of work or energy that can be expressed in many equivalent forms, such as heat energy (0.000948 BTU) and mechanical energy (10^7 ergs or 0.73756 foot-pounds). It is one of the derived units of the international system of units. The joule is commonly used in England in its electrical equivalent: A joule is equivalent to a watt-second, which is equal to 1 ampere at 1 volt flowing for 1 second. A joule is a small unit of energy; 3,600,000 joules equals one kilowatt hour of electrical energy. Joules are commonly used to rate the electrical power of electronic flash units, but because flash units vary in their ability to convert electricity into usable light, beam candlepower-seconds (BCPS) or effective candlepower-seconds (ECPS) ratings are more useful ratings for the evaluation of flash units or for finding exposures.

Judging Club Competitions

Many camera clubs have competitions. Depending on the club, competitions may have categories for prints (black-and-white and color), slides, stereo,

and movies. They may also divide competitions into subject classes such as pictorial, nature, portrait, and documentary.

The selection of judges is an important part of running a successful competition. In general, judges should not be members of the club. This will insure that impartial and objective decisions will be reached on the entries. It will also allow all members of the club to enter the competition if they wish.

Where can qualified judges be found? Sometimes, well-known photographers from other clubs may be willing to serve as judges. The Photographic Society of America offers a judging service to affiliated clubs. Once a year, the PSA Journal lists photographers who have been successful exhibitors in various photographic salons, and gives the names and addresses of PSA members. These lists can be used to find a nearby exhibitor who might be willing to serve as a judge. Where possible, it is generally thought to be better to have three judges to minimize the effects of the personal preferences for particular types of pictures that a single judge might have.

When no outside judge can be found, one workable way of judging is to have all the members of the club vote for the popular favorite. All the pictures in the competition are put on display, and each member is given a ballot form on which to express his choice of first, second, and third place. The votes can be quickly tabulated toward the end of the meeting, and the results announced at once.

Formal Judging

Where a formal judging is held, there may be just one judge, but more often there are three. The purpose of the odd number is, of course, to avoid tie votes.

The most common method of judging is the 1, 2, 3 system, sometimes called "In," "Hold," and "Out." Generally, this system is used for a competi-

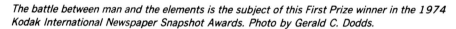

The battle between man and the elements is the subject of this First Prize winner in the 1974 Kodak International Newspaper Snapshot Awards. Photo by Gerald C. Dodds.

A good eye for composition and a fast camera won the photographer a First Prize in the black-and-white division of the 1977 Kodak International Newspaper Snapshot Awards. Photo by Rich Rollins.

tion in which there will not be just one or two winners. Rather, it is generally used to choose a given number of pictures to be shown at a forthcoming exhibit.

The pictures are displayed to the judges one at a time. An easel illuminated by a spotlight is one convenient way to show prints. Slides, of course, are projected. The judges may discuss each picture among themselves before voting on it. If a print gets either three or two "In" votes, it is in at once. One "In" vote puts it in the "Hold" category. Likewise, two "Holds" brings the print up again for another judging at a later time. Three "Out" votes or two "Out" votes and one "Hold" rejects a print; it will not be given a second viewing.

Of course, the judges may vary this procedure to suit themselves, or according to the instructions of the club committee. In any case, after all the prints have been judged, the "In" prints are counted. If there are not enough to make up the required number for the exhibition, then the judges go through the "Hold" prints again to see if any opinions have changed. At the end of this session, the voting is usually considered closed, even if there are not as many selected prints as had been desired for the exhibition.

To judge the winners of a competition, a similar system can be used, in which the judges first use the above system to winnow down the number of prints to a manageable quantity, then the remaining prints are re-examined until a consensus is reached on the winner and runners-up.

Slide Competitions

The only practical way to judge color slides is by projection; a good projector and screen are necessities. The projectionist will be given the slides in some kind of order, and all of them must have been numbered in advance for identification. As each slide is projected, the number is announced, and the judges may discuss it and proceed to vote "In," "Out," or "Hold" as before. The projectionist places the slide in one of three boxes, correspondingly marked. When judging is complete, the remaining procedure is the same as with prints.

Print Viewing

For a formal judging, prints should be shown one at a time, as mentioned. In order that each print may be seen at its best, it should be exhibited with a somewhat higher illumination level than the ambient room light. The Photographic Society of America has standards for displaying prints for judging. Since the illumination level determines, to a degree, how light or dark a print will look, it is important to be consistent so the print makers will have a standard to work to.

The print should be placed on an easel, which is illuminated by a small spotlight. It is important to check for evenness of illumination to be sure there

Judging Club Competitions

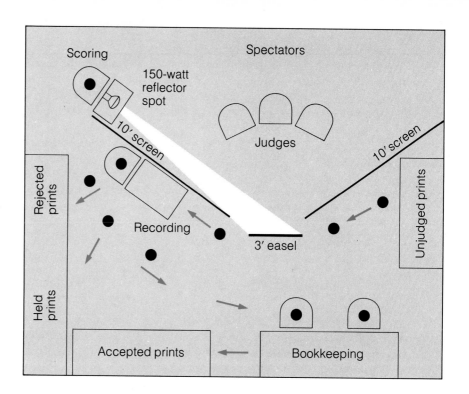

Scoring

150-watt
reflector
spot

Spectators

Judges

Rejected prints

10' screen

Recording

10' screen

Unjudged prints

3' easel

Held prints

Accepted prints

Bookkeeping

A formal print-judging arrangement, with the recommended lighting setup.

(Left) Sunlight reflected on waving grasses gives a spun-silver effect to this nature closeup, that won Second Prize in the 1977 Kodak International Newspaper Snapshot Awards. Photo by David W. La Haye.

are no hot spots or reflected glare on the surface of the print, and that the light unit itself does not interfere with viewing from the judges' position. The accompanying diagram shows the judging arrangement, with the recommended lighting.

A 150-watt reflector spot is the recommended light source, placed at an angle of about 35° to the print surface. This provides a color temperature of between 2800 K and 3200 K. For black-and-white and toned prints, the distance from the light to the print is adjusted to provide an illumination of 25± 3 footcandles at the print location. This is generally about 10 feet. For color prints, the distance is reduced to 7 feet, which should provide an illumination level of 70±20 footcandles. Both footcandle values include the ambient room illumination.

If you do not have a footcandle meter, you can use an incident meter centered in the print area of the easel, or a Kodak neutral test card (or the equivalent) with a reflection meter. Set the meter at ASA 125 and move the spotlight until the meter indicates an exposure between 2 and 3 seconds at *f*/16 for illimination of approximately 25 footcandles, or 1 second at *f*/16 for approximately 70 footcandles.

Basis of Judging

If experienced judges are available, they will have their own criteria by which to judge the entries. Where local people are used, it may be necessary to remind them that the bases of judgment are usually:

1. Subject interest or appeal.
2. Composition; arrangement of light and dark in black-and-white, or of colors in slides.
3. Technical excellence—sharpness, correctness of exposure, cleanliness of print, tonal quality of black-and-white prints. It is suggested that technical excellence *not* be considered a plus in advanced competition, but that poor quality result in demerits.

It is important to remember, especially for non-technical judges, that complete accuracy of color rendition is not always necessary or even desirable in color photographs. An altered color rendition may often add to the impact of a given picture.

• *See also:* CAMERA CLUBS; CONTESTS AND COMPETITION.

 Jump Cut

Jump cut is a motion-picture term. It is any cut made in a motion-picture scene without a change of camera viewpoint. For example, if a given action runs longer than desirable, one may be tempted to cut out some of the action from the middle of the scene, and show only the beginning and end.

Unless used with discretion, the effect of a jump cut can be disconcerting and annoying; jump cuts should always be avoided, except perhaps during part of a scene in which the action has stopped for a while. In this case, the static footage can be removed without causing an obvious jump.

In all other cases, every effort should be made to avoid the jump. If, for instance, the camera angle or distance is changed at the cut, then the jump will not be noticeable. For this reason, in making planned films it is always good to make two or three shots of a given action, either at different distances (such as close-up and medium shots) or from different angles. Then the editor can, if need be, use the beginning of one shot, the end of the other, and any missing action in between will not be noticed, being covered by the change of viewpoint.

When this cannot be done—in cases where the action is not repeatable, as in news events—there are two methods that can be used. One is to shoot the scene simultaneously with two cameras, either from noticeably different viewpoints or with lenses of different focal length.

The other method is to make sure that some more or less neutral material is photographed before or after the action in question. This film can be used by the editor for a "cut-away."

For example, a carpenter is sawing a board in half; this takes time and footage, which would simply bore the audience. If, however, you make a separate shot of sawdust falling on the floor, or even just a close-up of the carpenter's face or hands, then in editing, you start the sawing, after a few seconds cut to the sawdust build-up, and then cut back to the sawing scene just before the end, as the saw is about to finish its job. All the intervening sawing can be eliminated, and will not be missed by the audience.

• *See also:* EDITING MOVIES; MOTION PICTURE PRODUCTION.

Kallitype

An early silver printing process, generally attributed to W. W. Nicol, kallitype is similar to platinotype, except that the image is silver rather than platinum. It is a contact-printing process. The actual light-sensitive medium is ferric oxalate, which is reduced by the action of light to ferrous oxalate. This in turn causes a silver salt, included in the paper or cloth coating, to be reduced to metallic silver. Instructions for making kallitype prints follow.

Kallitype Sensitizer

Cloth or paper can be sensitized with the solution produced by following the formula below.

Distilled water	473.0 ml
Ferric oxalate	78.0 grams
Oxalic acid	5.2 grams
Silver nitrate	28.4 grams

CAUTION: Oxalic acid may cause local skin irritation or burns if you come in contact with the crystals or solutions. Avoid contact with the skin and eyes. Silver nitrate in either the dry chemical or solution form can cause burns of both the skin and the eyes. In handling dry silver nitrate, be careful not to inhale the dust. In case of contact with the skin or eyes, both the dry chemicals and solutions described above should be immediately flushed from the area of contact with water. If the eyes are involved, flush for at least 15 minutes and get medical attention.

Mixing. In a stainless steel, glass, or plastic container, dissolve the ferric oxalate and oxalic acid in the water at a temperature of about 38 C (100 F). Then add the silver nitrate to the solution and stir until dissolved. Pour the solution into a brown glass bottle, fit the bottle with a tight stopper, and allow the solution to ripen for a few days before you use it.

After you have mixed the sensitizer solution and left it to ripen, crystals will form in the solution. When you are ready to use the sensitizer, warm the container in a water bath at 38 C (100 F) in order to redissolve the crystalline material. Apply the solution at 38 C to the cloth or paper as described previously. Use the sensitized cloth or paper as soon as possible, because the sensitized coating will begin to deteriorate within a day or so.

Exposure

After it is dry, hold the sensitized cloth or paper in close contact with the negative you wish to print by placing a piece of clear glass over the negative. Then expose it to sunlight or very strong artificial light, such as a reflector photolamp, until details are visible in the highlight areas of the image. If you use a hinged printing frame, you can examine part of the print to determine when the exposure is adequate. Exposures require several minutes. Try an exposure of 2 minutes to 10 minutes or longer until you determine the best time to use. A correctly exposed print will appear as a faint brown image on a yellow background.

Development

To produce black tones, treat the print for about 2 to 8 minutes in the following solution at 38 C

(100 F). To mix the solution, dissolve the borax in water at 38 C while stirring, then add the Rochelle salts. If you are not going to use the developer soon after it is mixed, you will have to warm it up to the temperature recommended for mixing to redissolve crystalline deposits that may have formed.

Borax	57 g
Rochelle salts	
(sodium potassium tartrate) . . .	43 g
Water	591 ml

You can control the contrast of the image and enhance the highlight areas by adding a small amount of a 10 percent solution of potassium dichromate. If the negative you used was of normal contrast, add only a drop or two of the dichromate solution; but if the negative was flat—lacking in contrast—use 6 to 10 or more drops. For prints from very contrasty negatives, do not add any dichromate to the developer.

If you want purplish-brown tones in your print, change the proportions of the developer to 28 grams (1 ounce) of borax and 57 grams (2 ounces) of Rochelle salts. For a sepia or brownish effect, omit the borax and use only 28 grams (1 ounce) of Rochelle salts. Without the borax, you can mix and use the solution at 18.5 to 24 C (65 to 75 F), but at the lower temperature, you will have to develop your print for about 15 minutes. You can control the darkness of the print to some extent by removing it when the desired density has been obtained. For richer black tones use a different developer consisting of 85 grams (3 ounces) of sodium acetate to 591 millilitres (20 fluidounces) of water at 18.5 to 24 C. Mix the solution at the same temperature.

Clearing and Fixing

Clear the print in a solution of 28 grams (1 ounce) of potassium oxalate in 237 millilitres (8 fluidounces) of water at 18.5 to 24 C (65 to 75 F), and then fix for 3 to 5 minutes in the following bath at the same temperature. When mixing the solutions, dissolve the chemicals in the water at 18.5 to 24 C.

Water	591 ml
Sodium thiosulfate	
(hypo)	28 g
Household ammonia	7 ml

After fixing, wash the print thoroughly for 30 minutes in running water at 18.5 to 21 C (65 to 70 F). Then dry in the usual way.
• *See also:* FABRIC SENSITIZER; PLATINUM PRINT PROCESS.

Kelvin

After Lord Kelvin, English scientist, 1824–1907

A kelvin is the unit of temperature in the absolute scale. The absolute scale is so-called because it starts from theoretical absolute zero—the point at which all molecular motion stops. This is approximately −273 on the Celsius (formerly the Centigrade) scale. The kelvin is the same size as the degree Celsius, hence the freezing point of water, which is 0 C, is 273 K and the boiling point (100 C) is 373 K. The absolute scale is used in many scientific areas, and is used in photography for the measurement of color temperature.

NOTE: The unit is "the kelvin," not "degrees kelvin" nor "kelvin degrees," and the degree mark is not used with it. The name is spelled with the lower-case letter k (kelvin) but the abbreviation is capital K, not followed by a period, thus 3200 K and so on.
• *See also:* BLACK BODY; COLOR TEMPERATURE; MIRED; TEMPERATURE SCALES; WEIGHTS AND MEASURES.

Keystoning

When the image plane (film) is not parallel to the object plane, the shape of an object becomes distorted in the image. In the case of rectilinear objects, the effect is quite noticeable because the image shape is a trapezoid, similar to a keystone in an arch. To avoid keystoning, the two planes must be made parallel.

With a view camera, swing or tilt the film plane to move the largest part of the image toward the subject. This can be done either by moving the entire camera body, or by moving the back if it has independent swing and tilt adjustments.

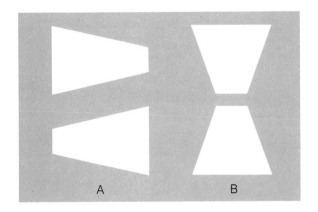

If keystoned images occur on the screen because of a slide or movie projector, horizontal keystoning can be corrected by swinging the side of the screen with the smaller part of the image away from the projector. Vertical keystoning is more easily corrected by tilting the projector up or down, as required.

• *See also:* CAMERA MOVEMENTS; VIEW CAMERA.

Kingslake, Rudolf

(Born 1903)
American lens designer

Born in London, Rudolf Kingslake studied science, electronics, and optics at the Imperial College of Science and Technology. After graduating, he worked for a year at the factory of Grubb, Parsons & Co., builders of telescopes. Following this, he worked as a research engineer at International Standard Electric Corporation.

In 1929, he began his association with the Optical Society of America. He served as president of the Rochester Section during 1932 and 1933, and president of the National Society from 1947–1949.

Until his retirement in 1969, Kingslake served as head of lens design at Kodak. During World War II, he found himself involved in the design of military optical instruments such as gunsights, telescopes, and height finders. Pre-war research at Kodak had resulted in the development of new optical glasses based on lanthanum oxide; these glasses were used extensively in military optics during World War II and later by Kingslake and his associates in developing a new series of photographic lens designs.

Until World War II, lens design was a matter of either pencil and paper computation using log and trig tables, or a marginally mechanized operation utilizing the mechanical desk calculators then available. In the 1950's, however, the rise of the electronic computer brought a whole new *modus operandi* to lens designing. Kingslake was instrumental in establishing the computer design system at Kodak, and training his staff in the new method.

Kingslake's publications are numerous; they include over 60 scientific papers and articles; in addition, he planned and edited the monumental 5-volume series *Applied Optics and Optical Engineering,* which is now the major reference work in the field. He also edited a new edition of Alexander Conrady's book *Applied Optics and Optical Design* and completed the second volume. Kingslake's latest book is *Lens Design Fundamentals.*

Kingslake continues to be active in the field of optics as teacher, writer, and consultant.

Kirlian Photography

Kirlian photography is the popular term for a method of electrophotography that records the luminous glow produced when a high-voltage, high-frequency electric potential is applied across a subject. Kirlian photography is named for two Russian researchers, Semyon and Valentina Kirlian, who began publishing results of their research on this phenomenon in the late 1950's. It has been variously referred to as electrophotography, corona-discharge photography, electroluminescence photography, and the photo-electrographic process.

Kirlian photograph of a leaf, made by direct contact on Ektachrome film. Photo by Lief Ericksenn.

While the phenomenon has frequently been adopted and displayed as a mystical or psychic "aura," the basic physical principles have been investigated and are explained in the following text. When a high-voltage charge is applied across electrodes arranged much like a large capacitor, a corona discharge can occur in the air space between. This discharge occurs well before high-current density will cause a spark to jump the gap. Corona discharge causes a luminous glow that can be observed and photographed either with a camera and film or with the film alone exposed directly by contact or close proximity to an object. The object, placed in the air gap or touching a dielectrically isolated electrode, or grounded and touching an electrode, will modify and channel the discharge.

Energy is radiated in the corona discharge at the ultraviolet and blue wavelengths. A sheet of film or photographic paper in the path will be exposed by the corona and will record the pattern of discharge around the object. When a transparent electrode is used, the corona may be observed visually and can be photographed in the normal manner with camera and film.

Many experiments have been conducted with both inanimate objects and living specimens. While some value has been seen in using the technique in physical testing of materials to detect surface ir-

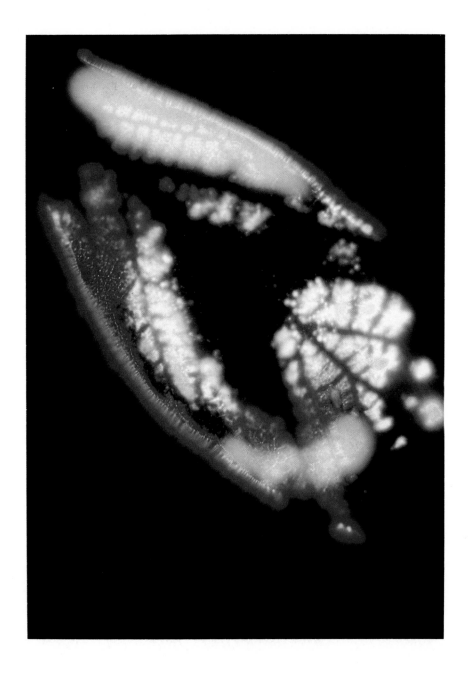

Another leaf photographed by direct contact, but at a different exposure. Corona discharge of electrical energy flowing over the surface of the object exposes the film. Photo by Lief Ericksenn.

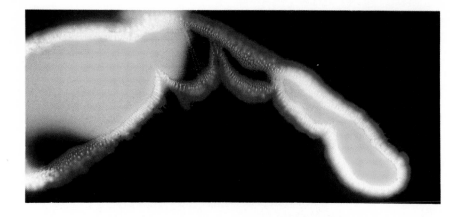

The little finger and side of the photographer's hand. Photo by Lief Ericksenn.

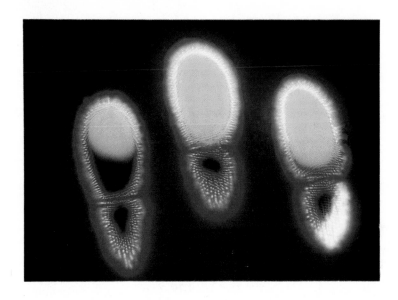

Kirlian image of the photographer's fingertips. Color and visible fringing are not predictable. Metallic objects such as coins seem to give the most dramatic effects. Photo by Lief Ericksenn.

regularities or internal flaws, the primary focus for investigation has been on living biological specimens. To date, the variations in the corona discharge appear to be closely related to the moisture around, on, or within the subject.

The production of startling and fascinating images has intrigued a wide range of investigators, both amateur and professional. Although it is relatively easy to assemble equipment and make images, the potential for mishandling high-voltage sources, especially in the dark, should cause most workers to consider their abilities before handling such equipment. The construction and use of high-voltage sources should be left to those with a background and experience in electrical and electronic devices. One or more of the reference sources gives some basic procedures, equipment, and safety precautions for the experimenter.

• *See also:* ELECTROPHOTOGRAPHY; RADIOGRAPHY; SCIENTIFIC PHOTOGRAPHY; THERMAL PHOTOGRAPHY.

Further reading: Dakin, H. S. *High-Voltage Photography,* 2nd ed. Barrington, NJ: Edmund Scientific Company, 1975. Krippner, Stanley and Daniel Rubin, eds. *The Kirlian Aura.* Garden City, NY: Doubleday / Anchor, 1974. Waite, M. *Projects in Sight, Sound, and Sensation.* Indianapolis, IN: Howard W. Sams & Co., 1974.

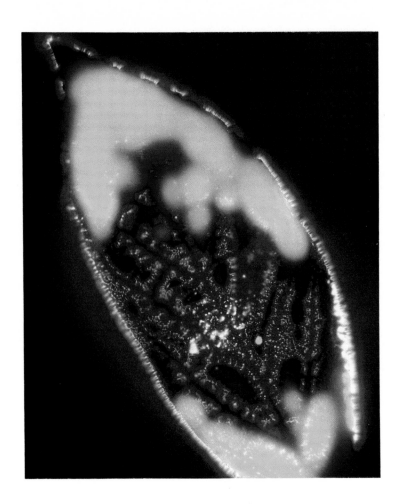

Leaf. A Kirlian image of a living specimen varies with moisture content and its general "healthiness" as well as with the energizing voltage and the distance from the film.

Kodachrome Film and Processing

Although Kodachrome film is similar in construction to other color films, the composition of its emulsion and the required processing are unique.

Because of the way Kodachrome films are made and processed, they are exceedingly sharp, extremely fine-grained color films. They are used widely in super 8, 16, 126, 110, and 35 mm formats. Kodachrome film is available as moderate and medium-speed daylight-balanced films, and as a 3400 K (type A) balanced film.

Modern color films basically have three emulsion layers with individual color sensitivities: red, green, and blue. The red-sensitive layer is next to the film base; the green-sensitive layer is above it; and the blue-sensitive layer is on top. There is a yellow filter layer just below the top layer to prevent blue light from reaching the green- and red-sensitive layers, which also have some blue sensitivity.

Dye-Forming Couplers

In all color films other than Kodachrome film, compounds called dye-forming couplers are incorporated along with the silver halides in each emulsion layer. The red-sensitive layer has cyan dye-forming couplers; the green-sensitive layer has magenta dye-forming couplers; and the blue-sensitive layer has yellow dye-forming couplers. In color reversal film, these couplers are triggered during development of the reversal (positive) image to produce visible dyes in proportion to the amount of silver being developed in each layer. The dyes are produced in all three layers simultaneously, during a single developing stage.

NOTE: The construction and processing of instant-print color films differ from that of the conventional films being described. (*See:* DIFFUSION TRANSFER PROCESS.)

Emulsion Layers of *Kodachrome* Film

The emulsion layers of Kodachrome film do not contain dye-forming couplers; the couplers are incorporated in various developing solutions. It is not possible to include couplers to form all three dyes in a single solution, because there is no practical way to be sure that a given coupler molecule will go to its own emulsion layer rather than either of the other two layers. Instead, separate solutions are used to develop the reversal image in each layer, one at a time; hence, each solution contains just one kind of color coupler.

Processing

The composition of Kodachrome film has been improved several times since its invention in 1935 by Mannes and Godowsky, and the processing chemistry has similarly been improved. Today, Process K-14 is used with the modern Kodachrome films. The basic procedures are as follows:

Rem-jet removal. A black antihalation backing on the film base is softened and removed so the red reversal exposure may be made through the film base.

First developer. The negative silver images are developed simultaneously in all three layers by a single black-and-white developer; no color is formed.

Red re-exposure. The film is exposed to filtered red light through the base so that the negative silver densities in the other layers do not interfere with the exposure. Only the previously undeveloped bottom-layer silver halides—which correspond to the red-record positive image—are exposed; the other two layers are not sensitive to red light.

Cyan developer. The exposed positive silver-halide image in the red layer is developed by a solution that contains a cyan coupler, so the cyan positive image is formed at the same time as the positive silver image.

Blue re-exposure. The film is exposed to blue filtered light from the emulsion side. Only the top layer is affected, because the yellow filter layer just below prevents any blue light from reaching the middle emulsion layer.

Yellow developer. The just-exposed blue-record positive silver-halide image in the top layer is developed, and a yellow dye-forming coupler in the developer forms the corresponding yellow dye image.

Magenta fogging developer. Re-exposure is not used to prepare the silver halides in the middle emulsion layer for development, because the developed silver in the top and bottom layers would block the light. Instead, a fogging developer is used. This solution renders the remaining halides in the green-sensitive layer developable by chemical action and then proceeds to develop the positive silver image there. Simultaneously, magenta dye-forming couplers in the developer form the positive magenta dye image.

Bleach. All silver has been developed; it is now bleached back to a silver-halide state, and the yellow filter layer, which is composed of collodial silver, is also converted to a silver halide.

Fixer. All silver halide formed in the bleach step is converted to soluble silver complexes by the fixer; these dissolve out in the fixing bath and wash. The positive dye images remain in the three layers to form a full-color subject representation.

Other Steps in Processing

There are rinse and wash steps between these processing stages that have not been indicated. Every step in the Kodachrome film process is controlled for time, temperature, and chemical balance with extreme precision. For this reason, processing cannot be accomplished manually or in small darkrooms. Only a complex, automatic, continuous-processing machine can assure controlled, repeatable results. The cost of such a processor makes it practical only for high-volume use, as in a large commercial-processing lab.

• *See also:* COLOR FILM PROCESSING; COLOR FILMS; DIFFUSION TRANSFER PROCESS; GODOWSKY, LEOPOLD; MANNES, LEO.

Kodalk Balanced Alkali

Kodalk is a trademark of Eastman Kodak Company for a proprietary alkali used in developers as an accelerator or activator. It is also occasionally used as a buffer in fixing baths. It is less strongly buffered than sodium carbonate, hence it produces an almost proportionate change in developer activity as its concentration is varied. In addition, it does not emit any gas when added to an acid stop or fixing bath, hence the danger of blistering a negative at elevated temperatures is reduced. When Kodalk alkali is not available, similar results can be obtained by the use of sodium metaborate in the same amount. It is the activator used in such commonly used Kodak developers as DK-50 and DK-60a, and in less commonly used developers such as DK-15 (tropical developer) and DK-20 (fine-grain developer).

Kohler Illumination

Kohler illumination is the most common system of illuminating a microscope specimen in photomicrography. It can be used in visual work, too, because it provides the best image quality and highest resolution.

Basically, Kohler illumination consists of using the field or lamp condenser to focus an image of the lamp filament on the substage condenser, which in turn focuses an image of the lamp condenser in the plane of the specimen. Thus, in effect, the lamp collector becomes the source of illumination.

The chief practical advantage of this technique is that, when the elements are properly aligned, a uniformly illuminated field is provided, with practically no restriction as to the structure of the light source. Hence, it is possible to employ a nonuniform source (such as a coil-filament tungsten lamp) or a high-intensity source of small area (such as a zirconium arc or a xenon arc).

Essentially, the method of producing Kohler illumination in photomicrography consists of focusing an image of the lamp collector in the plane of the object and an image of the lamp filament in the plane of the aperture diaphragm. (See the accompanying illustration.) In actual practice, the steps in establishing Kohler illumination are listed here:

1. Check alignment of the lamp with respect to the lamp collector. A quick check of alignment can be made by placing a piece of thin white paper over the field diaphragm and focusing the lamp collector to produce an image of the lamp on the paper. The image of the lamp should be centered within the outline of the diaphragm. The lamphouse —containing the lamp, collector lens, and diaphragm—should be placed about 10 inches from the microscope. The actual distance should be such that the image of the lamp filament projected onto the mirror is slightly larger than the maximum opening of the aperture diaphragm. The alignment of the lamp with respect to the lamp collector is necessary only once. When the lamp is changed, realignment is required.

2. Adjust the lamphouse so that the image of the lamp is centered on the mirror. Adjust the mirror so that the image reflected by it onto the aperture diaphragm is centered on the diaphragm. Focus the lamp collector to produce a sharp image of the lamp filament on the aperture diaphragm.

3. Stop down the field diaphragm to a small aperture. While looking into the microscope or at the ground glass of the camera, focus the condenser to obtain a sharp image of the field diaphragm in the specimen plane. For this step, the microscope must be in focus on a specimen.

4. The image of the field diaphragm should be centered in the observed field. If it is not centered, alignment of the lamp to the mirror or lamphouse adjustments were not properly made and should be corrected.

5. While still observing the diaphragm image, open the field diaphragm until its diameter is equal to, or just slightly greater than, the entire microscope field as seen.

A collector lens gathers an image of the lamp filament and projects this intense, uniform image through the field diaphragm and focuses it on the aperture diaphragm. After the light beam passes through the condenser, the uniform bundle of light passes through the specimen. Theoretically, an image of the filament is also formed at the exit pupil

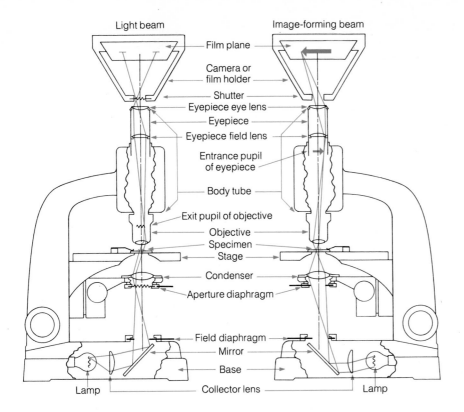

Light beam | Image-forming beam

- Film plane
- Camera or film holder
- Shutter
- Eyepiece eye lens
- Eyepiece
- Eyepiece field lens
- Entrance pupil of eyepiece
- Body tube
- Exit pupil of objective
- Objective
- Specimen
- Stage
- Condenser
- Aperture diaphragm
- Field diaphragm
- Mirror
- Base
- Lamp
- Collector lens
- Lamp

Kohler illumination is a method of brightfield illumination necessary to successful photomicrography. Establishing Kohler illumination provides a uniformly illuminated field from a nonuniform source such as a filament lamp. The paths of the light beam and image-forming beam are shown here.

of the objective. As the light beam continues through the microscope, it again forms an image of the filament, this time at the shutter or camera aperture. The accompanying diagram shows the path through the microscope of just two light rays originating at the same point on the filament. In actuality, the collector lens focuses an infinite number of rays on the aperture diaphragm.

Light rays are delivered to the field diaphragm by the collector lens. The condenser receives the rays from the field diaphragm and brings them into sharp focus in the plane of the specimen. By focusing an image of the field diaphragm in the specimen plane, the focused light picks up an image of the specimen and projects it into the objective. As these light rays travel through the microscope toward the eyepiece, an aerial image of the specimen is formed at the entrance pupil of the eyepiece. The eyepiece receives the image rays and focuses an image of the subject on the film plane for photography or on a viewing screen for visual purposes. The accompanying diagram shows the path of just two image-forming light rays through the microscope. Actually, the

image of the specimen is formed by an infinite number of light rays passing through the specimen.

• *See also:* PHOTOMICROGRAPHY.

Kostinsky Effect

When two small, heavily exposed images lie close together, a form of development inhibition known as the Kostinsky effect may take place. In the region between the two images, the developer is exhausted and the reaction products accumulate to a much greater extent than at other points around the image. As a result, development is inhibited where the images nearly touch, but proceeds normally elsewhere. The result of this asymmetrical inhibition is a warped shape that exaggerates the separation of the two images. This exaggeration can cause errors in scientific calculations based on photography. The Kostinsky effect is a specific form of edge or adjacency effects (Eberhard effects).

• *See also:* IMAGE EFFECTS.

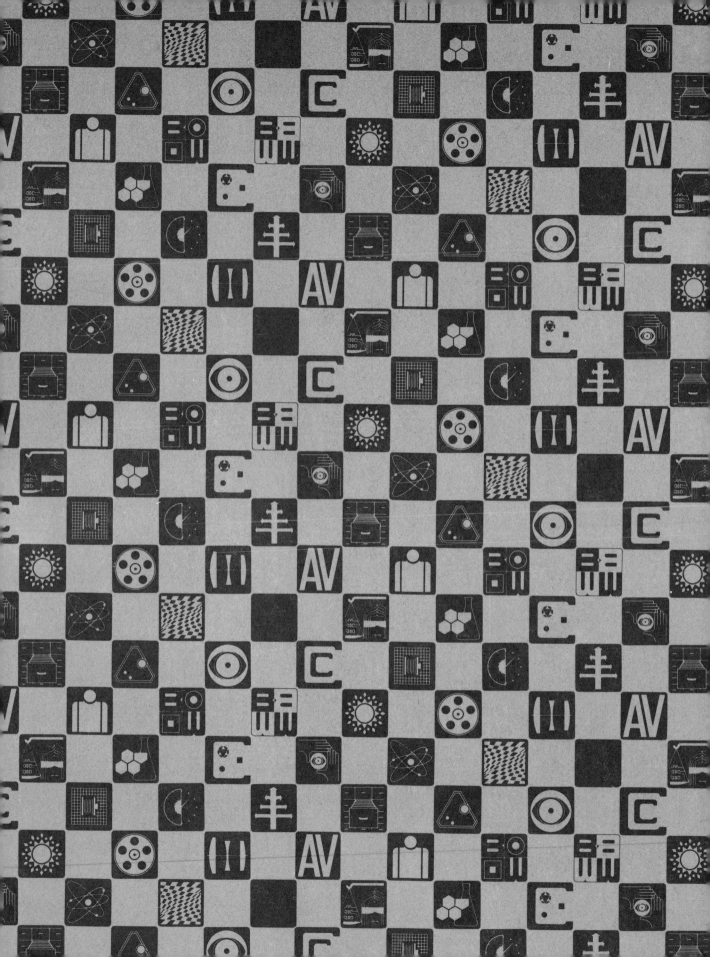